Archaeologies of P

WITHDRAWN

Archaeologies of Presence is a compelling exploration of how the performance of presence can be understood through the relationships between performance theory and archaeological thinking. Drawing together carefully commissioned contributions from leading international scholars and artists, this radical new work poses a number of essential questions:

- What are the principal signifiers of theatrical presence?
- How is presence achieved through theatrical performance?
- What makes a memory come alive and live again?
- How is presence connected with identity?
- Is presence synonymous with 'being in the moment'?
- What is the nature of the 'co-presence' of audience and performer?
- Where does performance practice end and its documentation begin?

Co-edited by performance specialists Gabriella Giannachi and Nick Kaye, and archaeologist Michael Shanks, *Archaeologies of Presence* represents an innovative and rewarding feat of interdisciplinary scholarship.

Gabriella Giannachi is Professor in Performance and New Media, and Director of the Centre for Intermedia at the University of Exeter, UK. Her book publications include: *Virtual Theatres: an Introduction* (2004), *Performing Nature: Explorations in Ecology and the Arts*, ed. with Nigel Stewart (2005), *The Politics of New Media Theatre* (2007), *Performing Presence: Between the Live and the Simulated*, co-authored with Nick

Kaye (2011), and *Performing Mixed Reality*, with Steve Benford (2011).

Nick Kaye is Dean of the College of Humanities and Professor of Performance Studies, at the University of Exeter, UK. His books include: *Postmodernism and Performance* (1994), *Art into Theatre: Performance Interviews and Documents* (1996), *Site-Specific Art: Performance, Place and Documentation* (2000), *Staging the Post-Avant-Garde: Italian Performance After 1970*, with Gabriella Giannachi (2002), *Multi-media: video – installation – performance* (2007) and *Performing Presence: Between the Live and the Simulated*, with Gabriella Giannachi (2011). He is co-director of REACT, an AHRC Knowledge Exchange Hub that will invest over £4 million in creating collaborations between academic researchers and the creative industries during 2012–16.

Michael Shanks is the Omar and Althea Hoskins Professor of Classics and Director of Stanford Archaeology Center's Metamedia Lab. His major book publications include: *ReConstructing Archaeology* (1987), *Social Theory and Archaeology* (1987), *Art and the Greek City State* (1999), *Classical Archaeology: Experiences of the Discipline* (1996), *Experiencing the Past: On the Character of Archaeology* (1992) and *Theatre/Archaeology*, with Mike Pearson (2001).

Archaeologies of Presence

Art, performance and the persistence of being

Edited by Gabriella Giannachi, Nick Kaye and Michael Shanks

Archaeologies of Presence
is supported by

Routledge
Taylor & Francis Group

LONDON AND NEW YORK

Arts & Humanities
Research Council

First published 2012
by Routledge
2 Park Square, Milton Park, Abingdon, Oxon OX14 4RN

Simultaneously published in the USA and Canada
by Routledge
711 Third Avenue, New York, NY 10017

Routledge is an imprint of the Taylor & Francis Group, an informa business

British Library Cataloguing in Publication Data
A catalogue record for this book is available from the British Library

Library of Congress Cataloguing in Publication Data
Archaeologies of presence : art, performance and the persistence of being
/ edited by Gabriella Giannachi, Nick Kaye and Michael Shanks.
p. cm.
Includes bibliographical references and index.
1. Performance art. I. Giannachi, Gabriella. II. Kaye, Nick. III. Shanks, Michael.
NX456.5.P38A73 2012
709.04'0755–dc23
2011041611

ISBN: 978-0-415-55766-5 (hbk)
ISBN: 978-0-415-55767-2 (pbk)
ISBN: 978-0-203-12673-8 (ebk)

Typeset in Sabon
by Saxon Graphics Ltd, Derby

Contents

Figures

Notes on contributors

Jon Erickson is Associate Professor in English at Ohio State University, USA. He is the author of *The Fate of the Object: From Modern Object to Postmodern Sign* (1995) and many essays on performance, including '"Presence," in *Staging Philosophy*, edited by David Saltz and David Krasner (2006), and "Defining Political Performance," in *Theatricality*, edited by Tracy Davis and Thomas Postlewait (2003). He is currently working on the ideal construction of the spectator by theorists and the resistance to textual authority in performance and performance theory.

Tim Etchells is best known for his work as artistic director and writer of Forced Entertainment, one of the UK's leading and influential performance and media ensembles who have been working together since 1984. He also creates diverse projects of his own in a variety of media, including SMS, video and installation. He has also collaborated with other artists in many disciplines, including the photographer Hugo Glendinning, the choreographer Meg Stuart/Damaged Goods and visual artists Vlatka Horvat, Franko B and Asta Groting. Under his direction, Forced Entertainment have toured widely in mainland Europe and beyond and have made projects that span theatre, durational performance, and other media. He has written widely about performance and contemporary culture, and has published three books: *The Dream Dictionary* (2001), *Endland Stories* (1999); and *Certain Fragments* – a collection of theoretical writing and performance texts (1999).

Josette Féral is full professor at the Drama Department of the Université du Québec à Montréal, Canada, where she has taught since 1981. She is presently teaching at Paris-Sorbonne Nouvelle. She has published several books including *Mise en scène et jeu de l'acteur*, volumes I, II and III (1997, 1999, 2007), *Teatro, Teoria y practica: mas alla de las fronteras* (2004), *Rencontres avec Ariane Mnouchkine* (1995) and *Trajectoires du Soleil* (1999), *La culture contre l'art: essai d'économie politique du théâtre* (1990). She has edited several books on the theory of the theatre, the most recent being *Pratiques performatives – Body Remix* (2011). Her publications in journals include 'Genetics of Performance' (*Theatre Research International*, 2008), 'The transparency of the text: Contemporary Writing for the Stage' (*Yale French* Studies, 2007) and 'Theatricality' (*Substance*, 2002). She has written extensively on the theory of theatre in Canada, the United States and Europe. Her most recent book, *Théorie et pratique, au-delà des limites*, will appear in *France à L'Entretemps* in 2011.

Erika Fischer-Lichte is Professor of Theatre Studies at Freie Universität Berlin. From 1995 to 1999 she was President of the International Federation for Theatre Research. She is a member of the Academia Europaea, the Academy of Sciences at Goettingen, and the Berlin-Brandenburg Academy of Sciences. Since 2008 she has served as director of the Institute for Advanced Studies on 'Interweaving Cultures in Performance' and since 2006 as Spokesperson of the International Research Training Group on „InterArt". She has published widely in the fields of aesthetics, theory of literature, art, and theatre, in particular on semiotics and performativity, theatre history, and contemporary theatre. Among her recent publications are *Theatre, Sacrifice, Ritual: Exploring Forms of Political Theatre* (2005), *The Transformative Power of Performance: A New Aesthetics* (2008) and *Global Ibsen. Performing Multiple Modernities* (2010).

Gabriella Giannachi is Professor in Performance and New Media, and Director of the Centre for Intermedia at the University of Exeter, UK. Her book publications include: *Virtual Theatres: an Introduction* (2004), *Performing Nature: Explorations in Ecology and the Arts*, ed. with Nigel Stewart (2005), *The Politics of New Media Theatre* (2007), *Performing Presence: Between the Live and the Simulated*, co-authored with Nick Kaye (2011), and *Performing Mixed Reality*, with Steve Benford (2011). From 2005–09 she was a principal investigator for *Performing*

Presence: from the live to the simulated, a large-scale collaborative research project funded by the UK Arts and Humanities Research Council, which she led in collaboration with Nick Kaye and Michael Shanks. She is an expert in performance documentation and is an investigator in the Research Councils UK (RCUK) funded Horizon Digital Economy Research Hub (2009–14) for which she developed a novel archiving tool, CloudPad.

Lynn Hershman Leeson has been called 'the most influential female in new media'. She works across platforms of photography, film, performance and computer-based installations. She is a recipient of many awards, including D.Digital, Sloan Foundation for Directing and Writing, John Simon Guggenheim Memorial Foundation Fellowship, amongst many others. Over the last three decades, artist and filmmaker Lynn Hershman Leeson has been internationally acclaimed for her pioneering use of new technologies and her investigations of issues that are now recognized as key to the working of our society: identity in a time of consumerism, privacy in a era of surveillance, interfacing of humans and machines, and the relationship between real and virtual worlds. In 2004 Stanford University Libraries acquired Hershman Leeson's working archive. Hershman Leeson is Chair of the Film Department at the San Francisco Art Institute and Professor Emeritus at the University of California, Davis, USA.

Amelia Jones is Professor and Grierson Chair in Visual Culture at McGill University in Montréal, Canada. Her recent publications include major essays on Marina Abramović (in *The Drama Review*), on feminist art and curating, and on performance art histories, as well as the edited volume *Feminism and Visual Culture Reader* (2003; new edition 2010). Her most recent book, *Self Image: Technology, Representation, and the Contemporary Subject* (2006), will be followed in 2012 by *Seeing Differently: A History and Theory of Identification in the Visual Arts* and her major volume, *Perform Repeat Record: Live Art in History*, co-edited with Adrian Heathfield, is also due out in 2012.

Simon Jones, Professor of Performance, University of Bristol, UK, is a writer and scholar, founder and co-director of Bodies in Flight, which has to date produced 16 works and numerous documents of performance that have at their heart the encounter between flesh and text, where *words move* and *flesh utters*. He has been visiting scholar at Amsterdam University (2001), a visiting artist at The School of the Art Institute of Chicago (2002) and Banff Arts Centre (2008). He has published in Contemporary Theatre Review, Entropy Magazine, Liveartmagazine, *Shattered Anatomies*, *The Cambridge History of British Theatre*, Performance Research: *on Beckett*, co-edited *Practice as Research in Performance and Screen* (2009) and his work with Bodies in Flight features in Josephine Machon's *(Syn)aesthetics? Towards a Definition of Visceral Performance* (2009).

Nick Kaye is Dean of the College of Humanities and Professor of Performance Studies, at the University of Exeter, UK. His books include: *Postmodernism and Performance* (1994), *Art into Theatre: Performance Interviews and Documents* (1996), *Site-Specific Art: Performance, Place and Documentation* (2000), *Staging the Post-Avant-Garde: Italian Performance After 1970*, with Gabriella Giannachi (2002), *Multi-media: video – installation – performance* (2007) and *Performing Presence: Between the Live and the Simulated*, with Gabriella Giannachi, (2011). Other publications include 'Acts of Presence,' an article, DVD-ROM and online publication, with Gabriella Giannachi, *The Drama Review* Winter 2011. From 2005–09 he was a principal investigator for *Performing Presence: from the live to the simulated*, a large-scale collaborative research project funded by the UK Arts and Humanities Research Council, which he led in collaboration with Gabriella Giannachi and Michael Shanks. From 2011–14, he is an investigator on another large-scale AHRC project, *Performing Documents: modelling creative and curatorial engagements with live art and performance archives*. He is co-director of REACT, an AHRC Knowledge Exchange Hub that will invest over £4 million in creating collaborations between academic researchers and the creative industries during 2012–16.

Mike Pearson trained as an archaeologist. He was a member of R.A.T. Theatre (1972–73) and an artistic director of Cardiff Laboratory Theatre (1973–80) and Brith Gof (1981–97). He continues to make performances as a solo artist and in collaboration with artist/designer Mike Brookes as Pearson/Brookes (1997–). In August 2010, he directed a site-specific production of Aeschylus's *The Persians* on the military training ranges in mid-Wales for the newly founded National Theatre

Wales. He is co-author with Michael Shanks of *Theatre/
Archaeology* (2001) and author of '*In Comes I': Performance,
Memory and Landscape* (2006), *Site-Specific Performance*
(2010) and *Mickery Theater: An Imperfect Archaeology* (2011).
He is currently Professor of Performance Studies, Department of
Theatre, Film and Television Studies, Aberystwyth University.

Nicholas Ridout teaches in the Department of Drama at Queen
Mary, University of London. He is the author of *Stage Fright,
Animals and Other Theatrical Problems* (2006), *Theatre &
Ethics* (2009) and co-editor, with Joe Kelleher, of *Contemporary
Theatres in Europe* (2006). He is the co-author, with Claudia
Castellucci, Romeo Castellucci, Chiara Guidi and Joe Kelleher of
The Theatre of Socìetas Raffaello Sanzio (2007).

Rebecca Schneider is the author of *Performing Remains: Art and
War in Times of Theatrical Reenactment* (2011) and *The Explicit
Body in Performance* (1997). She is co-editor of the anthology
Re:Direction (2001) and of numerous essays, including 'Solo
Solo Solo' in *After Criticism: New Responses to Art and
Performance* (2004) and 'Hello Dolly Well Hello Dolly' in
Psychoanalysis and Performance (2001). She is Chair of the
Department of Theatre Arts and Performance Studies at Brown
University, consortium editor for *TDR: The Drama Review*, and
co-editor of the book series 'Theatre: Theory/Text/Performance'
with University of Michigan Press.

Michael Shanks is the Omar and Althea Hoskins Professor of
Classics and Director of Stanford Archaeology Center's
Metamedia Lab. Two questions have driven his research into
prehistoric Europe: Design – from Classical antiquity to the
contemporary fine arts – How are we to understand people and
societies through the things they make and leave behind? And,
how are we to write the archaeological past on the basis of what
is left behind? – a question of the documentation of event. His
major book publications include: *ReConstructing Archaeology*
(1987), *Social Theory and Archaeology* (1987), *Art and the
Greek City State* (1999), *Classical Archaeology: Experiences of
the Discipline* (1996), *Experiencing the Past: On the Character
of Archaeology* (1992) and *Theatre/Archaeology*, with Mike
Pearson (Routledge 2001). From 2005–09 he was a principal
investigator for *Performing Presence: from the live to the*

simulated, a large-scale collaborative research project funded by the UK Arts and Humanities Research Council, which he led in collaboration with Gabriella Giannachi and Nick Kaye.

Phillip Zarrilli works internationally as a director, actor, and training actor/performers in psychophysical processes through Asian martial arts and yoga. As Artistic Director of THE LLANARTH GROUP, his most recent productions are *Told by the Wind*, co-created with Kaite O'Reilly and Jo Shapland, (2010/2011) and *The Echo Chamber,* co-created with Kaite O'Reilly, Peader Kirk and Ian Morgan (2012). Other recent productions include " *... sweet ... dry ...bitter ... plaintive ...* for SANKALPAM, part of *Corpo-realities* (2010); *Play* by Samuel Beckett with Gaitkrash and National Sculpture Factory (Cork, Ireland, 2011); and the world première of Kaite O'Reilly's *The Almond and the Seahorse* for Sherman Cymru (2008). In additional to running his private studio in West Wales, recent international residencies/workshops include the Grotowski Centre (Wroclaw), IMALIS project (Epidavros), Toronto, Taipei, and Seoul. His most recent book, *Psychophysical Acting: an intercultural approach after Stanislavski* (2009) received the 2010 ATHE Outstanding Book of the Year Award. He is Professor of Performance Practice at Exeter University, UK.

Acknowledgements

A book such as this rests on the interest and support of many individuals and organizations. We would like to extend our thanks first of all to our principal colleagues and collaborators in the Performing Presence project: Mel Slater, Professor of Virtual Environments, Department of Computer Science, University College London; and Dr David Swapp, Immersive VR Laboratory Manager at University College London. It has also been a particular privilege for us to develop the book in relation to the generous contributions of time, interest and assistance by the contributors to this volume. Of the contributors, Jon Erickson, Tim Etchells, Josette Féral, Lynn Hershman Leeson, Simon Jones, Mike Pearson and Phillip Zarrilli also played direct and important parts in the *Performing Presence* project itself, either by way of workshops, conversations and interviews, or contributions to the culminating conference in 2008. We would also like to thank Marco Gillies, Department of Computing, Goldsmiths, University of London, and Peter Hulton, Senior Research Fellow at the Department of Drama, University of Exeter, for their continual help and support throughout the project. During the development of the project we also benefited from the invaluable assistance of Henry Lowood, Curator for History of Science and Technology Collections and Film and Media Collections at Stanford University Libraries; Henrik Bennetsen, Associate Director at Stanford University's Stanford Humanities Lab; and Jeff Aldrich, Technology Director, Stanford Humanities Lab.

As a principal outcome of the *Performing Presence* project, this book has also received extensive institutional support. We are indebted in particular to the UK Arts and Humanities Research Council for a large research grant award to facilitate the research that underpins the volume. This award to *Performing Presence:*

from the live to the simulated provided for a large-scale interdisciplinary collaboration between the University of Exeter, Stanford University and University College London from 2005 to 2009. The University of Exeter also provided extensive financial and technical support to the project.

We would also like to acknowledge the invaluable support of the staff and resources of the following libraries and institutions: the New York Public Library for the Performing Arts at Lincoln Center; the Jerome Robbins Archive of the Recorded Moving Image at Lincoln Center; Electronic Arts Intermix. We would also like to thank the staff at the Stanford Libraries Special Collections unit.

With regard to the figures reproduced in the book, we are pleased to acknowledge the following credits: Figures 1.1, 10.1, 10.2, 10.3, 13.5 and 14.2 courtesy of Hugo Glendinning; Figure 1.2 courtesy of Marina Abramović Archives; Figures 2.1, 2.2 and 2.3 courtesy of Janet Cardiff and George Bures Miller, Luhring Augustine, New York and Barbara Weiss Gallery, Berlin; Figures 7.1, 7.2, 7.3 and 7.4 courtesy of Phillip Zarrilli and photographers as credited; Figures 8.1, 8.2 and 8.3 courtesy of Bodies in Flight and photographers as credited; Figure 11.1 courtesy of Marina Abramovic and Sean Kelly Gallery, New York and DACS; Figure 11.2 courtesy of Carolee Schneemann; Figure 11.3 courtesy of Yayoi Kusama; Figure 11.4 courtesy of Annie Sprinkle; Figures 12.1, 12.2 courtesy of Lynn Hershman Leeson; Figures 12.3 and 12.4 courtesy of Gabriella Giannachi; Figures 13.1, 13.2, 13.6 and 13.7 are © Chris Burden: courtesy of Gagosian Gallery; Figure 13.3 courtesy of the artist and Metro Pictures; Figure 13.4 courtesy of Doug Hall; Figure 14.1 courtesy of Mike Pearson.

We are happy to acknowledge that Chapter 4, 'Performance remains again' is altered and developed from Rebecca Schneider's 2001 essay 'Performance Remains' in *Performance Research*, 6:2, 100–08. Chapter 10, 'Looking Back: a conversation about presence, 2006' is developed from 'Tim Etchells Interviewed by The Presence Project', recorded and published online in 2006 by the authors in the Presence Project Collaboratory, at: http://spa.exeter.ac.uk/drama/presence/presence.stanford.edu_3455/Collaboratory/646.htm. Chapter 11, 'Temporal anxiety/"Presence" *in absentia*: experiencing performance as documentation' incorporates Amelia Jones' earlier essay, 'Presence' *in absentia*: experiencing performance as documentation' published in *Art Journal*, 56:4 (1997), 11–18. Chapter 12, 'Here and now', was originally published in *Seed*

Magazine as a streamed videocast, *Seed Salon: Lynn Hershman Leeson + Michael Shanks* in 2007, at http://salon.seedmagazine.com/salon_shanks_leeson.html, and as a text at http://seedmagazine.com/content/article/michael_shanks_lynn_hershman_leeson/ on 27 August 2007. The text is reproduced here courtesy of Seed Media Group.

Finally, we would like to thank Talia Rodgers for her interest and belief in this volume, as well as Niall Slater and Sam Kinchin-Smith for their patient and invaluable editorial support.

G.G.
N.K.
M.S.

Chapter 1

Introduction
Archaeologies of presence

Gabriella Giannachi, Nick Kaye and
Michael Shanks

This book is concerned with the location and speculation toward experiences and performances of presence. Posing the question of how, when and by which processes phenomena of presence are produced and received, this volume presents key analyses of the conditions, dynamics and dialectics that shape presence in – or in relation to – acts of performance. In so doing, this book approaches the theatrical performance of presence as both subject and framework. Addressing experiences of *being there* – and *being before* – the critical analyses of presence framed here engage firstly with dynamics fundamental to theatre, reflecting on relationships between actor and witness, as well as practices and concepts of ephemerality, liveness, mediation, and documentation. In turn, these theatrical practices offer lenses to approach and analyze acts of presence in which phenomena of self, other and place are defined.

Here, too, the critical examination of presence is approached in the convergence of performance theory and archaeological thinking. Occurring in relation to situated acts, 'presence' not only invites consideration of individual experience, perception and consciousness, but also directs attention outside the self into the social and the spatial, toward the enactment of 'co-presence' as well as perceptions and habitations of place. Presence implies temporality, too – a fulcrum of presence is tense and the relationship between past and present. In this context, the examination of presence and its performance is linked to inscriptions of the past into the present, even as performance theory may consider the cues and prompts in which a future sense of presence may come to be enacted. Here, then, speculations over a presence once performed (theatrically or socially), are confronted with questions over how we create relationships with that which remains. In this process, performance theory and archaeological thinking may productively converge in engagements with uncertainty, in documentation, and in the analyses of signs, remains and traces of dynamic and processual phenomena that once occurred in the consequences of an act, in recognition of otherness, or in the performance of specific configurations and ecologies of position, relation and place.

In turn, while relationships between performance theory and archaeology provide lenses to examine notions and processes of presence, so the concept of presence has also come to assert itself as a significant figure and question within these different fields.

In performance theory and practice, presence is both fundamental and highly contested. In theatre, drama and performance, debates over the nature of the actor's presence have been at the heart of key aspects of practice and theory since the late 1950s and are a vital part of the discourses surrounding avant-garde and postmodern performance. These discourses concerning the performance of presence have frequently hinged on the relationship between the live and mediated, on notions and effects of immediacy, authenticity and originality. More widely, presence prompts questions of the character of self-awareness, of the performance and presentation of self and role. Presence also implies witnessing and interaction – a *being before* or *being in* the presence of another. Such dynamics are deeply inflected in theatrical process and practice, and lend themselves toward analysis through frameworks of performance and performativity. In theatre, performance and visual art, the experience of presence has often been linked to practices of encounter and to perceptions of difference and relation with something or somebody, as well as the uncanny encounter with one's own sense of self.

At the same time, questions of presence have also gained ground in archaeological thinking, just as relationships between archaeology and performance have emerged as influential on performance theory and practice (Pearson and Shanks 2001). Archaeology is increasingly understood less as the discovery of the past and more in terms of different relationships with what is left of the past. This has foregrounded anthropological questions of the performance and construction of the past in memory, narrative, collections (of textual and material sources), archives and systems of documentation, in the experience of place. Concepts of 'presence', 'aura' and the 'uncanny' return of the past accompany an emphasis upon encounters with the cues or prompts of 'site' – with the sign or trace. Such thinking has led to radically new forms of archaeological investigation and documentation that draw on and advance theatre theory and practice.

In these contexts, recent theatre practice and theory has also come to re-emphasize the performance and experience of presence over its deconstruction and the associated tropes of postmodern theatrical practice (Kaye 1994). Within experimental theatre, such work can be configured as part of a broader response through 'live' performance to the growing ubiquity of technologies of presence, including virtual, augmented and mixed reality computing, as well as the increasingly common braiding of the live with the simulated, and the performance of personal and social presence, through network media. Coming to prominence from the mid-1990s in the work of theatre companies such as Forced Entertainment, The Builders Association, Blast Theory, 3-Legged Dog and Elevator Repair Service, among others, these generations of artists and theatre-makers have invested in the performance of presence as an integral part of their aesthetic. Thus Marianne Weems, artistic director of The Builders Association, for example, stresses that the company's blending of live, mediated and recorded performance in increasingly complex ways supports '[t]he pleasure of staging the idea of presence [...] how [the performers'] presence is either [...] extended in some ways and amplified or compromised and endangered' (Weems in Kaye 2007: 576). In this context, The Builders Association work explicitly to articulate the performance of presence across their multi-media theatre productions, as the signs of 'performer-presence' are overtly orchestrated through shifts across media and modes of representation (Kaye 2007). In this work, 'presence' is not associated with the unified occupation of a place or unmediated encounter, but is foregrounded in the self-reflexive construction of experiences of presence through multiple media, representational frameworks and performative lenses.

An analogous focus on 'presence' is evident also in recent live art installations, as well as events and performances in museum and gallery contexts. It is a tendency aligned, too, with a move toward the ephemeral that Adrian Heathfield identifies with the 'live' in art. Observing in 2004 that 'many of the "troubling" currents in visual art practice' are 'more about the presentation of some phenomena rather than the representation of some thing,'

Figure 1.1 Martin Creed, *Work No. 850*, Tate Britain (2008).
     Photo: Hugo Glendinning

Heathfield observes and anatomizes a 'drive to the live' in 'a hard to categorize space between sculpture, installation and Live Art' (Heathfield 2004: 7). Exemplified for Heathfield in Damien Hirst's installations combining objects, organic matter and living animals, such work confronts the viewer with their own presence before the 'live' phenomena of the work, so entwining their response and consciousness with that of the 'object' of their attention. In encountering Hirst's *The Pursuit of Oblivion* (2004) Heathfield recalls: 'A shiver runs through me. Facing this artwork time slides and I am gripped by an uncanny feeling. The sculpture is performing: the object is alive.' (Heathfield 2004: 7)

More recent work has extended this installation of 'live' presence within the museum. For Martin Creed's *Work No. 850* (2008), every thirty seconds during the opening hours of Tate Britain a person ran 'as if their life depended on it' through the 86-metre length of the neo-classical Deveen sculpture gallery. It is a run that continually repeats in alternation with caesura of equal time in which nothing is present. On this work, Creed comments that:

I like running. I like seeing people run and I like running myself … running is the opposite of being still. If you think about death as being completely still and movement as a sign of life, then the fastest movement possible is the biggest sign of life. So then running fast is like the exact opposite of death: it's an example of aliveness.

(Creed 2008)

Work No. 850 exhibits the paradox and desirability of 'presence' – as 'aliveness,' as the ephemeral act and so that which continually absents itself. In the event, the work flickers between presence and absence, resting on the rhythmic pause between runners in order to amplify and articulate the calculated intrusion and shock of the runner as an inappropriate performer within the gallery. In this context, too, the further dissemination of *Work No. 850* in video and photographic documentation complicates its assertion of the presence. Hugo Glendinning's image of Creed's work at once departs from its 'liveness,' yet participates in this work's energy and will to 'presence,' catching the run in a frame and moment unavailable to the gallery visitor. Indeed, in Creed's work neither the act nor the image can 'claim' the phenomena 'presence,' which is shaped palimpsestually in repetition, and so in absence; in the anticipation of the act, in its memory, and so also in its absence from the record and image of the 'live'. The experiential and ideological implications for the visitor of such stagings and re-staging of 'presence' in the museum is a topic of Amelia Jones' contribution to this volume, which engages with Marina Abramović's 2010 work *The Artist Is Present*, a new elaboration of her landmark durational work with Ulay, *Nightsea Crossing* (1985–89) and which rested on Abramović's continuous attendance in the work each day at MoMA New York over a four month period. This act and re-staging, which is related to Abramović's earlier *Seven Easy Pieces* (2005), in which she re-performed iconic and ephemeral performance art works by Vito Acconci, Joseph Beuys, Valie Export, Gina Pane and others at the Guggenheim Museum, New York, offer performances that play with the return or persistence of earlier acts, events and repetitions, as well as the economy of images and documentations by which they are known, and which become part of the fabric and claim to their 'being present' 'now'.

Figure 1.2 Marina Abramović, *The Artist Is Present* (2010).
Courtesy of Marina Abramović Archives. Photo: Marco Anelli.

This focus on the staging and modulation of presence in performance is in marked contrast to the emphasis of overtly postmodern critical narratives directed toward media-based theatrical performance in the late 1980s and 1990s, where presence was configured in relation to the deconstructive turn in critical practice and so as a locus of authority operating in elisions of social, cultural and historical contingencies to be challenged and displaced (Auslander 1994). Indeed, Phillip Auslander has identified a valorization of 'presence' as that which 'performance' rejected in favour of its deconstruction in the historical move from modern to postmodern, and which he reiterates explicitly in *From Acting to Performance: Essays in Modernism and Postmodernism* (1998). It is a skepticism toward presence also reflected in Peggy Phelan's location of the ontology of performance in its 'disappearance' and so in an eventhood and ephemerality that evades reproduction (Phelan 1993: 146–66). Yet in this very emphasis on processes of disappearance Phelan's celebrated formulation also reflects the processual nature of both performance and presence, where the experience of theatre becomes defined in the falling away of performance from its material traces, its remainder, the documentary image, and memory itself. Where Auslander thus identifies the mediatized theatre and performance of the 1980s and early 1990s with an overturning of the 1960s and 1970s valorization of the 'live' body in performance, more recent media art, theatre and performance has re-focused on processual understandings and practices of presence, in assertions, explorations and simulations of the experiences of presence.

Correspondingly, more recent critical engagements with the performance, experience and trace of presence in theatre, performance and media-based and visual art have also marked a resurgence of interest in the return, persistence or the production of experiences of presence. It is in turn signalled in the influence of Rebecca Schneider's implicit retort to Phelan that 'Performance Remains' (Schneider 2001a), as well as the function of documentation with regard to the ephemerality and persistence of performance (Auslander 2006; Kaye 2006). Similarly, the 'value' and transformative effect of 'live' theatrical and performed presence has been restaged in Erika Fischer-Lichte's *The Transformational Power of Performance* (Fischer-Lichte 2008). Such perspectives are also elaborated in a range of other monographs exploring *Presence in Play* (Power 2008), which re-examines the theatrical literature on presence, *Stage Presence* (Goodall 2008), and Joseph Roach's examination of charisma in *It* (Roach 2007). It is this new engagement with presence in theatre theory and practice, too, which *Archaeologies of Presence* works to reflect and capture, and to bring to this debate the processual character of presence, both in performance and its critical recovery.

In this re-focusing on presence in theatre theory and practice, questions over the tense of presence – and of the temporal ground, or flow, in which presence occurs have also come further to the fore. Indeed, throughout this volume, 'the present' is approached as always already subject to difference from itself, as the subject's occupation of the 'here and now' is imbricated with phenomena of memory and anticipation. This complicating of the present tense and the present moment of experience is consonant with the broadly post-structuralist perspective which underpinned the approach to presence within performance theory in the 1980s and 1990s, and in which 'presence' was approached firstly as an ideological and performative claim rather than a state, quality or experience. Yet the performance theory and practice encompassed

here tends to emphasize ways in which 'presence effects' or
'performer-presence' may gain ground in the performance of the
present moment, or in the very 'multipleness' this understanding of
'the present' implies. This tendency is also reflected in the broader
archaeological turn in contemporary performance practice evident
in the growing ubiquity of site-specific and site-sensitive theatre
and performance which invariably produce experiences of
'presence' by addressing the absences of place (Kaye 2000; Pearson
2010). It is an affinity between performance and archaeology also
directly evidenced in new strategies for documentation which have
increasingly come to emphasize the reader or viewer's relationship
with that which remains over the reconstruction of past events or
the transparency of one medium, context and time to another
(Auslander 2006).

This address to 'presence' through an engagement with
'multipleness' of time, place and performance is consonant also
with radical earlier avant-garde practice, which frequently sought
to interrogate and shape experiences of presence in the relationship
between differing representational schemes and the ostensibly
'real' circumstances of their performance. Such theatre frequently
approached the performance of presence through structures that
were explicitly multiple, aligning the performance of presence with
the articulation and crossing of thresholds and the doubling of the
fictive with the real. Thus, Richard Schechner, in recalling his
work with The Performance Group from 1967, remarks that:

> [a] performance can run according to several schemes at once.
> It can tell a narrative, but part of that narrative can be game-
> bound. So you can use game structure some of the time or in
> part of the space, and narrative structure at other times and in
> other parts of the space [...] *The Tooth of Crime* dealt with
> narrative structure, but also with performance in everyday
> life. That's what Spalding [Gray] meant, that some of his 'real
> self' was engaged directly, not used as in character-actor
> training as a way to invest the character, but side by side with
> the character.
>
> (Schechner in Kaye 1996: 165)

In one of The Performance Group's most celebrated performances,
Dionysus in 69 (1970), the principal performers thus negotiated
relationships between the canonical text, their own text and

improvised activity and choices, performing across differentiated, representational schemes (Schechner 1970). While the question of the revelation of the 'real self' of the performer may now be read as another layer of 'fiction' – or performance – it is nevertheless an effect of 'the real' orchestrated in steps between and across performative schemes – in moves from the theatrical to the 'social,' from the construction of the public to the 'private' act. Schechner's emphasis here, and elsewhere in relation to presence (Schechner 1988: 35–67), falls on the traversal of the 'fictional' toward the theatrical, social, and personal circumstances in which the act of performance and spectatorship occur, and so in a perceived excess or implication that the theatrical sign cannot easily contain.

Analogous strategies for the performance of presence are evident in both avant-garde and postmodern performance strategies. Thus, in Robert Wilson's early work, and in particular *Deafman Glance* (1970), the extreme slow motion executed by performers such as Sheryl Sutton served, Stefan Brecht recounts, to make 'our experience [...] pervasively dual: we are watching images and performers creating images' (Brecht 1982: 115) to create a heightened perception of performer presence simultaneously *in* and *in excess* of the image. Indeed, the modulation of perceptions and experiences of presence by operating across or between representational schemes is evident in a wide range of conventionally postmodern performance-related works. The Wooster Group's recent multi-media performance can be read as amplifying the performance of presence in conjugations of the live and mediated performance and a concomitant 'unfixing of the performer's place' (Kaye 2007a: 181) in a multiplying of media. For the Italian performance company, Societas Raffaello Sanzio, the use of animals onstage has served in part to articulate a presence that is disruptive of the representational apparatus of the theatre, such that the experience of 'being before' the performers is amplified and troubled (Giannachi and Kaye 2002: 150–64).

In these various strategies, phenomena of presence are advanced in the articulation of the performer's presence across ostensibly differing and differentiated schemes – or more recently, across differing media or representational frameworks. Such descriptions and effects of presence are also echoed in aspects of phenomenology, which support the mechanisms for the performance of presence outlined here. Thus, Martin Heidegger arrives at a description of 'being' and 'being present' inflected through notions of emergence and relation, and in which 'presence' to and of the other is articulated as process: as an act of persistence. He proposes that:

> [t]he word 'being' now no longer means what something is. We hear 'being' as a verb, as in 'being present' and 'being absent.' 'To be' means to perdure and persist. But this says more than just 'last and abide.' 'It is in being' means 'it persists in its presence,' and in its persistence concerns and moves us.
>
> (Heidegger 1971: 95)

Here, 'presence' is implicitly configured as *in movement*, as that which perceptibly exceeds the object and is more fittingly associated with dynamic and changing perceptions, and so the structures of consciousness. In 'The Nature of Language' (1959), Heidegger captures this relationship and movement of the self to the other in the concept of 'neighboring nearness,' which serves to describe the experience of investment, of 'dwelling in nearness' (Heidegger 1971: 93) to 'the other'. It is an act and experience that defines the co-performance of self and other, identity and presence. Heidegger notes that:

> Neighborhood, then, is a relation resulting from the fact that the one settles face-to-face with the other. Accordingly, the phrase of the neighborhood of poetry and thinking means that the two dwell face-to-face with each other, that the one has settled facing the other, has drawn into the other's nearness.
>
> (Heidegger 1971: 82)

It is a concept too that Heidegger derives from the relationship of language to poetry, and thereby reaches beyond the expression, limits and inter-relationship of identities and towards form, medium and practice. Here, if 'presence,' that which persists – and so is produced in movement and emergence – may be effected in the 'neighboring nearness' of poetry to language, so it may occur in the traversal of the live to the mediated, of the simulated to the real, each of which 'settles face-to-face with the other'. This notion of persistence also describes the processual characteristic of 'presence': that presence occurs as persistence between 'self' and 'other,' and so in a traversal of difference. In this context, division, separation, and differentiation form one condition for the performance and reception of phenomena of presence, which are provoked and shaped in acts of relation, in the performance of the network, in ecologies of differences. Presence, here, then, is not a function of unity and synthesis; not the untroubled occupation of place, or a definitive *being here* or *being there*; but is performed in the persistence of 'being' across division and differentiation.

The structure of *Archaeologies of Presence* reflects this emphasis on the processual and temporal. Thus this volume unfolds implicitly through steps into and out of conditions and terms of presence and performance. In turn, these steps align to terms fundamental to the theatrical event: to *being here*, to the performer's, or 'performing' viewer's, negotiation of the tenses of place and time; to *being before*, to the performer's subjection to the gaze, to the activity of witnessing, and to the reading of the body's signs of performance; and to ephemerality, to a presence encountered in the *traces* of performance. In each of these contexts, presence is approached as provoked and shaped within an ecology of relationships; in the realization of an environment; in the layered experience of temporality, 'presentness' or the present moment; in the tensions and investments implied by being seen; and in the persistence of performance through its representation and archival remains.

Within this framework, *Archaeologies of Presence* brings together essays that approach the object of performance and the processual nature of presence in radically differing ways and from different disciplinary perspectives, referencing performance theory, semiotics and philosophy, visual art, reception theory, and inter-cultural practice as well as new media practice and theory. Reflecting on this book's archaeological turn toward performance, each of its three sections is prefaced with a brief contextualizing essay that sets out the core issues and debate around which contributions cluster. In turn, each of these three sections begins with an essay emphasizing the theatrical, cultural, philosophical or environmental frameworks in which practices of presence are produced and received and is followed by detailed examinations of performance or performative practice. In their different perspectives and engagements with principle and practice, these essays nevertheless converge on the analysis of presence as an ephemeral, emergent phenomenon provoked and shaped in dynamic networks of action, response, perception and witnessing. It is here, too, that the specificity of this book's interrogation of performances of presence is defined, and in which the detailed narrative of this volume unfolds.

Section one, 'Being Here,' then, approaches the conditions – the networks, layers and ecologies – that form the various nexus of relations in which experiences of presence may be enacted. Beginning with questions of place, Josette Féral sets out taxonomies of 'presence effects,' while Gabriella Giannachi defines the performance of presence as and in environment. Both Féral and Giannachi write against the background of discourses of presence in virtual reality, and specifically the capacity of immersive virtual reality environments and contemporary media to simulate experiences of place and provoke the 'effect' of the 'present' body in its absence.

Setting out a taxonomy of presence and 'presence' and 'reality' 'effects,' Féral goes on to examine in detail experiences of presence in the work of Janet Cardiff. In Cardiff's sound works created, variously, for immersive installations and peripatetic walks through found sites, Féral attributes experiences of presence to the blurring of 'the fictitious and the real'. It is an analysis that draws Féral implicitly toward a reading of the experience of presence in relation to the functioning of virtual reality and immersive media. Arguing that the 'presence effects' in Cardiff's work operates in 'a carnal coefficient,' expressed in the sensation of the real body's place in this 'fictional' sound world. In the viewer's subsequent engagement with the resulting 'friction point between the self and the world,' the experience of Cardiff's practice might best be captured in Féral's account of '[p]resence as an intermittent state,' in which it is 'alternating moments of presence and absence that create the state of presence'. It is an analysis and performance of presence that emphasizes the spectator's mobility of position, of the importance of 'rupture' and 'absence,' even of 'frustration,' to the evocation and modulation of phenomena of presence.

In contrast to Féral, Giannachi explores the experience of 'environmental presence' in ecologies of inter-linked effects and qualities of presence, with reference to environmental and ecological art practices. Citing presence research in computer science, Giannachi approaches 'presence' in 'real' environments, whilst 'not synonymous,' as nevertheless entailing 'a shift in perspective over the same territory'. Where Féral identifies Cardiff's provocation of alternating and shifting positions as a key to effect of presence within her sound environments, Giannachi identifies 'environmental presence' as 'the continuous unfolding of the subject into what is other to it,' while locating 'the environment' as that which occurs or is experienced as in excess or persistently 'other' to this process. It follows, Giannachi concludes, that 'presence' is 'an ecological process that marks a moment of awareness of the exchanges between the subject and the living environment of which they are a part'. As phenomena, 'presence,' here, arises in the individual's sense of doubling or division in relationship to their context and place, while the perception of 'environment' at once participates in and is experienced as other to this emergent sense of one's own sense of being. It follows, Giannachi notes, that 'it is through the operation of presence that environments are generated,' and thus, as phenomena, 'environments are always *in fieri*, pending, changing, evolving'. It is a process and dynamic that Giannachi goes on to elaborate through analyses of environmental work by John Cage, Allan Kaprow, Robert Smithson, Gilberto Zorio, and others, while ranging across music, performance, sculpture and new media.

Where Féral and Giannachi focus on the complexities and layers of place or site, Rebecca Schneider and Jon Erickson elaborate loci for presence in relation to temporality, and in doing so return implicitly to the question of the archaeological as a fulcrum between past and present. Schneider, in 'Performance Remains Again,' further elaborates her signal essay of 2001 (Schneider 2001a), which challenges and qualifies Peggy Phelan's influential claims over the ontology of performance. Emphasizing the processual nature of disappearance, and resisting the construction of performance as the 'vanished' object or as 'of' disappearance, Schneider thus emphasizes the multiple and dispersed encounters with the signs of disappearance and preservation, between the 'absence' of the live performance and valorization in contemporary 'archive culture' of the 'presence' of the document. Here Schneider observes the remains in which the 'performance' is constituted, persists and may be performed again. Challenging the binary between absence and presence in which the complexity of Phelan's position is sometimes elided, Schneider considers the archive as the locus of the presence of performance's remainder and, in this, the performance of presence itself.

In the context of Schneider's argument, the link between the ontology of performance and its 'disappearance' might be better understood as processual; as the ebb and flow between absence and presence analogous to Féral's 'alternating moments of presence and absence.' Crucially, here, 'performance' is not a stable state or position, nor does the act of performance succumb to a simple state of 'being present' or being 'in absence': presence is an emergent and processual phenomena, while the act of performance is never simply in the present moment. Thus Schneider's interrogation of performance's relationship to absence or presence arrives at a position where 'performance challenges loss,' for: 'performance becomes itself through messy and eruptive re-appearance. It challenges, *via* the performative trace, any neat antinomy between appearance and disappearance, or presence and absence through the basic repetitions that mark performance as indiscreet, non-original, relentlessly citational, and remaining'.

Performance, it follows, presents itself perpetually in acts of construction and reconstruction. Unable to fall back on an essential absence, as the 'vanished' antithesis of what remains, the space, time and tense of performance becomes more complex, subject to – and inseparable from – the relationship(s) we make with it. In memory, too, just as in its 'material' or archival presence persists, performance has not 'disappeared,' but remains, as Schneider suggests, 'differently,' within a play of acts, signs, views and understandings to which performance was always already subject.

Where the material remainder invites reflection on the persistence of presence, Jon Erickson pays attention to the performance of temporality itself as a locus for experiences of presence. Here, Erickson shares Schneider's implicit sense that the time of performance is encountered in a flow of tenses, *as* past, present and future; or in memory, attention and expectation. Indeed, Erickson's account of the performance of time draws on phenomenological approaches to presence, reflecting Husserl's concepts of 'retention' and 'protention' (Husserl 1964), in which the 'now' point of experience is defined as a temporal flow invested in that which belongs to the past and future. It follows that performance, and the realisation of presence in the act of performance, is formed in a layering of the times and tenses operating in or as the present. Erickson thus proposes that 'time is actually produced in the theatre for the spectators by the performance' and that 'the experience of time arises out of the creation of instances of tension and release, at multiple levels, which produces rhythms that either carry along the spectator, or produces resistances'. This analysis of the multiple times and tenses of performance is in accord with analyses of time in music. Thus, Jonathon Kramer argues in *The Time of Music*, where music should be understood as 'a series of events, events that not only contain time, but also shape it' (Kramer 1988: 5), so, he proposes, the experience of music arises in a phenomenological distinction 'between the time a piece *takes* and the time which a piece *presents* or *evokes*' (Kramer 1988: 7, original emphasis). In this regard, Kramer concludes, the time-structure characteristic of all music is defined by:

> at least two temporal continua, determined by order of succession and by conventionalized meanings of gestures. This duality makes musical time quite special: The past-present-future qualities of events are determined by their gestural shapes as well as their placement within the absolute-time succession of a performance.
>
> (Kramer 1988: 161)

Where performance, as Erickson argues, 'actually *produces* time,' and where this production of time is itself subject to 'the time differential between performer and audience,' then phenomena of presence in performance cannot simply be resolved into the occupation of a 'now,' of a 'liveness' that uniquely confronts the viewer with the occupation of the 'present'. Instead, acts of performance engage in constructing and in constructed ecologies of time; in the production, layering and negotiation of inter-connected temporal experiences, which might be captured as acts of 'presencing' – as acts that modulate and engage with experiences of 'being (in the) present' in the performance of temporal rhythms that engage with and shape the experience of memory, attention and expectation. Indeed, elsewhere, Erickson has articulated the effect of 'performer-presence' as arising precisely in the disjunction of these tenses and experiences, arguing in *The Fate of the Object* (1998) that:

> 'Presence' in the theater is physicality in the present that at the same time is grounded in a form of absence. It is something that has unfolded, is read against what has been seen, and presently observed in expectation as to what will be seen. It means that the performer is presenting herself to the audience, but at the same time holding something back, creating expectation [...]. In other words, not only does the notion of presence in performance imply an absence, but that absence itself is the possibility of future movement; so paradoxically,

presence is based not only in the present, but in our expectation of the future.

(Erickson 1998: 62)

It follows that the articulation of 'presence' in performance is an enactment of this layering, while the capacity to 'be present' *in* the act is itself subject to the ecology of times and tenses in which the experience of the 'present moment' is constituted; that is, enacted, experienced and read.

Where these interrogations of 'Being Here' articulate the complexities of the 'present tense' performance of place and time, the second part of this volume, 'Being Before,' explores the divisions within the theatrical relationship itself as productive of experiences of presence. These essays focus on the negotiation of spectator and audience gaze in the theatrical construction of presence; on the body-mind as an instrument and catalyst of experiences of presence; on presence as the fulcrum of the relationship between watcher and watched; on the commodification of performance and the construction of charisma, and 'stage presence'; as well as the articulation of presence in the exposure of mechanisms of representation and illusion in theatre, performance and media.

Here, then, Erika Fischer-Lichte's opening essay defines a weak, strong and radical concept presence. In doing so, however, Fischer-Lichte divides the performing body into phenomenal and semiotic aspects. Analyzing the dialectic in which these dimensions of the performing body define each other, Fischer-Lichte goes on to account for the effects of a presence performed in an emphasis on the quality of the phenomenal body, in its *becoming* and on the act of embodiment, even as 'the body is ultimately elusive'. In contrast, the 'radical concept of presence' – PRESENCE – sees a merging of the phenomenal and semiotic body, as 'the mind is embodied and the body is "en-minded" '. In turn, this assertion of the body 'as embodied mind' confronts the spectator's own bodily presence and act, such that 'the spectator experiences the performer and himself as embodied mind in a constant process of becoming'. Here, evidently, in achieving this act of 'radical presence,' Fischer-Lichte presents a vision of the persistence of the actor's presence (and embodied being) across this dialectical relationship between the phenomenal and the semiotic, a traversal to which, she concludes, 'spectators might become addicted' in its revelation of 'human beings as embodied minds'.

Referring directly to Fischer-Lichte's elaboration of presence, Phillip Zarrilli 'interrogates "presence" from the performer's perspective inside a performance event' – *Told by the Wind*, which Zarrilli co-created for première in 2010. Identifying 'presence' as an emergent possibility, a 'perception shared between the performer(s), the performance score and its dramaturgy, and the audience,' Zarrilli emphasizes the processual effect of presence, where it '*should* only exist for the actor *as a question*' (original emphasis). Here, Zarrilli explicitly directs the question of presence from the act, or intention, of the performer, and toward the ecology of acts and perceptions *in performance* into which his or her awareness of its 'emergent possibility' is displaced. Locating this proposition within the principal literatures on a theatrical presence, Zarrilli focuses on the phenomenological co-presence of audience and performers, to provide an anatomy of the practice of presence, where this possibility is realized in the actor's commitment to detail, to process and technique, and, simultaneously, to uncertainty '*in the moment of each enactment*'.

Where Zarrilli focuses on the act and attitude in performance, Simon Jones extends this focus toward the question of the 'preservation' of the aesthetic construction and so identity and presence of the artwork, '*within* the co-presence of that work and its participants'. Here, Jones questions the growing emphasis on interactivity in art and performance, and its link to experiences of presence, with reference, among others, to Claire Bishop's critique of Nicholas Bourriaud's 'relational aesthetics' and the concomitant dissolution of aesthetic construct into participatory acts and 'staged personal experiences' (Bishop 2004: 52). Drawing on the phenomenology of Emmanuel Levinas, Martin Heidegger and Maurice Merleau-Ponty, Jones reflects on his collaborations through the performance company Bodies in Flight, to examine and advance performance strategies that while challenging conventional audience/performer relationships, work to 're-sensitize each individual audience–spectator to their own embodied experience of the performance-event' and so to experiences of presence *within* their occupation of the performance work. To this end, Jones emphasizes the phenomenological encounter with difference, whereby, in the immediacy of being 'face-to-face' within the work, or within an interaction with another, experiences of presence are provoked and shaped in a sense of otherness or separation from oneself. Here, after Levinas, Jones argues that:

In inter-'acting,' one is fully occupied in this to-and-fro of exchanging: in effect, one acts or plays the part of being inbetween – 'inter'. One is not dwelling in the space-time of the event as oneself, but explicitly as *not*-oneself, as *an-other* (any-other) who only appears to the extent that their qualities can be interactive, that is, expressed as turns taken in the exchange, moves made explicitly in order to sustain that exchange, the commun(e)-icating … .

The engagement with presence, by contrast, is provoked in performance's complexity rather than this mechanism toward consensus, and so, after Levinas, in the performance of 'out-standing standing-within': in acts that implicate the self *in* the other, and in which the self is defined 'face-to-face' with the other. With regard to presence, it is also precisely this relationship and dynamic of otherness that performance complicates. Thus performance, Jones notes, 'puts an individual before another before a host of others' which, he argues, opens the potential of actualizing Levinas' proposition that '*The individual and the personal are necessary for Infinity to be able to be produced as infinite*' (Levinas 1969: 218, original emphasis). The 'participatory aesthetics' of performance, Jones concludes, 'must be by way of and about presence,' while presence, by implication, is a function of these ecologies of implication and difference: of the recognition of the other in the self, of the experience of difference *from* oneself.

Where, by implication, Jones' reads the divisions implicit in the act of performance before and toward others as a dynamic and mechanism by which a 'presencing' of the self may occur, Nicholas Ridout considers the presence of the 'mis-spectator,' setting out a questioning of the study of the 'presence' of the theatrical audience. In doing so, Ridout calls on Jacques Ranciere's critique of consensus – of 'the distribution of the sensible' – with regard to the imagined spectator, whose position and subjectivity this consensus, in its implicit assumption of audience expertise and conformity, serves to centre, in its effort to answer the question of what the performance 'is'. In contrast, Ridout takes Proust's portrait of Marcel as 'mis-spectator' in *Remembrance of Things Past, Volume One* to demonstrate a redistribution of the position and sensibility of the audience, with a view to interrupting 'the machinery of the theatre'. Proposing that, 'there is nothing whatsoever wrong with the mis-spectator,' such that the performance formed in his or her view, is continually subject to radical and unpredictable re-composition and to conflicting and unstable presences. Thus, the mis-spectator's view unpacks the performance of presence in uncertain apprehensions of the rules and operations of the theatrical apparatus. Here, then, where 'the thousand strong audience looks on and listens in silence' as '[t]wo angry men appear on stage, arguing,' for the mis-spectator 'two "insolent fellows" invade the stage and appropriate the space and attention of the public'. Ridout's analysis proceeds to unpack, through the mis-spectator's eyes, the various presences in performance: 'the presence of the star presence'; the 'barely present' star; the 'confusion over who is real and who just has someone else's face and voice'. Made aware of the gaps and modes of presence, becoming witness to their shifts and changes according to his assumptions, or changing understandings, the mis-spectator's own position is correspondingly rendered unstable. In these dynamics, 'presence' becomes a radical variable in performance, and, regardless of the suppositions of the performer, is modulated by the uncertainties of spectating itself: the mis-spectator, then, is witness to and stands in for the lack of any single subjectivity or position by the 'audience'. In these operations, Ridout departs from the security of the audience's perception or collusion in the actor's performance of presence, while opening a view of the spectator to the very uncertainties and variable phenomena the performance theorist may wish to stabalize: thus, here, the mis-spectator joins the economy of views, perceptions and mis-perceptions in which presence is emergent.

Finally, in this section, Tim Etchells of the UK-based media and performance company Forced Entertainment discusses with Gabriella Giannachi and Nick Kaye the play of these very uncertainties in the work of Forced Entertainment and the company's sustained address to performer-presence. For Etchells, this begins in a paring down of performance to a looking back, or a return of the view of the audience, which seeks to foreground, examine and operate in the uncertainties implied in Jones' and Ridout's analysis of the theatrical relation. Etchells suggests that for Forced Entertainment: 'a definition of theatre – of performance – we often invoke – that as performers we are people at one end of a room, who are paid to do something for a bunch of other people in the same room'. In turn, Etchells identifies a base line of performance – and performer-presence – from which the company's work frequently emanates, 'simplicity' whereby 'a lot of the live work that we have done – a sort of peeling away of things to the point where we are often stood in a line at the front looking back at the audience – and very much measuring this body on the stage and this bunch of people watching; measuring the distance between the two'. It is from this essential uncertainty, in the relation of witnessed and witnessing, and in the promise or potential of the act that, for Etchells, the performance of presence begins. Etchells concludes:

> Being present is always a kind of construction. Perhaps we could think of presence as something that happens when one attempts to do something, and whilst attempting to do that thing you become visible; visible in not quite succeeding in doing it, visible through the cracks or the gaps.

The final cluster of essays in this volume returns to overtly archaeological readings of the performance of presence in analyses of the trace, the recollection, record, or document. Here the question of presence is approached as a fulcrum of relationships between present and past: as a means of interrogating the persistence of ephemeral and performative acts in memory, trace and remains; and as a conceptual framework for understanding performance and its documentation. Yet these approaches to the document are informed, also, by the complexities and uncertainties of the performance processes in which 'presence' is both emergent and uncertain.

Fittingly, this section begins in Amelia Jones' revisiting – and reintroduction, in 2010 – of her 1996 essay 'Presence *in Absentia*,' which re-examines her earlier proposition that in addressing critically performances she did not attend 'the problems raised by my absence (my not having been there) are largely logistical rather than ethical or hermeneutic'. Here, Jones presents a critical point, which in her re-contextualisation in 2010 she considers in relation to Marina Abramović's retrospective exhibition at MoMA New York, January to April 2010, *The Artist Is Present*; that 'documentation,' far from establishing an absolute difference from the embodied act of performance, provides one point within an economy or mutual exchange and interdependence between act and artefact within which the event, remainder and identity of performance is configured. Thus, Jones proposes in her original essay, '[t]he body art event needs the photograph to confirm its having happened: the photograph needs the body art event as an ontological 'anchor' of its indexicality'. It is a proposition that flows from Jones' core assertion, that:

> there is no possibility of an unmediated relationship to any kind of cultural product, including body art. Although I am respectful of the specificity of knowledges gained from participating in a live performance situation, I will argue here that this specificity should not be privileged over the specificity of knowledges that develop in relation to the documentary traces of such an event.

Jones' approach to documentation complicates the question of presence further. Locating the photographic image within 'reciprocity' between the act and its recollection and representation, Jones elides the opposition between the fullness of the 'presence' of the performed act, and its 'elision' in the image. Thus, in her re-framing of this essay, Jones states unequivocally that 'performance, as a time-based act, points to the impossibility of ever fully knowing embodied experience, and thus of ever fully encompassing past events in the present'. It is a position in accord, also, with the archaeological perspectives and discussion of ephemerality subsequently offered by Lynn Hershman Leeson and Michael Shanks in the exploration of the re-animation of Hershman's archive. Indeed, if the 'embodied act' is constructed in reciprocal relationships between performance and image, in differentiations between 'present' and future spectators or readers, then documentation 'itself' becomes part of the dynamic in which 'presence' is performed. Such a position calls into question the possibility of ever 'fully encompassing' the present embodied act, which, it follows, operates in and out of the time of its performance and reception: the 'embodied act' is never complete, 'self-present' or 'fully present' or manifest. Indeed, it is constructed in reciprocities: in processes of exchange and difference over time. It is a view and construction of embodied 'presence' that complicates not only documentation, but the museological memory, recovery and, increasingly, re-performance of 'past' works and acts.

Focusing on Lynn Hershman Leeson's 1972 site-specific and durational work, *Dante Hotel*, staged firstly within the real Hotel Dante in North Beach, San Francisco, then re-animated in Second Life as *Life Squared* in a collaboration with the Presence Project and Stanford Humanities in 2006, Michael Shanks and Lynn Hershman extend this discussion of this reworking of 'what remains'. Centred on the question of 'how to reanimate the archive' (Shanks), this debate considers not only the 'forensic sensibility' (Shanks) enacted in archaeological turns in thinking that, rather than 'discover the past,' 'work on what remains [...] to bring it forward, first into the present, through our interpretation of it'. It is a paradigm, too, that not only counters the assumption that archaeology 'discovers the past' (Shanks) but that implicitly questions the assumption of 'the present' and so the experience of 'presence' as singular, available and therefore to be recovered or reconstructed. It is a sensibility resonant also in Hershman's practice, exemplified in the temporal layers and play of memory and interpretation in the re-animation of the documentary traces of *Dante Hotel*. Thus, where, in this conversation, Shanks questions the capacity of any documentation – or remembering – to access an event uninflected by interpretation and selection – and so of 'the politics of presence. What is made present and what is kept absent and invisible,' Hershman questions the self-identity of the event and the onlooker. Noting that, in reproduction or simulation, '[t]he closer you get to what you think something is, the more evident it becomes that it's also an illusion,' Hershman turns this thinking toward that of the agent or subject, whose identity and unity of experience, even if only in a specific time, forms a ground of a 'sense of being there'. In a digital world, of fluid identities, or in the multiple performance of identities, Hershman states:

[n]ow we're spawning a different kind of mutation, because we're able to reconceive ourselves virally and instantly put that morphed and evolving regeneration into the world specifically so that it can be adapted and changed. So, where does that mutation leave us? Is our sense of presence, and who we are, an appendage to how we are perceived?

Here, where the 'inside' and 'outside' of the subject seems indefinite, where experience of the 'past' is performed and realized only in a present temporal flow, then the difference between identities and lives forms the ecology in which we make and perform our own presence: where the archaeological traces of others become, for Hershman, 'the relics of ourselves'.

Turning such perspectives toward performance installation and 'performed photography,' Nick Kaye then considers the capacity of performance and the image to provoke experiences of presence through engagements with the interval or delay, and in anticipation and expectation. Focusing on problematizing of time in the photographic image's use of delay and interval in relation to performance documentation, Kaye draws attention to performance artist Chris Burden's capture of processual and performative presence, analyzing the performance frame that is operational in marking the viewer's entry into a 'situation' set up by the artist, the artist's use of anticipation and delay in establishing presence, and the potential co-location, co-presence, of viewer and artist. Drawing from Maurice Blanchot, Kaye then shows how Burden's *White Light/White Heat* (1975) offers the visitor 'an encounter defined in displacements of the image in favour of the viewer's agency and emergent presence that anticipates and so precedes the spectacle of "performance",' suggesting that where presence is processual, occurring over time, presence is generated by these mechanisms of refusal and delay. In turn, Kaye outlines analogous photographic strategies that amplify a sense of the recovery and representation of 'presence,' where the photograph, or image, 'provokes experiences of presence in the very lack in which it obtains its relationship to its object'. Discussing images by Cindy Sherman, Doug Hall, as well as Hugo Glendinning and Tim Etchells' *Empty Stages* (2003–), he concludes that it is in these images' refusal to bring performance to appearance that the persistence of presence is felt and in which the potential of the performance event is most powerfully recalled and reproduced.

Finally, Mike Pearson writes '*for* performance' and '*about* performance' in 'Neither Here Nor There...' in a critical recollection and documentation of his 2008 performance, *something happening, something happening nearby* in which he remembers his mother's passing: 'On sitting with the dying'; 'On sitting with the dead'. The last in a series of works, begun in 1992 with *From Memory*, 'that have addressed and involved interpenetrating themes of dwelling, place, memory and landscape,' through these events Pearson has worked to situate himself, as 'agent' and 'subject', at distance from himself, as 'performer'. In this gap and dialogue, Pearson peforms toward his own 'presence,' filtering and creating, in his present act, the interpretation of 'what remains' – in relation to '*his*' memory, past emotion and places. The outcome is a series of displacements in the act of performance, whereby Pearson works toward being neither here nor there. It is an act evoking the constellation of tenses, of the present reworking of memories and constructions of lost subjectivities. Here presence is evoked in speculations and connections over self and other; where the performance of that which is lost doubles and brings forward the presence of the performer, enacting an archaeological turn, embodying an animation and interpretation of the trace, relic and sign, 'to bring it forward, first into the present, through our interpretation of it' (Shanks), thereby to enact the presence of that which cannot be recovered.

It is finally this notion of a processual, enacted presence around which the essays in this volume cluster. Presence, here, is a phenomenon always in the process of being enacted and remembered, an experience never resolved but always a persistent, relational *effect*. Phenomena of presence thus occur in these acts of investment of one time, place and position in another – and so in temporary, performed acts of reciprocity. It is in this figure and process of reciprocity, too, that the essays here find common ground, in their various moves toward a definition of the performance – and recovery – of presence.

Works cited

Auslander, P. (1994) *Presence and Resistance: Postmodernism and Cultural Politics in Contemporary American Performance*, Ann Arbor MI: University of Michigan Press.
——(1998) *From Acting to Performance: Essays in Modernism and Postmodernism*, London: Routledge.
——(2006) 'The Performativity of Performance Documentation', *PAJ: A Journal of Performance and Art*, 28:3, 1–10.
Bishop, C. (2004) 'Antagonism and Relational Aesthetics', *October*, 110, 51–79.
Brecht, S. (1982) *The Theatre of Visions: Robert Wilson*, London: Methuen.
Creed, Martin (2008) 'Tate Britain Duveens Commission 2008: *Work No. 850*' (Press Release). Online. Available: www.tate.org.uk/about/pressoffice/pressreleases/2008/15818.htm (accessed 22 July 2011).
Erickson, J. (1998) *The Fate of the Object: From Modern Object to Postmodern Sign in Performance, Art, Poetry*, Ann Arbor MI: The University of Michigan Press.
Fischer-Lichte, E. (2008) *The Transformative Power of Performance: A New Aesthetics*, translated by S. I. Jain, London: Routledge.

Giannachi, G. and Kaye, N. (2002) *Staging the Post-Avant-Garde: Italian Experimental Performance After 1970*, Oxford: Peter Lang.

Goodall, J. (2008) *Stage Presence: The Actor as Mesmerist*, London: Routlege.

Heathfield, A. (2004) *Live: Art and Performance*, London: Tate Publishing.

Heidegger, M. (1971) *On The Way to Language*, New York: Harper and Row.

Husserl, E. (1964) *The Phenomenology of the Consciousness of Internal Time*, Bloomington IN: Indiana University Press.

Kaye, N. (1994) *Postmodernism and Performance*, Basingstoke: Palgrave MacMillan.

——(1996) *Art into Theatre: Performance Interviews and Documents*, London: Routledge.

——(2000) *Site-Specific Art: Performance, Place and Documentation*, London: Routledge.

——(2006) 'Displaced Events: Photographic Memory and Performance Art' in A. Kuhn and K.E. McAllister (eds) *Locating Memory: Photographic Acts*, Oxford: Berghahn Books, 173–200.

——(2007) 'The Builders Association and dbox, SUPER VISION (2005)' *Contemporary Theatre Review*, 17:4, 557–77.

——(2007a) *Multi-Media: Video – Installation – Performance*, London: Routledge.

Kramer, J.D. (1988) *The Time of Music: New Meanings, New Temporalities, New Listening Strategies*, New York: Schirmer Books.

Pearson, M. and Shanks, M. (2001) *Theatre/Archaeology*, London: Routledge.

Levinas, E. (1969) *Totality and Infinity: An Essay on Exteriority*, translated by A. Lingis, Pittsburgh PA: Duquesne University Press.

Pearson, M. (2010) *Site-Specific Performance*, Basingstoke: Palgrave MacMillan.

Phelan, P. (1993) *Unmarked: The Politics of Performance*, London: Routledge.

Power, C. (2008) *Presence in Play: A Critique of Theories of Presence*, Amsterdam: Rodopi.

Roach, J. (2007) *It*, Ann Arbor MI: University of Michigan Press.

Schechner, R. (1970) *Dionysus in 69: The Performance Group*, New York: Farrar, Strauss and Giroux, Inc.

——(1988) *Performance Theory*, revised edn, London: Routledge.

Schneider, R. (2001a) 'Performance Remains', *Performance Research* 6:2, 100–08.

Part I

Being here
Place and time

Written by researchers in theatre and performance studies engaging with phenomenology, philosophy, performance and documentation, anthropology, neuroscience and environmental studies, 'Being here' interrogates presence in its spatio-temporal constitution, addressing it *hic et nunc* in its emergence. In this section presence is seen as presentness and presencing. Temporally, it is discussed as tense, in its temporality, availability, immediatedness, both in terms of retention and protention. Spatially, it is discussed as occurrence, place, area, site, environment and ecology. Epistemologically and phenomenologically presence is discussed as effect and legacy. Presence here is seen not only a state or appearance but also a mapping tool. More specifically, 'Being here' interrogates presence 'in itself,' as liveness, as a phenomenon that is able to affect the subject in terms of their own spatio-temporal perception and impression of themselves and others in the present moment between past and future points in time. In this sense presence becomes an affective fictional and rhythmic tool that is able to generate its own legacies and that is crucial to human orientation. At the same time, in each of these contributions, the experience of the 'present tense' occupation of a place and time is revealed as layered, so at once complicating the idea of 'presence' while deflecting attention toward the individual's enactment and performance of place and time. The experience of 'Being here,' it follows, is subject to the spatial dislocations and anachronisms of any specific place or location, for the occupations of a site are always in process, always being defined by others, always subject to other histories, times and narratives that cannot be fully recovered. In these contexts, these essays come together in accounts of acts of occupation of 'real' and 'fictional' sites, of the individual's sense of the occupation of place within an ecology and environment, and within temporal structures, that explicitly defer the sense of presence toward processual acts.

Chapter 2

How to define presence effects

The work of Janet Cardiff[1]

Josette Féral

To speak about presence effects is, paradoxically, to think right away about absence, since there can be no presence (effects) unless there are bodies present. This is obvious. By 'presence effects,' one means the feeling of a body's (or an object's) presence – that these bodies or objects create the impression of really being there, even if the audience rationally knows that they are not. What constitutes this presence or presence effect? Consequently, I would like to try to disentangle the different meanings of the concept through the various disciplines: from the performing arts (theatre and dance) to the media and digital arts, including avatars.

To begin with, we must distinguish between the various epistemic fields of envisioning the concept of presence:

1

An existential field refers to *a person's 'being there'*. I, you, we are present. We must discover the characteristics of this vast concept. How can we classify and analyze this presence? What distinguishes it? Is it palpable? What does is signify to 'be there,' and what of the expressions 'be present,' or 'be in the moment,' that are frequently used by directors addressing actors?

2

This slight deviation in syntax indicates a second level of meaning, a level which touches on *the quality of my being*: a way of being present that not only affirms my presence but underlines the particular aspect that I am not only present, but that I also have presence, which is not the same thing. We have moved from the *verb 'to be'* ('to be present') to the *verb 'to have'* ('to have presence'). This analysis of the quality of presence aims to seek out that which, in the case of an actor (or a performer), can give the spectator the impression that certain actors, more than others, have presence. It is this quality of presence that researchers such as Eugenio Barba attempt to recreate in the actor (Barba 2005), and that colloquiums, such as that which resulted in the publication of the book *Crever les Planches, Brûler l'Écran. La Présence de l'Acteur* (Farcy and Prédal 2001), attempt to discern. This preoccupation has also been at the root of certain questions addressed to directors in my published series of interviews titled *Mise en Scène et Jeu de l'Acteur* (Féral 1997, 1998 and 2006).

3

A third meaning is derived from these two precedents and yet is distinct from them. It is that which touches on the *impression of presence*, or one might say, on an *'effect of presence,'* which is not the same thing (see Michel Lemieux and Victor Pilon's *Norman* or *La Tempête* and Janet Cardiff's *The Paradise Institute*), or even daydreams (see the studies at the Sha Xin Wei laboratory at Concordia which create immersive environments aimed at recreating the same type of presence that exists in daydreams ...)[2]. These are experiences that give the impression that someone is there, when in truth, no one is there[3]. In this third case, the impression of presence is due to the fact that the same sensations and perceptions that occur in the real presence of another person (or object) are invoked. To investigate this meaning is to attempt to analyze the conditions under which this effect of presence emerges, to analyze what makes it possible. What is it? How does it manifest itself? What techniques do artists use to establish it? What parameters regulate the spectators' perception of it?

The junction point of these three different manifestations of presence is that, in one case as in the others, 'presence' means the feeling that a body is present – generally a living body (often a person, but this can also be applied to objects) that the subject has the impression is really there. I will not treat here further the field of presence analysis, although this would be worth doing, since it clearly underlies presence effects. In what follows, it is not a question of analyzing a presence's quality by investigating what in a performer's bearing may convey to the audience the impression that some actors have more 'presence' than others[4]. Here, it is rather a matter of analyzing the conditions that make possible this presence effect. Therefore, as a starting point, I will assert that a presence effect is the feeling the audience has that the bodies or objects they perceive are really there within the same space and timeframe that the spectators find themselves in, when the spectators patently know that they are not there. It is a question of the perception of a physical presence that puts the subject's perceptions and their representations into play. This temporality and common space shared by the spectator and the presence being evoked (a character, an avatar, or an object) is fundamental.

Perception of presence

Of course, the question that immediately arises is that of the perception of this presence, its manifestation. Should presence therefore be affirmed and analyzed in terms of corporeal presence (the simple fact of being there)? Perception (with respect to the individual spectator)? Or rather in terms of mental state (being intellectually present, not merely physically present)?

All of this plays out between the assertive (I am there) and the qualitative (a given quality or modality of being there). The notion is both obvious and hazy, as reflections by Maurice Merleau-Ponty and others (Weissberg 1999; Noël 1988) have shown.

Physically present but intellectually absent

The first stance is to define presence in comparison with absence. Presence would be what is here, what is not absent. That is to say, present within the subject's space and time. This relation with respect to space and time is fundamental. This has to do with a physical presence, or better still, with a physical presence effect. The question of mental presence – that of bodies that are present but whose minds are wandering elsewhere – is put aside. Indeed, if physical presence is relatively easy to grasp, 'mental spaces,' as Jean-Louis Weissberg says, 'are multiple. Their topo-chronologies cannot be described. One is never where and when one believes he is. One is continually expatriating oneself [...] particularly when in a state of immobility, of rest' (Weissberg 1999: 19-20). Much could be said on this point, but this question, however fascinating, does not seem relevant to the presence effects that I wish to discuss here.

I will leave this question in abeyance, simply echoing Richard Schechner's observation that the spectator practises a 'selective inattention,' which we could, of course, describe as mental absence. Peter Sloterdijk has also written on this question, revaloring *unwakedness*[5].

Presence as an intermittent state

We often conceive of presence as the uninterrupted state of a subject or object, which the audience would apprehend as a continuum, a linear phenomenon, but it could also be defined, following Weissberg, as an intermittent state that is strongest at the moments of its apparitions and disparitions. Weissberg speaks of 'multiple suggestions of apparitions and disparitions of the infinite layers which made up the State of Being Present' (Weissberg 1999: 52). It is these alternating moments of presence and absence that create the state of presence.

In support of his approach, Weissberg offers Edmond Couchot and Michel Bret's films *La Plume* (1988) [*The Feather*] and *Le Pissenlit* (1990) [*The Dandelion*][6] as examples during which the viewer blows on the screen in order to cause the digital feather or the downy seeds of the dandelions to fly away. The presence effect comes from the apparent effect of this blowing on the flying dandelion seeds. It is in the process the films establish, in the medium made visible between the spectators' breath and the digital effect on the screen (the flight of the dandelion fluff and the feather), that the distance that separates them becomes visible through their interaction. Paradoxically, it is this division, this gulf, the make-believe, the 'as-if,' the play of the illusion, that creates presence.

Absence of presence

A third view states, on the contrary, that presence is more strongly felt when there is a rupture, a straying away or a failing of presence, an absence of presence, a '*défaut de présence*'. This point is made by Gregory Chatonsky[7] in his work. He shows that the feeling of a presence is stronger when accompanied by frustration (the invisible interlocutor in Cocteau's *La Voix Humaine* [*The Human Voice*], the interlocutors on the phone in Robert Lepage's one man shows: *Needles and Opium, The Far Side of the Moon, The Andersen Project*.

Presence at a distance and telepresence

Mention should also be made of presence at a distance, an idea developed by Weissberg according to Deleuze's concept: the 'crystal presence' (see Deleuze 1985: 92–128), and perhaps of telepresence as well (for example, Paul Sermon's *Rêve Télématique* [1992]).

Presence as representation: thought and memory

Resonance

Experimentation with a presence effect situates mankind in the midst of his own representations. Through it, the subject experiences his being in the world (to speak in phenomenological terms). His experience relies on both thought and memory. On the one hand, experience arouses a resonance within our being; on the other hand, there is a resonance of our being upon the world (so to speak). There is the object we are seeing (the object's apparition), and the idea of this object in our thought. On the one hand, the mind absorbs the real, thereby becoming sensitive to it; on the other hand, the subject locates within himself the remembered objects or beings, recognizes them, and associates them with other features, other 'mental images'.

In his book *Le lieu des signes*, Bernard Noël has attempted to describe what experiencing the presence of objects might be. He has experimented with the impression of an object's presence from the very apparition of the object to the internal of the object in one's thought. This process entails all the paradox of representing an object (as image and mental action) as well as the taking over of reality. This interaction calls upon the body (and the memory). This is how Noël describes a glass ashtray:

> It is radically whole and alien. It has no innerness. It is what it appears to be, and yet it could pass for a form without appearance. Its volume is not impervious to the space surrounding it, or at least: we can see through it. Although it is a spread out body, yet it is stealing away – to the extent that it drags the eye farther away within time wherein it dissolves. [...] Nothing organic, nothing for relationship: it is there and

nothing more. It leaves me to my own fluctuations, my own mobility, which will only cease with life.

(Noël 1998: 21)

Yet this involvement of the body is twofold: it is connected to thought which is activated by the sensory organs, but also with the field of awareness and with the reactions, sensations and perceptions connected to the physical body. In effect, by recognizing a presence (of a being or an object), the intellect is focused, and thus becomes sensitive to reality, a reality that inhabits it even as it inhabits reality. In this process, the body and the intellect see the beings and objects that surround them in unison.

In order to grasp this presence, the intellect seeks the object or being within themselves, in memory, recognizes it, and associates it with other qualities, other 'mental images,' so to speak. This analysis of presence should be completed with an analysis of the returning memories or daydreams, where the individual has the impression of a genuine presence in the room[8].

Perception

This brings a second point. Presence effect has to do with perception. It is sensation more than representation. Indeed, man's very being is defined by his presence, by the sensation of his presence. In this quest, the world stands as perception rather than as representation. It is an experimentation of this effect. Presence effect no longer resides in the act of apparition, but rather in the perception of this apparition. It is perception itself that creates the synthesis of this multiplicity of beings constituting a being. Prior to analyzing any relation with other people, the body itself realizes all the paradoxical situation that belongs to perception. The body is both obstacle and necessary element for this perception.

It is a perception which, according to Henri Bergson, is no longer centripetal (from perception to idea) but centrifugal (idea determines perception). Perception operates by 'the external projection of an actively conceived image, analogous to the object that fits its form. Perception is a prediction mobilizing memory, a prediction that seeks in a real test its adjustment to the object: to see is to see again and to foresee' (Weissberg 1999: 210). So, for Bergson, perceptive recognition could be compared to a membrane that is sensible on its two faces: the front one imprinting the image of a real object, while the inner one proposes 'the influence of a virtual object' (Bergson 2007: 167).

Sensations are on the alert, are 'solicited'. Among solicited senses, the most important is vision, whether 'effective' (confirming the impression), or 'by default,' when seeing or knowing that there is nothing may amplify the state of being present. As Merleau-Ponty notes in his study on the visible and invisible, sight allows the subject to think of himself thinking, to picture himself thinking. In perceiving, in seeing, the subject not only sees things and creates them for himself, but at the same time he creates himself. Sight makes up being, the subject's presence and presence effect creates through him, for him; in him it becomes both revelation of the surrounding world and realization of his own universe. It then becomes the very condition of the being's presence in the midst of reality. And art stands exactly there; it realizes more exactly this interspace (see Merleau-Ponty 1985). Then sight becomes parallel, if not similar, to illusion and dream.

We will deal again with this importance of vision when we analyze Janet Cardiff's work, since it is this vision that demarcates the divide between effective presence and presence effect; indeed, the characters are present for the ear alone, and it is only because sight clearly indicates their absence that the presence effect takes place.

With the presence effect, the image grows more and more autonomous as it is revealed as an apparatus and no longer as a product. The visibility of the imagination process creates a presence effect since it reveals the apparatus of perception. In fact, all contemporary art uses the realization of this presence effect to question us. It uses troubles, effects, and ruptures, and works upon all these confused zones that show our perception in action, whether the artist is asking us to try new forms of perception, or is deceiving us with some simulation. In all cases, the spectator must question himself about the process. He is caught in the game of his own deluding senses. The hiatus between reality and imagination has been abolished. The presence effect has therefore to do with a 'reality effect'[9].

Figure 2.1 Janet Cardiff and George Bures Miller, *The Paradise Institute* (2001). Wood, theater seats, video projection, headphones and mixed media Edition of 4. 118 x 698 x 210 inches (299.72 x 1772.92 x 533.4 cm). Courtesy of the artist, Luhring Augustine, New York and Barbara Weiss Gallery, Berlin. Photo by Markus Tretter

A case study. Janet Cardiff: between memory and fiction

Known for her work in creating audio walks, Cardiff is an Ontarian artist, who chanced upon the concept that was to become the basis of her art form. 'While walking through a cemetery in Banff, Cardiff used a portable tape recorder to log the names engraved on headstones. She hit the rewind button by accident, and found herself listening to the ambient sounds produced by her walking and her voice. This recording formed the basis of Cardiff's first "audio walk," entitled *Forest Walk*'. From this sprang her 'audio and video walks,' during which the spectators (who are both visitors and actors), 'while listening to a portable CD player or watching the screen of a camcorder, follow her directions through a chosen site, and become "participants" in her stories.' Cardiff's recorded voice guides them along a pre-determined path. 'Her spoken and whispered words are intercut with bits of ambient sound or sound effects recorded in a binaural technique. These recordings appear to be three-dimensional and create [on the part of the visitor] a dislocating uncertainty concerning what is recorded "fiction" and what is "reality."' Her stories 'lay the ground for an active course that combines map and memory.' During the audio walk, the visitor/participant 'is guided through a sonic "virtual" journey,' using recorded voices and sounds delivered via a headset. 'Cardiff, in effect, creates virtual spaces anchored in reality. She takes her participants to the crossroads of fiction and reality, the actual and the virtual, things remembered and newly experienced'[10].

On the www.thecanadianencyclopedia.com website, Marnie Fleming writes:

> Cardiff, in effect, creates virtual spaces anchored in reality. She takes her participants to the crossroads of fiction and reality, the actual and the virtual, things remembered and those newly experienced. [...] Participants listen to what is spoken, as she reinvents a location charged with mythical and symbolic forces (her walks often take place in gardens, around a few clusters of homes, or inside museums). She does not offer merely a simple geographic tour, but also the discovery of an interior space. [...] The sounds associated with treading the textured surfaces of the walk (cement, grass, cobblestones, bridges, woodchips, stairs, and steep slopes) stage the interrelation between the interior self and the exterior self, and make physical and mental actions 'apparent'.
>
> (Fleming 2011)

Piece by piece, Cardiff has added visual elements to her works (natural panoramas, films, sculptures, and installations). She currently chooses to work with a variety of methods of expression (videos, installations, and recorded sound) and shows her work throughout North America and Europe in museums and other appropriate spaces. But two of her more significant pieces – and doubtless those that are better known – are: *Forty Part Motet* (awarded the Millennium Prize from the National Gallery of Canada) and *The Paradise Institute,* both created in 2001. *Forty Part Motet* is an entirely musical installation that is a reworking of

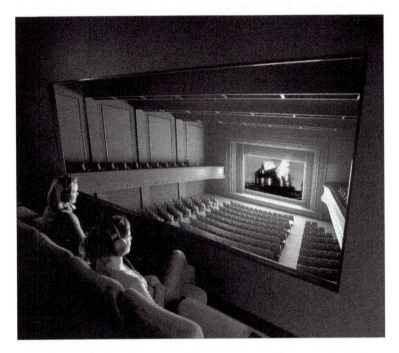

Figure 2.2 Janet Cardiff and George Bures Miller, *The Paradise Institute* (2001). Courtesy of the artist, Luhring Augustine, New York and Barbara Weiss Gallery, Berlin. Photo by Markus Tretter

a particularly complex 16th century polyphonic choral piece (*Spem in Alium* by the English composer Thomas Tallis) recorded by the Salisbury Festival Choir. Cardiff arranges forty audio speakers within a space (most often a chapel) and the spectator moves through this space experiencing a perfect illusion of a singing choir. The singers are in harmony but attentive spectators who approach the separate audio speakers one at a time can also hear each individual voice quite distinctly.

More complex is *The Paradise Institute*, presented at the 49th Venice Biennale and for which Cardiff won the Special Award, together with her partner George Bures Miller[11]. This installation is set up in the hall of a museum. It is a rather small, soundproofed space enclosed with plywood, inside a museum. Access to the room is by a stair, and the doors are shut once the visitor has entered. Within this closed space, sixteen red seats arranged in two rows, are set as in a theatre. Screenings take place every seventeen minutes. Each spectator (having been provided with a headset), sits in front of a small miniature stage and theatre (*en trompe l'oeil*), separated by a railing. Before him is a stilllife of scenery and a complete theatre. He then watches a ten-minute video, while hearing ambient noises from his headset (narration connected to the film, dialogue, characters, sirens, cries ... but also ambient noise whisperings from neighbours, unwrapped candies, comments from spectators behind and all the other stray noises usual in theatres). Cardiff creates sound effects that give the spectator the impression that he or she is elsewhere, in a real space surrounded by others, though the spectator knows that he or she is in reality alone[12].

Besides the aesthetic pleasure these installations afford, the interesting feature of this work lies in that:

I

Cardiff plays on the relations between fiction and reality by using techniques that restore the feelings the spectator may have had in facing real surroundings, thereby causing him to no longer know how to distinguish between the fictitious and the real. She therefore blurs the boundary between illusion and reality, compelling the spectator to seesaw between the two. At times he is completely within reality (when the installation is outdoors, he witnesses the other spectators, the streets, houses, fields in the case of walks – when they take place outside of more traditional exposition spaces) at other times he stands in fiction. He knows it: the entire installation proclaims it, displays it, underlines it. Although he perceives the illusion of those sounds and images he recognizes as fictitious, he is simultaneously calculating their proximity to those same sounds and images in real surroundings.

In the case of *Forty Part Motet*, one could question the difference between this reworking of a Renaissance choral piece, and the same piece presented in concert form.

• Beside the almost perfect quality of the sound, which eliminates noises and places the audience closest to the source (arousing concert-like attention), the difference comes from the spectator's knowing that what he listens to is an artifice. Or more exactly, not what he is 'listening' to, but what he is thinking is the source of this music.

Figure 2.3 Janet Cardiff and George Bures Miller, *The Paradise Institute* (2001). Selected film still. Courtesy of the artist, Luhring Augustine, New York and Barbara Weiss Gallery, Berlin.

- There is in this case a dissociation between eye and ear, vision and hearing.
- The 'presence effect' is grounded on this dissociation.

It seems that the presence effect is produced by these situations that make the spectator feel that he is where he knows very well he is not, and that he hears or sees things 'as if' they were there, while knowing they are not present. In this manner, Cardiff's installations make the spectator feel that the words he hears behind him are really uttered by his neighbour, which is impossible since his headset prevents him from hearing all these ambient noises usual during a show. Whence this 'presence effect' that we are trying to grasp.

2

This presence effect therefore comes from a reconstitution process of the (auditory and visual) presence: the 'binaural effect,' for Cardiff. This allows an almost perfect game of illusion for the spectator. We do not stand within the 'as if' of Stanislavski, but within the 'just as'.

In order to create this presence effect, Cardiff uses a technique that she did not discover, but that she uses in an entirely original way. It is the binaural effect. This effect was first identified in 1973 by Doctor Gerald Oster at the Mount Sinai School of Medicine in New York. The principle is simple.

In order to create a binaural effect, Cardiff employs a technique that places miniature microphones in the ears of a person or mannequin, which allows her to record and then reconstitute a given sound in a spatial environment with stunning accuracy, thus making the sound three-dimensional. Cardiff also notes that all her recordings superimpose multiple layers of sound, sometimes including as many as eighteen layers, which results in a more complex environment for voices and helps to spatialize them[13]. The sounds are offered to the listener cut off from their source, and this source is the result of a purely technical apparatus that reconstitutes a reality that is more real than reality itself.

3

Yet at the same time, the artist is foregrounding and illuminating the process that 'deludes' the spectator. Spectators are aware that their senses are deceiving them (everything in the artist's installation emphasizes this fact) and that where they have the impression there is being, there is only illusion. The sounds offered are cut from their source. And this source is the result of a purely technical montage that restores a reality more real than reality itself.

4

Thus the habitual functioning of the spectator's perceptions, which usually proceeds from sensation to representation, is held in check. Indeed, phenomenology has taught us that perception has as its basis an obvious link between sensation and representation. In order to perceive, one has to find in one's memory a concordance between the sounds one hears and an image, a representation. This representation proceeds through thought.

Now with Cardiff, there is a dissociation between a given perception and the thought of the thing that this perception is usually connected with, as if Cardiff were unfolding thought – separating perception from representation – and were inscribing a rupture, a hiatus, at the heart of that unfolding. Sight and

hearing are thus made autonomous; the installation creates this dissociation, which confounds the spectator and gives him a playful pleasure.
In order to create this dissociation:

- Cardiff cheats (swindles) the spectators' perceptions by disorganizing the information received by their senses. 'We hope to invoke basic philosophical questions by playing with our perceptual tools. We try to fool people about which reality they are actually in by screwing up the information reaching their senses'... 'We're trying to fool people's perceptions. You hear someone walk up to you and then someone is very close to you, you can almost feel them' she observes[14].
- She appeals to the senses of the participants (to their 'sensorial body,' one might say). As Daniela Zyman notes, she uses them separately, not only to create quasi extensions of the body, but also to intensify the spectators' self-consciousness. For the spectator, this evokes an intense feeling of being alive[15]. In fact, he is subject to a powerful interplay of relationships between exterior surroundings and his inner universe[16]. A tension operates between his visual, auditory and proprioceptive senses.
- Cardiff allows one to see by means of one's hearing (and not only through the eye). The ear guides perception, permits identification, provides the presence effect and magnifies the perception of reality. Cardiff demonstrates how we not only hear through our ears but with our whole body, and proves that the power of hearing activates an invisible world that becomes more real than reality. As she describes it:
- Because the sound is recorded in binaural audio we can push people's perception of the reality around them. Sometimes the characters from the movie are close to you; sometimes the audience is laughing or clapping around you. Someone beside you offers you popcorn. (Kölle in Baerwaldt 2001: 11)
- Her collaborator and life partner, George Bures Miller, adds: 'I like the idea that we are building a *simulated experience* in the attempt to make people feel more connected to real life' (Kölle in Baerwaldt 2001: 11).
- She creates surroundings in which the spectator can immerse himself (Baerwaldt 2001: 3). As George Bures Miller notes, technically: 'Everyone listening to the headphones is at the

centre of the recording, where the binaural head was placed originally. Everyone feels like the action is happening around them' (Kölle in Baerwald 2001: 15). For example, 'In *The Paradise Institute*, the viewers move into and through enveloping, sequenced stages of illusion, and a series of experiences that the artist have edited like a film' (Kölle in Baerwald 2001: 4).

CONCLUSIONS

What conclusions about presence effects can be drawn from Cardiff's works?

I

Cardiff helps us better understand presence effects because she places us in ideal conditions in which to experiment with and analyze these effects. She is working at this friction point between the self and the world. She fictionalizes sensations of space and time.

2

Presence effects originate in the friction point between the self and the world outside, in a place where the sense of space and time is fictionalized. In unfolding reality and making the soundscape and sound itself palpable, Cardiff makes spectators aware of the different layers that typically make up reality. She extends (and modifies) their state of consciousness. Reality is absorbed, rendered, in a hyper-personalized space that intensifies self-consciousness to an even greater degree than the awareness of outward reality. What emerges is an other, hybrid reality, simultaneously constructed of the virtual and the real. She makes space sonorous and sound concrete.

3

It becomes equally clear that presence effects call upon memory and are connected to the different modalities of representation that authorize the operation of 'recognition' in the absence of the object. Thus, there is a superposition of the idea and the sound.

4

Lastly, while they appeal to all of the senses and engage the body, Cardiff's works paradoxically render the body transparent, as if its opacity disappears, allowing everything to pass through the sole conduit of the ear (belied by sight). This unique relationship to the body in this context merits further examination.

I would say that the presence effect seems more and more to be the result of experimentation that:

- puts man, at the very core of his own representations, into play. Through him, the subject experiences his existence in the world. This experience engages thought and memory at the same time. On one hand, it calls on a resonance within our being, and on the other, on a resonance of our being upon the world (to speak in phenomenological terms). A rapt attention becomes sensitive to reality, but at the same time the intellect seeks the object or being within himself, in memory, recognizes it, and associates it with other qualities, other 'mental images' [17].

- calls upon a carnal coefficient. In every 'presence effect' on the spectator, there is a carnal coefficient brought into play. The body is interpellated by way of the sensory organs (eye, ear), and also by the spectators' sensations, a body which is simultaneously an essential element and an obstacle because it has some opacity. It is the body that perceives, but it is equally the body that filters. Through the body's mediation, the act of recognizing 'presence' achieves the same experience as the subject within the world. Thus, at the same time, the body is an obstacle, but an essential element of this perception.

- evokes the feeling that there is a genuine sharing of a common space and time. It takes place in the present. One can imagine a presence effect with figures that are inscribed within the past, but in this case it is the spectator who is transported into that distant reality. In his 'literary fiction,' Guillaume Apollinaire spoke of long-distance touch leading to a 'disruption of the spatial situation' (Apollinaire in Weissberg 1999: 38).

- demonstrates that presence effects have to do with perception. It is sensation rather than representation. One might say that the presence effect is not in the advent of the object, but in the perception of this advent. It is this primary relation to perception that gives the spectator the feeling that there is a real sharing of a common space and time (that of the present).

- allows the senses to be awake, to be 'on call' (*en appel*). Among the sensory organs involved, the most important are the eyes, whether vision is 'effective' and serves as a caution to the impression received[18], or whether it is a vision 'by default,' serving to remind the spectator of a gap, an absence, a play of illusion. For example, such a play of illusion might make a voice heard by the spectator – a voice endowed with a striking realism and proximity, such as those in *The Paradise Institute* – the voice of someone absent that is also utterly present. By this I mean to say that seeing (knowing) that nothing is there can amplify the state of presence. The importance of vision should be emphasized because it is what allows one to mark the dividing line between effective presence and a presence effect (in effect, the characters are present only to the ear; the presence effect can only occur because vision clearly indicates their absence)[19].
- demonstrates that with the presence effect, there is an escalating process of automation of the image by showing it as the focus, not the product. This is the visibility of the imaginative process in its truest sense; the image's revelation creates the presence effect because it makes the focus of perception palpable.
- allows spectators to find themselves at the heart of a 'performative' experiment where, first and foremost, they understand that there is a gap between their perceptions and the reality the installation offers their senses, hence a powerful presence effect. The importance of vision allows one to draw the dividing line between effective presence and presence effects.

In fact, all contemporary art plays on this phenomenon, calling this presence an artistic value, particularly where interdisciplinary forms play on the duality of presence/presence effects, with the achievement of a presence effect as a type of questioning. Contemporary art plays on the disturbances, the effects, the ruptures, and uses all of these areas of disorder which show our perception in action, whether the artist calls upon us to experiment with specific forms of perception, or whether the artist subjects us to trickery. In either case, spectators are called upon to question the process. They are caught in the interplay of their own senses deceiving them.

Cardiff helps us to better understand presence effects. She is working at this friction point between the self and the world.

Works cited

Baerwaldt, W. (ed.) (2001) *The Paradise Institute – Janet Cardiff and George Bures Miller*, Winnipeg: Plug In.

Barba, E. and Savarese, N. (eds) (2005) *A Dictionary of Theatre Anthropology: The Secret Art of the Performer*, London and New York: Routledge.

Bergson, H. (2007) *Matter and Memory*, New York: Cosimo.

Deleuze, G. (1985) *L'image-temps: Cinéma 2*, Paris : Éditions de Minuit.

Farcy, G.-D. and Prédal, R. (eds) (2001) *Crever les Planches, Brûler l'Écran. La Présence de l'Acteur*, Vic-la-Gardiole: L'Entretemps.

Féral, J. (ed.) (1997) *Mise en Scène et Jeu de l'Acteur, vol. 1 (L'Espace du Texte)*, Carnières & Montréal: Lansman and Éditions Jeu.

——(ed.) (1998) *Mise en Scène et Jeu de l'Acteur, vol. 2 (Le Corps en Scène) and 3 (Voix de Femmes)*, Carnières & Montréal: Lansman and Éditions Jeu.

——(ed.) (2006) *Mise en Scène et Jeu de l'Acteur, vol. 3 (Voix de Femmes)*, Montréal: Québec-Amérique.

Fleming, M. (2011) 'Janet Cardiff' in *The Canadian Encyclopedia Online*. Online. Available: *www.thecanadianencyclopedia.com/index.cfm?PgN m=TCE&Params=A1ARTA0009772* (accessed 25 July 2011).

Merleau-Ponty, M. (1985) *L'œil et l'esprit*, Paris: Gallimard.

Noël, B. (1988) *Le lieu des signes*, Périgueux: Editions Unes.

Schaub, M. (ed.) (2005), *Janet Cardiff – The Walk Book*, New York: D.A.P./ Distributed Art Publishers.

Sloterdijk, P. (1993) *Weltfremdheit (Unwordliness)*, Frankfurt/Main: Suhrkamp Verlag.

Weissberg, J.L. (1999) *Présences à distance, déplacement virtuel et réseaux numériques, pourquoi nous ne croyons plus à la télévision*, Paris: L'Harmattan.

Notes

1 This work originates from a Social Sciences and Humanities Research Council (SSHRC) research group made up of six professors and fifteen students and concerned with the notions of presence effects. Born from previous research on notions of theatricality and performativity, the research group endeavours to bring to light the several forms of interpenetration between virtual and real, and to measure the reality effects produced. It studies, more particularly, productions where virtual characters must interact with real actors according to several

modalities or techniques (projections, telepresence, morph, interpolation, incrustation, chroma key, etc.) and according to given scenarios and desired effects. The notion of 'presence,' as treated in several theoretical works, whether in its relation to voice, bodily bearing, breathing, or movement, lies therefore at the centre of this research. What is it that creates a feeling of presence when we are face to face with some virtual character or with no character at all? The following text is a step in this reflection. A shorter version of this text was read at the forum of the CRI (*Centre de recherche sur l'intermédialité, Université de Montréal*) in May 2007. I would like to thank Edwige Perrot for having helped with this research.

2 See http://topologicalmedialab.net (accessed 5 May 2011).

3 The observation that 'no one is there' requires further thought. The person who has the impression that someone is there may either know that no one is there – as, for example, in Janet Cardiff's immersive environment – it is a case of technological or numerical effects and the spectators' enjoyment stems precisely from the fact that they see the deception being practiced on them; or be unaware no one is there and yet have the impression of a presence – as in a daydream or in the experiments of certain researchers like Sha Xin Wei, who attempts to induce a sense of presence in the 'visitors' to his laboratory.

4 Regarding this, see the works by Eugenio Barba and other stage theoreticians and practitioners, especially the interviews I conducted with several contemporary stage directors where this question is analysed (Féral 1997).

5 'One punchline of post-metaphysical thinking is that subjects today, after thousands of years of experiments with the phantasms of eternal wakefulness, can return in active resignation to a positive theory of the impossibility-of-staying-awake-all-the-time' (Sloterdijk 1993: 294–325).

6 See www.numeriscausa.com/pages/artistes.html Accessed 5 May 2011.

7 In a lecture entitled '*Flußgeist: En présence des flux*' held at the Performativité Effets de présence research group on 7 February 2007.

8 See Sha Xin Wei's research again at http://topologicalmedialab.net (accessed 5 May 2011).

9 One question remains: how to evaluate presence? Can we ascribe different degrees to presence? Or different intensities? Can we say that a given person has more or less presence, and if so, what does that mean in concrete terms? This question seems to make more sense in the context of the theatrical arts, a domain which draws upon actors and dancers whose training is often centered on the idea of presence. Yet it becomes less clear when applied to a virtual presence. Can it be said that the presence resulting from an effect of Pepper's Ghost effect has a greater density (*La Tempête*) than another on-screen or otherwise projected presence (Gladyszewsky)? I will not attempt to answer the question here but from this brief typology and the questions that accompany it, it is apparent that as soon as one begins to examine the notion of presence in depth, it becomes progressively more complex.

10 Summary based on, and quotations drawn from, www.collectionscanada.
ca/women/002026-505-f.html and www.thecanadianencyclopedia.com/
index.cfm?PgNm=HomePage&Params=A1 (accessed 5 May 2011).
11 In an interesting way, *Forty-Part Motet* and *The Paradise Institute*,
both created the same year, are two works standing in counterpoint.
While *Motet* suppresses all stray noises in order to restore pure sound,
The Paradise Institute makes use of the background noises preceding
a show as well as of stray noises accompanying it (unwrapped candies,
whisperings from a spectator to his neighbour...).
12 In fact, they are surrounded by other silent spectators like themselves.
13 'All of my walks are recorded in binaural audio with multi-layers of
sound effects, music, and voices (sometimes as many as 18 tracks)
added to the main walking track to create a 3D sphere of sound.
Binaural audio is a technique that uses miniature microphones
placed in the ears of a person or dummy head. The result is an
incredibly lifelike 3D reproduction of sound.' (Cardiff in Schaub
2005: 15). Also 'I use different methods to record the voices not only
to suggest other characters but also to give a more complex and
spatial relationship to the voices. A voice recorded normally with my
binaural head will sound very clear, intimate, and real. It reads as
though it is on the same physical level as your own head. A voice
recorded on a small dictaphone playing back from a tiny speaker
recorded again by the binaural head about two feet away will give
the physical illusion of being that far away. So then you have the
strange situation of the recorded main voice listening to her own
voice on a different machine from a different time period. Because
the one voice is clear and the other is scratchy and grainy, it creates
the illusion of two different characters' (Cardiff in Schaub: 172). 'On
a technical level, when a sound wave of one frequency enters one ear,
and a soundwave of a very different frequency enters the other ear,
the brain tends to compensate by attempting to synchronize its two
hemispheres. It reacts by creating a very characteristic type of sound,
called binaural beats, whose frequency corresponds to the difference
between the frequencies of the two initial sound waves. [...] For
example of an initial soundwave of 400 Hz directed at one ear, and
a second soundwave of 404 Hz directed at the other. The brain will
progressively adjust the frequency until it registers a sound at 4 Hz.
However, the lower limit of human hearing is approximately 20 Hz.
Thus this process allows one to "hear" very low sounds in the
frequency range of beta, alpha, delta or theta states of consciousness.
It is important to note that, in order to be effective, the listening
experience must occur through a headset, and the difference in
sound frequency between right and left must not exceed 30 Hz.' (The
Monroe Institute. *Brain Wave Generator*, www.ledepot.info/archives/
index.php?2006/04/18/46-binaural-beats verified 5 May 2011).
Cardiff reminds us that the first binaural experiment occurred in 1881
at the Paris Opera. 'There is a community that is obsessed with
creating three-dimensional sounds. You'll find out that the first
binaural experience took place at the Paris Opera in 1881. They used

microphones installed along the front edge of the stage.' (Cardiff in Schaub: 4).

14 'I Wanted to Get Inside the Painting: Brigitte Kölle in conversation with Janet Cardiff and George Bures Miller' (Kölle in Baerwaldt 2001: 15–17).

15 'She also exploits the ability to trigger our five senses separately and uses them not only to create an extension of our own body but also to intensify our self-awareness and, ultimately, to make us feel alive' (Zyman in Schaub 2005: 11).

16 'A Cardiff site is not static; instead, it is a net of possible references and relationships between the inner space of the walker and their external environment. The body moving through space is not guided by the controlling discipline of the eye (as de Certeau has argued). The walker uses his 'blind eye,' a corporeal and visceral form of knowledge. [...] It is a dualistic experience that takes place on two intertwined levels of the body's movement in space and the continuity of the narrative form' (Zyman in Schaub 2005: 11).

17 In his book, *Le Lieu des Signes* [*The Place of Signs*], as we have mentioned earlier, Bernard Noël attempts to describe experiments on the presence of objects. He has experimented with the impression of an object's presence from the advent of the object to the internal idea of the object in thought. This process encapsulates the paradox of representing an object (as an image and as a mental action) as well as the predominance of reality.

18 The spectator is, in effect, seeing an avatar. For example there are certain characters in Michel Lemieux's *La Tempête* [*The Tempest*], staged at the TNM which the spectator knows to be avatars, but their stage presence ultimately gives the impression of a real presence.

19 As Merleau-Ponty notes in his research on the visible and the invisible, vision allows the subject to think of themselves as thinking, to represent themselves as thinking (*L'Œil et l'Esprit*).

Chapter 3

Environmental presence

Gabriella Giannachi

Presence is constituted in the complex network of relationships the subject establishes with the physical and/or digital world they inhabit. Integral to presence, as Nick Kaye and I discussed in our monograph *Performing Presence: between the Live and the Simulated,* is what is before or in front of the subject, both spatially and temporally (Giannachi and Kaye 2011: 4–9). Also integral is the performance the subject undergoes as part of this process. Discourse on environment and ecology should therefore play a crucial role in the analysis of presence. As we know, environment indicates the surroundings or conditions in which a person, animal, or plant lives or operates. On the other hand, ecology indicates a branch of biology that is concerned with the relations of organisms to each other and to their surroundings. So, an environmental interpretation of presence foregrounds the set of circumstances that surround the occurrence of presence, while an ecological reading of presence foregrounds how presence may operate as a relational tool between organisms. In this chapter I will present an analysis of presence from environmental and ecological perspectives, propose a framework for the interpretation of presence within this context, and offer an interdisciplinary reading of a number of artworks that can be broadly categorized as environmental and/or ecological, and that are significant in terms of presence research.

I will start by revisiting the notion of environment. Anthropologist Tim Ingold points out that environment is a 'relative' term and that just as one cannot conceive of an organism without an environment, one should not conceive of an environment without an organism (Ingold 2000: 20). It follows for Ingold that an environment is never complete because it is forged by living things

(Ingold 2000: 20) and that the relationship between organisms and their environments cannot be other than a process. This of course suggests that one is never simply 'present,' but rather that one is present in a given environment and ecology. In fact presence could be read as the network formed by the subject and the environment they are in through a set of ecological exchanges. We know from Giorgio Agamben that the term environment indicates something highly subjective, so much so that, for example, a forest is not 'an objectively determined environment' but rather it is constructed in the dweller's experience of it, so that the environment of a given forest is different for the hunter, the botanist, the carpenter, etc. who encounter it (Agamben 2002: 46). For Agamben each environment should therefore be considered as 'a closed unity,' although, influenced by Jakob von Uexküll, he describes these unities as being in 'musical' dialogue with each other (Agamben 2002: 46). As an example of his hypothesis, Agamben cites the relationship between the spider and the fly. The spider, he states, whilst being unaware of the environment of the fly, is able to build a cobweb that is 'proportionate' to the fly's flight-speed in such a way that the fly cannot see the cobweb and so inexorably flies towards its death (Agamben 2002: 46). This suggests that there is not an identity between the subject and an environment within which it is located, but rather that the subject is simultaneously part of a number of environments (including those generated by others) and may be 'present' within multiple environments. This indicates a subject who does not have one identity, but rather, paying tribute to Gilles Deleuze and Felix Guattari, exists in rhizomatic multiplicity (Deleuze and Guattari 1999).

Yet whilst environments may be closed entities, in the sense that they are subjective, they are nevertheless open to change, or, in Ingold's words, they are 'alive' (Ingold 2000: 66). Incidentally, Ingold notes a difference between what he calls environmental conservation, practiced by hunter-gatherers and scientific conservation advocated by Western wildlife protection agencies. Whereas the latter presumes a homocentric view, in which humans change an environment by inhabiting it, and thus presuming a kind of ur-nature, the former sees the human as an integral part of nature. Ingold cites societies' understanding of wilderness to explain this difference. We know from Roderick Nash's study of wilderness that wilderness is not a 'specific material object' (Nash 1967: 1) and cultures have very different understandings of what constitutes wilderness. Thus Nash reports his conversation with a Malaysian hunter-gatherer in which he was trying to identify what wilderness meant to him by asking him to comment on the expression 'I am lost in the jungle' to which the hunter-gatherer replied that the question made little sense to him 'as would asking an American city dweller how he said "I am lost in my apartment". Lacking a concept of controlled and uncontrolled nature, the Malaysian had no conception of wilderness' (Nash 1967: xiv). So whereas, for hunters and gatherers 'there is no contradiction between conservation and participation' (Ingold 2000: 68), for the Western conservationist participation implies the modification of a wilderness that precedes human presence within it.

These considerations are crucial if one is to analyse presence in an environmental and ecological context. Presence, as we discussed elsewhere (Giannachi and Kaye 2011), is the medium through which the subject engages with an environment. I do not by this mean to say that presence, indicating that which is in front of or before the subject, coincides with the environment, rather that it is the inter-relational tool through which the subject networks (and is networked by) the external world. We have seen how some societies may have utilized presence and dwelling as a means to separate the subject from the environment they inhabit. The majority of studies in presence research published so far focus on virtual environments and whilst they provide us with a wealth of information about how humans construct the digital world around them as present to them, they rarely offer insight into how presence is used as a relational tool rather than a sign demonstrating that a given subject is treating a digital world as if it was 'real' (Sanchez-Vives and Slater 2005). Here I argue that presence and environment, whilst not synonymous, entail a shift in perspective over the same territory: where presence indicates what is in front of the 'I am' (Giannachi and Kaye 2011), environment indicates what is around ('environ'). In this context, we can see that presence includes the position of the subject, whereas environment does not. This suggests that while presence is about the continuous unfolding of the subject into what is other to it, environment defines the surroundings, that is, what remains other to it, that is however necessary for presence to occur. The environment, in this sense, hosts the archaeological traces left by the remains of what was excluded in the construction of presence. In other words, the environment does not exist prior to the subject, it is what remains from its construction. This indicates that the environment entails traces of the operation of presence. This also implies that the environment is a condition for presence to occur since it is the environment that presence draws from. Crucially, this does not exclude relationships with the other-than-human. In other words, presence is also an ecological process that marks a moment of awareness of the exchanges between the subject and the living environment of which they are part. I will now introduce the operation of presence in a number of environmental and/or ecological artworks spanning from John Cage, the Italian movement *arte povera* and land art to locative media.

A number of early environmental works utilized recorded sound as a tool to draw the audience's attention to their environment and to the operation of presence necessary to engage with it. John Cage's *alla ricerca del silenzio perduto* (1977 [*Researching Lost Silence*]), a happening consisting of the broadcasting of environmental sounds recorded on a train journey through Italy, and *Five Hanau Silence* (1991), where ambient sound was recorded in five different parts of the German town of Hanau as indicated by the I Ching, as well as his well-known 'silent' composition, *4'33"* (1952), in which a pianist is on stage for four minutes and thirty-three seconds, opening and closing the piano's lid for the three movements of the piece, without, however, playing the instrument, reflect Cage's interest in silence as a form of performance of environmental sound within a musical frame. All three pieces play with the complex relationships between place, space/time, environment and presence. This is crucial to understand the operation of presence in this context. Before analysing the works, we must, however, devote attention to some of the salient characteristics of environmental art. Kathan Brown notes that whereas 'environmental art is made for a particular space,' situationist art is made for a particular *place* (cultural or social) and usually involves action instead of, or as well as, installation' (Brown in White 1980, original emphasis). This points to a distinction between environmental art and other forms of art invested in site, place, or nature. For Brown, environmental art is not so much invested in a place as it is made for or out of a particular space. To explain this further, it is important to consider Allan Kaprow's thesis that environmental works make no attempt towards unity of representation: 'the field [...] is created as one goes along, rather than being there *a priori*, as in the case of a canvas of certain dimensions. It is a process, and one that works from the inside-out, though this should be considered merely metaphorical, rather than descriptive, since there actually exists no inside, a bounded area being necessary to describe a field' (Kaprow 1966: 159, original emphasis). Environmental works are not merely a snapshot or representation of an existing site, as landscape paintings might be, but rather constitute an engagement with, or itinerary through space (rather than place), often foregrounding the operation of presence that occurs within it with respect to another site (or place) within which the work was constructed. Arguably then, it is through the operation of presence that environments are generated, not vice versa, as is suggested by computer scientists, such as Jonathan Steuer, who states that presence indicates 'the sensation of being in an environment,' rather than its generation (Steuer 1992: 75), or by Mel Slater who suggests that presence is 'a perceptual mechanism for selection between alternative hypotheses: "I am in this place" and "I am in that place" ("I am confused")' (Slater 2002: 435), again presupposing the existence of a number of environments *a priori* from the subject.

Five Hanau Silence consists of five ambient recordings. In a correspondence about the piece, Cage describes the instructions for its realisation as follows: '(send me a map of the city; I will mark the points specified by chance operations) I will also specify the "times" of day or night when the recordings are to be made. They should then be superimposed (made into a single record), or even better, played separately from separate points in space' (Cage 1991). The instructions reveal that Cage recommended the creation of a space within which the five environmental sound recordings were to cohabit. This was also the space of the listener. Similar processes occurred in *4'33"*, though here the listener became the subject *and* the object, as well as the medium, of the broadcast. As Nick Kaye has suggested, in *4'33"* Cage 'strips the musical work of everything but a context and the listener's experience of her own presence' (Kaye 1994: 93). While *Five Hanau Silence* excluded the listener from the original recording, in *4'33"* the listener 'audits' themselves. The operation of presence in *4'33"*, therefore, is not only one that facilitated the encounter with another environment, as in *Five Hanau Silence*, but one that drew attention to the listener's own presence precisely by staging the very process of the creation of an environment, and so the operation of presence. For Cage it was crucial to devote attention to this process:

You say: the real, the world as it is. But it is not, it becomes! It doesn't wait for us to change... It is more mobile than you can imagine. You are getting closer to reality when you say that it 'presents itself'; that means it is not there, existing as an object. The world, the real, is not an object. It is a process.

(Cage in Cage and Charles 1981: 80)

Similarly, *alla ricerca del silenzio perduto,* also known as *il treno* [the train], had the structure of a musical composition (it had a timetable and stops) which coincided with a section of the timetable and stops of a train. Here, the listener was on a journey in which, again, their search of the 'lost silence,' a pun on Marcel Proust's masterpiece *In Search of Lost Time,* occurred in the discontinuities produced by the overlay of environmental sound with music played on and off the train. As in the previous two works, environmental sound prompted listeners to reposition, that is 're-present,' themselves between the various spaces, places and environments generated by the work.

Another important environmental work is Robert Smithson's *Enantiomorphic Chambers* (1965), which consisted of two chambers cancelling out the viewers' reflected image via the use of two mirrors. The term, 'enantiomorphic' refers to 'a pair of crystalline chemical compounds whose molecular structures have a mirror-image relationship to each other' (Hobbs 1981: 61). When the viewers stood in front of the mirrors they saw nothing but reflections of reflections. The mirrors in fact reflected mirror images dispersing the viewers' vision so that 'one's sight is reflected but one is not' (Hobbs 1981: 61). According to Smithson:

The two separate 'pictures' that are usually placed in a stereoscope have been replaced by two separate mirrors [...] thus excluding any fused image. This negates any central vanishing point, and takes one physically to the other side of the double mirrors. It is as though one were being imprisoned by the actual structure of two alien eyes. It is an illusion without an illusion.

(Smithson in Flam 1996: 359).

Like Cage, who drew attention to the operation of presence through the use of environmental sound, whether broadcast *in situ* or in a separate space, here the occurrence of presence was turned into a non-referential process. As pointed out by Robert Hobbs, 'sight in his sculpture becomes the nonreferential act of seeing instead of the usual unconscious looking at something' (Hobbs 1981: 61). This points to an important difference between the works considered so far. Whereas for Cage art is the medium that re-introduces 'life' (Cage and Charles 1981: 52), for Smithson, in his own words, art 'becomes a tautology, a reflexive statement of its supposed function' (Smithson in Hobbs: 1981: 13). In both cases, however, it is the operation of presence that is scrutinized to make a statement about the role of art in relation to the subject.

We have seen how the above-cited works play with the uncanny environmental shifts that occur during the operation of presence. To explain the complexity of these terms it is worth looking at Kaye's definition of the relationship of space and place. While Kaye draws on de Certeau to propose a linguistic model of the relationship between space and place whereby space 'is like the word when it is spoken' and thus unable to 'manifest the order and stability of its place' (Kaye 2000: 5), environment is the cacophony or entropy that is excluded by the operation of presence. Environment thus entails, as we have said, the surroundings and conditions under which the subject operates and presence occurs. This explains why the concepts of environment and organism are interdependent. This also shows why environments are always *in fieri,* pending, changing, evolving. We have seen that silence in Cage is where the operation of presence should occur, that is where the listener is made to encounter what is in front of or before them, so that they may become alert to what is around them, meaning their environment. This is also where the subject re-locates, or re-presents, in space and time in order to re-encounter themselves in the other or as an other. In Smithson, there is a questioning of the subject's ability to exert control over this process. Here, through an interrogation of sight, and the collapse of its ability to generate a perspectival view, with the two chambers standing for the subject's own eyes (Shapiro 1995: 67), unable to synthesize the image, Smithson reminds us that in the operation of presence the subject is not in control of the environment, nor at the centre of it, but rather caught in a truncated, non-referential presencing process.

Trace and shadow have also been used by a number of environmental artists in work that is relevant to presence research. A well-known example of *arte povera* engaging with trace is

Claudio Parmiggiani's *Delocations* (1970–71), which consisted of the imprints of removed canvasses left by shadows of dust and smoke. Another example of environmental art that adopted trace is Robert Irwin's *Fractured Light – Partial Scrim Ceiling – Eye-Level Wire* (1970–71), an installation shown at the Museum of Modern Art in New York, which focussed on light, space and ambiance. Irwin described the work as follows:

> [the gallery's personnel] never announced [the piece]; they never acknowledged it. But they wanted to put up a label so people wouldn't think it was an empty room. Jenny would go in each day and she would take the label down ... One of the things that [the room] did was challenge you at every level. You would walk in there, and the first question [you had] was: 'Is this intended?' Then 'Is it finished?' – even *before* you got to the question of whether it was *Art* or not. The question was whether or not it was even *there,* and on what grounds it was there. [...] People would go in there, see nothing, leave and go into the next gallery.
> (Irwin in Butterfield 1993: 24, original emphases).

Both works utilize shadows to visualize traces left by events that either, as in Parmiggiani's case, mark the passing of time, or, as in Irwin's case, note the effects of the passing of time on space. To better understand the role of shadows in these works I need to open a parenthesis on the use of shadow in two of the most famous paintings in the history of art. In his study of shadows, Ernst Gombrich points out that whilst shadows belong to landscapes, they constitute an ephemeral and changing aspect of it (Gombrich 1996: 14). The inclusion of shadows in painting, therefore, draws attention to the environment's mutability but also to the effect of the human presence within it. Gombrich cites Masaccio's *La guarigione dello storpio* (1425 [Healing of the Cripple]), showing an episode in the life of St Peter, in which the shadow of the saint heals the cripple. On the other hand in Caravaggio's *Cena in Emmaus* (1601 [Supper at Emmaus]) Jesus' gesticulation, probably an act of blessing the supper, reveals him as mortal, covered in shadows, about to disappear into darkness. In both these paintings, shadow is used to mark the operation of someone's presence, in the sense that in the former it denotes the effect of Jesus' presence over the cripple and in the latter his imminent death. Similarly, in the

two environmental works by Parmiggiani and Irwin, shadows were used to draw attention to a 'delocation,' or displacement, of presence in the environment, visualizing the remains of the unfolding of place into space, and thus drawing attention to the processes that the subject is invested in when being confronted with what is in front of or before them. Shadow here is used to create another space, and time, which has not yet occurred in the world of the painting but that we know is imminently present, that is, before or in front of the subject. As in Caravaggio's *Cena in Emmaus* and Adalbert von Chamisso's well-known *Peter Schlemils wundersame Geschichte* (*[Peter Schlemil's Remarkable Story]* 1814), a novel about a man who sold his shadow to the devil only to find out that shadowless humans are shunned by society, shadow is used here as a form of spatio-temporal augmentation, to visualize the implications of its operation on the environment.

Arte povera engaged, in Kaye's words, 'with exchanges between material, body and action that revealed an ecological logic, a logic of interdependency and transformation between "object", environment and organism' (Kaye 2005: 270). For him, a work that exemplifies these processes is Gilbero Zorio's *Rosa – Blu – Rosa (Pink – Blue – Pink)* (1967), consisting of an eternit semi-cylinder of cobalt chloride whose reaction to changes of humidity in the environment in which it is located caused gradual changes in its colour. Kaye notes that the work 'articulates a material exchange, as the viewer's bodily presence affects the ambient environment, precipitating an event and sculptural operation in which the form of the work evolves, so expressing, as Zorio proposes, a "concept of transition or identification between body and sculpture" (Celant 1991: 43)' (Kaye 2005: 271). Here, we witness the ecological processes that the viewer's presence induces over a contained environment. For Nehama Guralnik, 'this is, therefore, a time-system responding to changes that affect it. It is outside intervention which changes its formal balance, there being no optimal state, or state of rest; to experience the work the viewer needs to be present, his presence perforce changing the appearance of the work' (Guralnik in Eccher and Ferrari 1996: 208). As Gregory Bateson proposed in *Steps to an Ecology of Mind* (1972), an organism is always an 'organism-in-its-environment' (Bateson 1972: 451). In *Rosa-Blu-Rosa*, breath causes humidity, which in turn causes the work of art to change colour. Presence here is not just an operation of self-identification but one of biological change. In facing what is before or in front of them, the subject not only sees himself or herself as an other, but undergoes *and* generates biological change in this other. In this sense the operation of presence is always also biological, chemical and even genetic. Thus trace, in this context, becomes both what occurred in the past and what is likely to occur in the future since we know that, medically, a trace is a symptom, and a symptom can be the sign of a transformational condition.

To explain the relationship between presence and ecology, I will open a parenthesis on the biological operation of cells. I have discussed elsewhere that cells do not just perform in isolation, they also respond to their context (Giannachi 2007). In fact, cells act on the information they receive from their neighbouring cells (Johnson 2002: 86). Moreover:

> the extracellular matrix (ECM), once thought to be merely 'stuff between the cells' and a structural support for tissues, induces embryonic changes in tissues and plays a role in directing gene expression. Cellular interactions with ECM affect the way cells proliferate, adhere to surfaces, and migrate to other areas, which means that these signals affect the three-dimensional organisation and form of various tissues and organs. Without the right clues from other cells and from the material between cells, cells may not differentiate, perform specialized functions, or organize into larger structures. Thus the microarchitecture and spatial configurations of cells, as much as their cellular mechanisms, seem to be responsible for organ function.
>
> (Hogle in Franklin and Lock, 2003: 73–4).

Hence each cell is not just individually responsible for its behaviour and function, it also depends on the in-between-cells. In other words, a cell's environment is just as responsible for its behaviour and function as its own content and architecture. In this sense, a cell is a network, storing, transmitting, receiving and elaborating information. While we still know little about the neurological operation of presence, it is established that agency plays a significant role in the acquisition of a sense of presence in childhood development and for some this inextricably ties the two, so much so that Gerardo Herrera *et al* suggest that presence is in part rooted into agency (Herrera *et al* 2006), and Giuseppe Riva states: 'humans develop intentionality and Self by evaluating prereflexively their agency in relation to the constraints imposed by the environment: they are "present" if they are able to enact their intentions.' Likewise, others are present to us 'if we are able to recognize them as enacting beings (Riva 2008: 103), leading Riva to conclude that presence is the mechanism by which the subject 'prereflexively' controls his/her action through a forward-inverse model: the prediction of the action if compared with perceptual inputs to verify its enaction' (Riva 2008: 111). Other research in the neurological foundation of presence has hypothesized that what are known as place cells, which are located in the hippocampus and parahippocampal formation, create a cognitive map of our environment that 'integrates information about location, multi-sensory inputs and internal information'. These neurons constitute 'the roots of spatial presence,' although other areas of the brain are also involved (Brotons *et al* 2005: 499). Unquestionably more research is needed in these areas to explain the function of presence within an ecological context, but it is clear even at this early stage of research that presence is also a mechanism for mapping and orientation that allows the subjects to reposition themselves both environmentally and ecologically.

We have hypothesized that presence is the operation through which the subject witnesses itself as other and then recycles this 'other' so that it may become part of itself. Not only does this uncanny operation occur at the level of consciousness, but also biologically, chemically and genetically. In this context trace, as we have seen, is both a footprint left by that which has already occurred (as in Parmiggiani's *Delocations*), and a symptom leading to fundamental change (as in Zorio's *Rosa-Blu-Rosa*). This relationship between presence and ecology is crucial here. As Alphonso Lingis suggests, 'there is perhaps no species of life that does not live in symbiosis with another species' (Lingis in Wolfe 2003: 166). Presence then becomes a key concept in understanding the operations through which the subject experiences this symbiosis between species.

To conclude, a few more words need to be devoted to the way that ubiquitous computing is facilitating the creation of environmental and ecological works that influence our reading of presence. One of these works was developed by Ryoko Ueoka, Hiroki Kobayashi and Michitaka Hirose from the University of Tokyo. *Wearable Forest* (2008) is a work consisting of a 'clothing system that bioacoustically interacts with distant wildlife in a remote forest through a networked remote-controlled speaker and microphone' (Kobayashi *et al* 2009: 300). This work, according to the authors, was based on the concept of a human-computer biosphere interaction (HCBI) aiming to express 'the unique bioacoustic beauty of nature' and allowing 'users to interact with a forest in real time through a network and acoustically experience a distant forest soundscape, thus merging human beings and nature without great environmental impact' (Kobayashi *et al* 2009: 304). The piece, which was inspired by Zen Buddhism's view of deep meditation 'to achieve a sense of being at one with nature,' allowed for the creation of a hybrid human-computer that was networked with a subtropical forest of the southern Ryukyu Islands of Japan. Equipped with embedded speakers, LEDs, an embedded CPU system and a wireless internet connection, the dress played the soundscape of the forest through the speakers and used the LEDs to create patterns reflecting the activity level of forest life. Sensors also let the user transmit pre-recorded acoustic data back to the forest installation, creating what has been described as 'a bioacoustic loop' (Kobayashi *et al* 2009: 301). *Wearable Forest* allows for the creation of human-computer environment, which facilitates new forms of communication between humans and plants and allows for the direct personal experience of a particular ecology. Here, presence is also telepresence and the subject is no longer just experiencing the environment in which they are physically located but also one that is remote to them. Here the subject is not so much choosing between different hypotheses (Slater 2002) as utilizing their tool to relate to the external world (presence) to perceive different environments simultaneously. In this context it will not only be traces, footsteps, shadows, and soundscapes, but also digital, contextual footprints that will mark the remains of the operation of presence between digital and physical worlds.

Works cited

Agamben, G. (2002) *L'aperto: L'uomo e l'animale,* Torino: Bollati e Boringhieri.

Bateson, G. (1972) *Steps to an Ecology of Mind,* New York: Ballantine.

Brotons, J., O'Mara, S., Sanchez-Vives, M. (2005) 'Neural processing of Spatial Information: What We Know About Place Cells And What They Can Tell Us About Presence', *Presence,* 15:5, 485–99.

Butterfield, J. (1993) *The Art of Light + Space,* New York: Abbeville.

Cage, J. (1991) *Five Hanau Silence*. Online. Available: www.sterneck.net/john-cage/hanau-silence/index.php (accessed 30 June 2010).

Cage, J. and Charles, D. (1981) *For the Birds*, London: Marion Boyars.

Celan, G. (1991) *Gilberto Zorio*, Florence: Hopeful Monster.

Deleuze, G. and Guattari, F. (1999; [1980]) *A Thousand Plateaus: Capitalism and Schizophrenia*, translated by B. Massumi, London: the Athlone Press.

Eccher, D. and Ferrari, R. (eds) (1996) *Gilberto Zorio*, Torino: Hopefulmonster.

'environ' The Concise Oxford Dictionary of English Etymology. Ed. T. F. Hoad. Oxford University Press, 1996. Oxford Reference Online. Oxford University Press. Online. Available at: http://www.oxfordreference.com.lib.exeter.ac.uk/views/ENTRY.html?subview=Main&entry=t27.e5122 (subscription-only; accessed 28 June 2010).

Flam, J. (ed.) (1996) *Robert Smithson: The Collected Writings*, Berkeley CA: The University of California Press.

Franklin, S. and Lock, M. (eds) (2003) *Remaking Life & Death: Towards an Anthropology of the Biosciences*, Santa Fe NM: School of American Research Press.

Giannachi, G. (2007) *The Politics of New Media Theatre: Life®™*, London and New York: Routledge.

Giannachi, G. and Kaye, N. (2011) *Performing Presence: Between the Live and the Simulated*, Manchester: Manchester University Press.

Gombrich, E.H. (1996) *Ombre*, Torino: Einaudi.

Herrera, G., Jordan, R., Vera, L. (2006) 'Agency and Presence: a Common Dependence on Subjectivity?', *Presence: Teleoperators and Virtual Environments*, 15:5, 539–52.

Hobbs, R. (1981) *Robert Smithson: Sculpture*, London: Cornell University Press.

Ingold, Y. (2000) *The Perception of the Environment: Essays in Livelihood, Dwelling and Skill*, London: Routledge.

Johnson, S. (2002) *Emergence: the Connected Lives of Ants, Brains, Cities and Software*, London: Penguin.

Kaye, N. (1994) *Postmodernism and Performance*, Basingstoke: Palgrave MacMillan.

——(2000) *Site Specific Art: Performance, Place and Documentation*, London: Routledge.

——(2005) 'Performed Ecologies: Body, Material, Architecture', in G. Giannachi and N. Stewart (eds) *Performing Nature: Explorations in Ecology and the Arts*, Oxford: Peter Lang, 269–84.

Lingis, A. (2003) 'Animal Body, Inhuman Face', in C. Wolfe (ed.) *Zoontologies: The Question of the Animal*, Minneapolis MN: University of Minnesota Press, 165–82.

Kaprow, A. (1966) *Assemblages, Environments and Happenings*, New York: H. N. Abrams.

Kobayashi, H. *et al* (2009) 'Wearable Forest Clothing System: Beyond Human-Computer Interaction', *Leonardo*, 42:4, 300–06.

Nash, R. (1967) *Wilderness and the American Mind*, New Haven and London: Yale University Press.

Riva, G. (2008) 'Enacting Interactivity: The Role of Presence', in Morganti, F., Carassa, A., Riva, G. (eds) (2008) *Enacting Intersubjectivity: A Cognitive and Social Perspective on the Study of Interactions*, Amsterdam: IOS Press, 97–114.

Sanchez-Vives, M. V. and Slater, M. (2005) 'From Presence to Consciousness through Virtual Reality', *Nature Reviews Neuroscience*, 6:4, 332–9.

Shapiro, G. (1995) *Earthwards: Robert Smithson and Art After Babel*, Berkeley: University of California Press.

Slater, M. (2002) 'Presence and the Sixth Sense', *Presence: Teleoperators and Virtual Environments*, 11:4, 435–9.

Steuer, J. (1992) 'Defining virtual reality: Dimensions determining telepresence', *Journal of Communications*, 42, 73–93.

White, R. (1980) *Music, Sound, Language, Theater*, Santa Cruz NM: Crown Point Press.

Chapter 4

Performance remains again

Rebecca Schneider

The peculiar burden and problem of the theatre is that there is
no original artwork at all. Unless one maintains that the text is
the artwork (which repudiates the entire history of the theatre),
there seems no way of avoiding this difficult fact. Every other art
has its original and its copies. Only music approximates the
theatrical dilemma, but notation insures that each musical
performance will at least come close to the composer's intention.
(Schechner 1965: 22, 24, original emphasis)

Dance exists at a perpetual vanishing point. [...] It is an event
that disappears in the very act of materializing.
(Siegel 1968: 1)

In theatre, as in love, the subject is disappearance.
(Blau 1982: 94)

Performance originals disappear as fast as they are made. No
notation, no reconstruction, no film or videotape recording can
keep them. [...] One of the chief jobs challenging performance
scholars is the making of a vocabulary and methodology that
deal with performance in its immediacy and evanescence.
(Schechner 1985: 50)

Performance cannot be saved, recorded, documented, or
otherwise participate in the circulation of representations of
representations: once it does so it becomes something other
than performance. [...] Performance [...] becomes itself
through disappearance.
(Phelan 1993: 146)

> We need a history that does not save in any sense of the word;
> we need a history that performs.
> (Blocker 1999: 134)

This essay is about performance and the archive, or the positioning of performance in archival culture.[1] It takes up the long-standing invitations of many in performance studies to consider performance 'always at the vanishing point' (Blau 1982: 28)[2]. Taking up these invitations, I've set myself the following question: If we consider performance as 'of' disappearance, if we think of the ephemeral as that which 'vanishes,' and if we think of performance as the antithesis of preservation[3], do we limit ourselves to an understanding of performance predetermined by a cultural habituation to the patrilineal, West-identified (arguably white-cultural) logic of the archive?

Troubling disappearance

The archive has long been habitual to Western culture. We understand ourselves relative to the remains we accumulate as indices of vanishment, the tracks we house, mark, and cite, the material traces we acknowledge as remaining. Jacques Le Goff stated the Western truism quite simply, noting that history, requiring remains, has been composed of documents because 'the document is what remains.' Even as the domain of the document has expanded to include 'the spoken word, the image, and gesture,' the fundamental relationship of remain to documentability remains intact (Le Goff 1992: xvii). But the 'we' of this mode of history as material remains is not necessarily universal. Rather, 'archive culture' is appropriate to those who align historical knowledge with European traditions, or, even more precisely, those who chart a (mythic) descent from Greek antiquity[4]. As Derrida reminds us in *Archive Fever,* the word archive stems from the Greek and is linked at the root to the prerogatives of the archon, the head of state. Tucked inside the word itself is the house of he who was 'considered to possess the right to make or to represent the law,' and to uphold, as Michel Foucault has written, the 'system of its enunciability' (Derrida 1995: 2)[5].

In the theatre the issue of remains as material document, and the issue of performance as documentable, becomes complicated – necessarily imbricated, chiasmically, with the live body. The theatre, to the degree that it is composed in live performance, seems to resist remains. And yet, if live theatre in the West is approached as that which refuses to remain, as performance studies scholars have quite fulsomely insisted, it is precisely in live art and live theatre that scores of late twentieth-century and early twenty-first-century artists explore history – the recomposition of remains in and as the live[6]. If we consider performance as of disappearance, of an ephemerality read as vanishment and loss, are we perhaps limiting ourselves to an understanding of performance predetermined by our cultural habituation to the logic of the archive?

According to the logic of the archive, what is given to the archive is that which is recognized as constituting a remain, that which can have been documented or has become document. To the degree that performance is not its own document (as Schechner, Blau, and Phelan have argued), it is, constitutively, that which does not remain. As the logic goes, performance is so radically 'in time' (with time considered linear) that it cannot reside in its material traces and therefore 'disappears.'

The definition of performance as that which disappears, which is continually lost in time, is a definition well suited to the concerns of art history and the curatorial pressure to understand performance in the museal context where performance appeared to challenge object status and seemed to refuse the archive its privileged 'savable' original. Arguably even more than in the theatre, it is in the context of the museum, gallery, and art market that performance appears to primarily offer disappearance. Particularly in the context of visual art, performance suggests a challenge to the 'ocular hegemony' that, to quote Kobena Mercer, 'assumes that the visual world can be rendered knowable before the omnipotent gaze of the eye and the 'I' of the Western cogito' (1996: 165). Thus there is a political promise in this equation of performance with dis-appearance: if performance can be understood as disappearing, perhaps performance can rupture the ocular hegemony Mercer cites. And yet, in privileging an understanding of performance as a refusal to remain, do we ignore other ways of knowing, other modes of remembering, that might be situated precisely in the ways in which performance remains, but remains differently? The ways, that is, that performance resists a cultural habituation to the ocular – a thrall that would delimit performance as that which cannot remain to be seen.

The predominant performance-studies-meets-art-history attitude toward performance as disappearance might overlook different ways of accessing history offered by performance. Too often, the equation of performance with disappearance reiterates performance as necessarily a matter of loss, even annihilation. Curator Paul Schimmel made this perspective clear in his essay 'Leap into the Void,' writing that the orientation toward 'the act,' which he historicizes as a post-World War II preoccupation, is an orientation toward destruction. 'Although there are instances of lighthearted irreverence, joy, and laughter in this work, there is always an underlying darkness, informed by the recognition of humanity's seemingly relentless drive toward self-annihilation' (Schimmel 1998: 17). In his analysis, performance becomes itself as void. It may be a medium of creation, but a creation subservient to a disappearance understood as loss, 'destruction,' and 'darkness.'

If we adopt the equation that performance does not save, does not remain, and apply it to performance generally, to what degree can performance interrogate archival thinking? Is it not the case that it is precisely the logic of the archive that approaches performance as of disappearance? Asked another way, does an equation of performance with impermanence, destruction, and loss follow rather than disrupt a cultural habituation to the imperialism inherent in archival logic? A simple example may serve us well: on a panel at a Columbia University conference in 1997 on documentation, archivists Mary Edsall and Catherine Johnson bemoaned the problems of preserving performance, declaring that the practices of 'body-to-body transmission,' such as dance and gesture, mean that 'you lose a lot of history'[7]. Such statements assume that memory cannot be housed in a body and remain, and thus that oral storytelling, live recitation, repeated gesture, and ritual enactment are not practices of telling or writing history. Such practices disappear. By this logic, being housed always in the live, 'body-to-body transmission' disappears, is lost, and thus is no transmission at all. Obviously, the language of disappearance here is hugely culturally myopic. Here, performance is given to be as antithetical to memory as it is to the archive.

Should we not think of the ways in which the archive depends upon performance, indeed ways in which the archive performs the equation of performance with disappearance, even as it performs the service of 'saving'? It is in accord with archival logic that performance is given to disappear, and mimesis (always in a tangled and complicated relationship to the performative) is, in line with a long history of antitheatricality, debased if not downright feared as destructive of the pristine ideality of all things marked 'original'[8].

Performing the archive

> It is thus in [...] domiciliation, in [...] house arrest, that archives take place.
>
> (Derrida 1995: 2)

If the twentieth century was famous for, among other things, criticizing the concept of historical facticity, such criticism has not resulted in the end of our particular investments in the logic of the archive. Rather, we have broadened our range of documents to include that which we might have overlooked and now practice the stockpiling of recorded speech, image, gesture in the establishment of 'oral archives' and the collection of 'ethnotexts.' The important recuperation of 'lost histories' has gone on in the name of feminism, minoritarianism, and its compatriots. In light of this, what does it serve to remind ourselves that this privileging of site-able remains in the archive is linked, as is the root of the word archive, to the prerogatives of the archon, the head of state? In what way does the housing of memory in strictly material, quantifiable, domicilable remains lead both backward and forward to the principle of the archon, the patriarch? The Greek root of the word archive refers to the archon's house and, by extension, the architecture of a social memory linked to the law. The demand for a visible remain, at first a mnemonic mode of mapping for monument, would eventually become the architecture of a particular social power over memory[9]. Even if the earliest Greek archive housed mnemonics for per-formance rather than material originals themselves, archive logic in modernity came to value the document over event. That is, if ancient archives housed back-ups in case of the failure of localized knowledge, colonial archives participated in the failure of localized knowledge – that failure had become a given. The document, as an arm of empire, could arrest and disable local knowledges while simultaneously scripting memory as necessarily failed, as Ann Laura Stoller has amply illustrated. The archive became a mode of governance against memory[10]. The question becomes: Does the logic of the archive, as that logic came to be central to modernity, in fact demand that performance disappear in favor of discrete remains – material presented as preserved, as non-theatrical, as 'authentic,' as 'itself,' as somehow non-mimetic? In the archive, flesh is given to be that which slips away. According to archive logic, flesh can house no memory of bone. In the archive, only bone speaks memory of flesh. Flesh is blind spot[11]. Dissimulating and disappearing. Of course, this is a cultural equation, arguably foreign to those who claim orature, storytelling, visitation, improvisation, or embodied ritual practice as history. It is arguably foreign to practices in popular culture, such as the practices of US Civil War reenactors who consider performance as precisely a way of keeping memory alive, of making sure it does not disappear. In such practices – coded (like the body) primitive, popular, folk, naïve – performance does remain, does leave 'residue'[12]. Indeed the place of residue is arguably flesh in a network of body-to-body transmission of affect and enactment – evidence, across generations, of impact.

In scholarly treatments, the question of the performance remains of history, or more specifically history that remains in performance practice (versus written or object remains) generally falls under the rubric of memory versus history, and as such it is often labeled 'mythic.' Oral history also often falls under the rubric of ritual. In turn, 'ritual' generally (or historically) has fallen under the rubric of 'ethnic' – a term which generally means race- or class-marked people but which Le Goff cites as 'primitive' or 'peoples without writing' (Le Goff 1992: 55)[13]. Clearly, concatenations of primitivism and attendant racisms attach, in turn, to attempts to acknowledge performance as an appropriate means of remaining, of remembering. Is this perhaps because performance threatens the terms of captive or discrete remains dictated by the archive? Is this in part why the logic of the archive – that utopic 'operational field of projected total knowledge' – scripts performance as disappearing? (Thomas 1993: 11) Because oral history and its performance practices are always decidedly repeated, oral historical practices are always reconstructive, always incomplete, never in thrall to the singular or self-same origin that buttresses archontic lineage. In performance as memory, the pristine self-sameness of an 'original,' an artifact so valued by the archive, is rendered impossible – or, if you will, mythic.

Performance practice has been routinely disavowed as historical practice[14]. Though historiographers such as Pierre Nora claim that this attitude has shifted in favor of a 'new' history that incorporates collective memory and performative practices, nevertheless that 'new' history is manifested in the constitution of 'radically new kinds of archives, of which the most characteristic are oral archives' (Le Goff 1992: 95–6). The oral is not here approached as already an archive, a performance-based archive. Rather, oral histories are constituted anew, recorded and 'saved' through technology in the name of identicality and materiality. Though this 'new' archiving is supposedly against loss, doesn't it institute more profoundly than anything the loss of a different approach to saving that is not invested in identicality? Doesn't it further undo an understanding of performance as remaining? Do not such practices buttress the phallocentric insistence of the ocularcentric assumption that if it is not visible, or given to documentation or sonic recording, or otherwise 'houseable' within an archive, it is lost, disappeared?

It is interesting to take the example of battle reenactment into account and look at the particular case of Robert Lee Hodge – an avid Civil War enthusiast who participates in reenactments. As Marvin Carlson described him in an essay on theatre and historical reenactment, Hodge has attained significant notoriety among reenactment communities for his 'ability to fall to the ground and contort his body to simulate convincingly a bloated corpse' (Carlson 2000: 237–48)[15]. The question is obvious: under what imaginable framework could we cite Hodge's actions as a viable mode of historical knowledge, or of remaining? Is Hodge's bloat not deeply problematic mimetic representation, and wildly bogus and indiscreet at that? Does Hodge, lying prone and fake-bloating in the sun, attempt to offer index of – as well as reference to – both the material photograph and the photographed material of Civil War corpses? Is the live bloater only offering a mimetic and perhaps even ludicrous copy of something only vaguely imagined as a bloated corpse? Yet, within the growing 'living history' and reenactment movement, Hodge's bloating body is, for many enthusiasts, evidence of something that can touch the more distant historical record, if not evidence of something authentic itself[16]. In the often-ridiculed 'popular' arena of reenactment, Hodge's bloat is a kind of affective remain – itself, in its performative repetition, a queer kind of evidence. If the living corpse is a remain of history, it is certainly revisited across a body that cannot pass as the corpse it re-calls. If it cannot pass, what kind of claim to authenticity can such a faulty corpse demand?

I am reminded of Charles Ludlam's queer Theatre of the Ridiculous in which the replaying of classics or the 'camp' reenactment of the folk art of 'vulgar' commercial entertainment (such as B-movies) offers a different though perhaps related kind of 'living history.' Ludlam's parodic evenings offered a fractured re-entry of remainders – a history of identifications, of role-playing and its discontents. In Ludlam's theatre, as Stefan Brecht described it in 1968, 'Removal of cadavers, necessitated by the high onstage death-rate, is done with exaggerated clumsiness, the corpse does not cooperate – but mostly the dead just sit up after a while, walk off, reparticipate in the action' (Brecht 1968: 120).

When we approach performance not as that which disappears (as the archive expects), but as both the act of remaining and a means of re-appearance and 'reparticipation' (though not a metaphysic of presence) we are almost immediately forced to admit that remains do not have to be isolated to the document, to the object, to bone versus flesh. Here the body – Hodge's bloated one – becomes a kind of archive and host to a collective memory that we might situate with Freud as symptomatic, with Cathy Caruth with Freud as the compulsory repetitions of a collective trauma, with Foucault with Nietzsche as 'counter-memory,' or with Fred Moten with Baraka, Minh-ha, and Derrida as transmutation[17]. The bodily, read through genealogies of impact and ricochet, is arguably always interactive. This body, given to performance, is here engaged with disappearance chiasmically – not only disappearing but resiliently eruptive, remaining through performance like so many ghosts at the door marked 'disappeared.' In this sense performance becomes itself through messy and eruptive re-appearance. It challenges, via the performative trace, any neat antimony between appearance and disappearance, or presence and absence through the basic repetitions that mark performance as indiscreet, non-original, relentlessly citational, and remaining.

Indeed, approached in this way, performance challenges loss. Still, we must be careful to avoid the habit of approaching performance remains as a metaphysic of presence that fetishizes a singular 'present' moment. As theories of trauma and repetition might instruct us, it is not presence that appears in the syncopated time of citational performance but precisely (again) the missed encounter – the reverberations of the overlooked, the missed, the repressed, the seemingly forgotten. Performance does not disappear when approached from this perspective, though its remains are the immaterial of live, embodied acts. Rather, performance plays the 'sedimented acts' and spectral meanings that haunt material in constant collective interaction, in constellation, in transmutation.

Death and living remains

Let us not too rapidly dispose of the issue of disappearance. If Schechner, Blau, Phelan, and others are correct and performance is given to become itself through disappearance – to resist document and record, to deny remains – we find ourselves in a bit of an awkward bind regarding the argument so far. In fact, Blau's work on this bind, particularly his *Take Up the Bodies: Theatre at the Vanishing Point,* has been particularly trenchant:

> Whatever the style, hieratic or realistic, texted or untexted – box it, mask it, deconstruct it as you will – the theatre disappears under any circumstances; but with all the ubiquity of the adhesive dead, from Antigone's brother to Strindberg's Mummy to the burgeoning corpse of Ionesco's Amedée, it's there when we look again.
>
> (Blau 1982: 137)

Upon any second look, disappearance is not antithetical to remains. And indeed, it is one of the primary insights of poststructuralism that disappearance is that which marks all documents, all records, and all material remains. Indeed, remains become themselves through disappearance as well.

We might think of it this way: death appears to result in the paradoxical production of both disappearance and remains. Disappearance, that citational practice, that after-the-factness, clings to remains – absent flesh does ghost bones. We have already noted that the habit of the West is to privilege bones as index of a flesh that was once, being 'once' (as in both time and singularity) only after the fact. Flesh itself, in our ongoing cultural habituation to sight-able remains, supposedly cannot remain to signify 'once' (upon a time). Even twice won't fit the constancy of cell replacing cell that is our everyday. Flesh, that slippery feminine subcutaneousness, is the tyrannical and oily, invisible-inked signature of the living. Flesh of my flesh of my flesh repeats, even as flesh is that which the archive presumes does not remain.

As Derrida notes, the archive is built on the domiciliation of this flesh with its feminine capacity to reproduce. The archive is built on 'house arrest' – the solidification of value in ontology as retroactively secured in document, object, record. This retroaction is nevertheless a valorization of regular, necessary loss on (performative) display – with the document, the object, and the record being situated as survivor of time. Thus we have become increasingly comfortable in saying that the archivable object also becomes itself through disappearance – as it becomes the trace of that which remains when performance (the artist's action) disappears. This is trace-logic emphasizing loss – a loss that the archive can regulate, maintain, institutionalize – while forgetting that it is a loss that the archive produces. In the archive, bones are given not only to speak the disappearance of flesh, but to script that flesh as disappearing by disavowing recurrence or by marking the body always already 'scandal' (Schneider 2006).

An instituted loss that spells the failure of the bodily to remain is rife with a 'patriarchal principle.' No one, Derrida notes, has shown more ably than Freud how the archival drive, which he labels as a 'paternal and patriarchic principle,' is both patriarchal and parricidic.

> The archival drive posited itself to repeat itself and returned to reposit itself only in parricide. It amounts to repressed or suppressed parricide, in the name of the father as dead father. The archontic is at best the takeover of the archive by the brothers. The equality and liberty of brothers. A certain, still vivacious idea of democracy.
>
> (Derrida 1995: 95)

Ann Pellegrini has stated this Freudian schema succinctly: 'son fathers parent(s); pre- is heir to post-; and "proper" gender identification and "appropriate" object choices are secured backward' – a 'retroaction of objects lost and subjects founded' (Pellegrini 1997: 69). Elsewhere, I have discussed this parricidal impulse as productive of death in order to ensure remains (Schneider 2001). I have suggested that the increasing domain of remains in the West, the increased technologies of archiving, may be why the late twentieth century was both so enamored of performance and so replete with deaths: death of author, death of science, death of history, death of literature, death of character, death of the avant-garde, death of modernism, and even, in Suzan-Lori Parks's brilliant and ironic rendition, *Death of the Last Black Man in the Whole Entire World* (1995). Within a culture that privileges object remains as indices of and survivors of death, to produce such a panoply of deaths may be the only way to insure remains in the wake of modernity's crises of authority, identity, and object. Killing the author, or sacrificing his station, may be, ironically, the means of ensuring that he remains.

For the moment let me simply suggest that when we read this 'securing backward' Pellegrini discusses, this 'retroaction' of objects, we are reading the archive as act – as an architecture housing rituals of 'domiciliation' or 'house arrest' – continually, as ritual, performed. The archive itself becomes a social performance space, a theatre of retroaction. The archive performs the institution of disappearance, with object remains as indices of disappearance and with performance as given to disappear. If, in Derrida's formation, it is in domiciliation, in 'house arrest' that 'archives take place' we are invited to think of this 'taking place' as continual, of house arrest as performative – a performative, like a promise, that casts the retroaction of objects solidly into a future in which the patriarchic principle Derrida cites will have (retroactively) remained.

To read 'history,' then, as a set of sedimented acts that are not the historical acts themselves but the act of securing any incident backward – the repeated act of securing memory – is to rethink the site of history in ritual repetition. This is not to say that we have reached the 'end of history,' neither is it to say that past events didn't happen, nor that to access the past is impossible. It is rather to re-situate the site of any knowing of history as body-to-body transmission. Whether that ritual repetition is the attendance to documents in the library (the physical acts of acquisition, the physical acts of reading, writing, educating), or the oral tales of family lineage (think of the African-American descendents of Thomas Jefferson who didn't need the DNA test to tell them what they remembered through oral transmission), or the myriad traumatic reenactments engaged in both consciously and unconsciously, we refigure 'history' onto bodies, the affective transmissions of showing and telling[18]. Architectures of access (the physical aspect of books, bookcases, glass display cases, or even the request desk at an archive) place us in particular experiential relations to knowledge. Those architectures also impact the knowledge imparted. Think of it this way: the same detail of information can sound, feel, look, smell, or taste radically different when accessed in radically different venues or via disparate media (or when not told in some venues but told in others). In line with this configuration, performance is the mode of any architecture or environment of access (one performs a mode of access in the archive; one performs a mode of access at a theatre; one performs a mode of access on the dance floor; one performs a mode of access on a battlefield). In this sense, too, performance does not disappear. In the archive, the performance of access is a ritual act that, by occlusion and inclusion, scripts the depreciation of (and registers as disappeared) other modes of access.

Remaining on the stage

Artists such as Suzan-Lori Parks attempt to unpack a way in which performance (or actions, or acts) remain – but remain differently. Such works are interested in the ways in which history is not limited to the imperial domain of the document, or in which history is not 'lost' through body-to-body transmission. Is this less an investigation of disappearance than an interest in the politics of dislocation and relocation? The idea that flesh memory might remain challenges conventional notions of the archive. By this reading, the scandal of performance relative to the archive is not that it disappears (this is what the archive expects, this is the archive's requirement), but that it remains in ways that resist archontic 'house arrest' and 'domiciliation.'

To the degree that it remains, but remains differently or in difference, the past performed and made explicit as (live) performance can function as the kind of bodily transmission conventional archivists dread, a counter-memory – almost in the sense of an echo (as Parks's character Lucy in *The America Play* might call it). If echoes, or in the performance troupe Spider-woman's words 'rever-ber-berations,' resound off of lived experience produced in performance, then we are challenged to think beyond the ways in which performance seems, according to our habituation to the archive, to disappear[19]. We are also and simultaneously encouraged to articulate the ways in which performance, less bound to the ocular, 'sounds' (or begins again and again, as Stein would have it), differently, via itself as repetition – like a copy or perhaps more like a ritual – like an echo in the ears of a confidence keeper, an audience member, a witness.

Arguably, this sense of performance is imbricated in Phelan's phrasing – that performance 'becomes itself through' disappearance. This phrasing is arguably different from an ontological claim of being (despite Phelan's stated drive to ontology), even different from an ontology of being under erasure. This phrasing rather invites us to think of performance as a medium in which disappearance negotiates, perhaps becomes, materiality. That is, disappearance is passed through. As is materiality.

Works in which the political manipulations of 'disappearance' demand a material criticism – works such as Diana Taylor's *Disappearing Acts* or José Esteban Muñoz's 'Ephemera as Evidence' – thus create a productive tension within performance studies orientations to (and sometime celebrations of) ephemerality. It is in the midst of this tension (or this 'pickle' as Parks might put it) that the notion of performance as disappearance crosses chiasmically with ritual – ritual, in which, through performance, we are asked, again, to (re)found ourselves – to find ourselves in repetition.

Pickling
[performance] iz trying to find an equation
for time *saved*/saving time
but theatre/experience/performing/
being/living etc. is all about
spending time. No equation or...?
(Parks 1995: 13, original emphasis)

Works cited

Agnew, V. (2004) 'Introduction: What is Reenactment?', *Criticism* 46: 3, 327–39.

Barish, J. (1981) *The Antitheatrical Prejudice*, Berkeley: University of California Press.

Bernal, M. (1989) *Black Athena*, New Brunswick, NJ: Rutgers University Press.

Blau, H. (1982) *Take Up the Bodies: Theater at the Vanishing Point*, Urbana: University of Illinois Press.

Blocker, J. (1999) *Where Is Ana Mendieta: Identity, Performativity, and Exile*, Durham, NC: Duke University Press.

——(2004) *What the Body Cost*, Minneapolis: University of Minnesota Press.

Brecht, S. (1968) 'Family of the f.p.: Notes on the Theatre of the Ridiculous', *The Drama Review*, 13:1, 117–41.

Carlson, M. (2000) 'Performing the Past: Living History and Cultural Memory', *Paragrana*, 9:2, 237–48.

Connerton, P. (1989) *How Societies Remember*, Cambridge: Cambridge University Press.

Derrida, J. (1995) *Archive Fever: A Freudian Impression*, translated by E. Prenowitz, Chicago, IL: University of Chicago Press.

Elam, H. and Rayner, A. (1994) 'Unfinished Business: Reconfiguring History in Suzan-Lori Parks's *The Death of the Last Black Man in the Whole Entire World*', *Theatre Journal*, 46:4, 447–61.

Foucault, M. (1972) *The Archaeology of Knowledge*, translated by A. Sheridan, London: Tavistock.

Halbwachs, M. (1992) *On Collective Memory*, Chicago, translated by L. A. Coser, IL: University of Chicago Press.

Horwitz, T. (1999) *Confederates in the Attic: Dispatches from the Unfinished Civil War*, New York: Vintage.

Jarman, N. (1997) *Material Conflicts: Parades and Visual Displays in Northern Ireland*, Oxford: Berg Publishers.

Kammen, M. (1993) *Mystic Chords of Memory: The Transformation of Tradition in American Culture*, New York: Vintage Books.

Kirshenblatt-Gimblett, B. (1998) *Destination Culture: Tourism, Museums, and Heritage*, Berkeley: University of California Press.

Le Goff, J. (1992) *History and Memory*, New York: Columbia University Press.

Mercer, K. (1996) 'To Unbury the Disremembered Past: Keith Piper', in M. Kalinovska (ed.) *New Histories*, Boston, MA: Institute of Contemporary Art, 161–6.

Moten, F. and Rowell, C. H. (2004) "Words Don't Go There': An Interview with Fred Moten', *Callaloo* 27, 4, 954–66.

Muñoz, J. E. (1996) 'Ephemera as Evidence: Introductory Notes to Queer Acts', *Women and Performance: A Journal of Feminist Theory*, 8:2, 5–18.

Nyong'o, T. (2009) *The Amalgamation Waltz: Race, Performance, and the Ruses of Memory*, Minneapolis: University of Minnesota Press.

Ong, W. (1982) *Orality and Literacy*, New York: Methuen.

Parks, S-L. (1995) *Death of the Last Black Man in the Whole Entire World*, in *The America Play and Other Works*, New York: Theatre Communications Group.

Pellegrini, A. (1997) *Performance Anxieties: Staging Psychoanalysis, Staging Race*, New York: Routledge.

Phelan, P. (1993) *Unmarked: The Politics of Performance*, New York: Routledge.

Schechner, R. (1965) 'Theatre Criticism', *The Tulane Drama Review*, 9: 3, 13–24.

——(1985) *Between Theatre and Anthropology*, Chicago, IL: University of Chicago University Press.

Siegel, M. B. (1968) *At the Vanishing Point. A Critic Looks at Dance*, New York: Saturday Review Press.

Schneider, R. (1997) *The Explicit Body in Performance*, New York: Routledge.

——(2001) 'Hello Dolly Well Hello Dolly: The Double and Its Theatre', in P. Campbell and A. Kear (eds) *Psychoanalysis and Performance*, New York: Routledge, 94–114.

——(2001a) 'Performance Remains', *Performance Research*, 6:2, 100–108.

——(2006) 'Judith Butler in My Hands', in E. Armour and S. St Ville (eds) *Bodily Citations: Religion and Judith Butler*, New York: Columbia University Press, 225–52.

——(2011) *Performing Remains: Art and War in Times of Theatrical Reenactment*, New York: Routledge.

Schimmel, P. (1998) 'Leap Into the Void: Performance and the Object', P. Schimmel (ed.) *Out of Actions: Between Performance and the Object*, Los Angeles, CA: Museum of Contemporary Art, 17–120.

Sickinger, J. P. (1999) *Public Records and Archives in Classical Athens*, Chapel Hill: University of North Carolina Press.

Stoller, A. L. (2002) 'Colonial Archives and the Arts of Governance', *Archival Science*, 2:1-2, 87–109.

——(2009) *Along the Archival Grain: Epistemic Anxieties and Colonial Common Sense*, Princeton, NJ: Princeton University Press.

Taylor, D. (1997) *Disappearing Acts*, Durham, NC: Duke University Press.

——(2003) *The Archive and the Repertoire*, Durham: Duke University Press.

Thomas, R. (1992) *Literacy and Orality in Ancient Greece*, Cambridge: Cambridge University Press.

——(1993) *The Imperial Archive: Knowledge and the Fantasy of Empire*, New York: Verso.

Weber, S. (2004) *Theatricality as Medium*, New York: Fordham University Press.

Yates, F. (1966) *The Art of Memory*, Chicago, IL: University of Chicago Press, 1966.

Notes

1 The essay is here altered somewhat from the original 2001 publication – modifications that bear the marks of the essay's promiscuous afterlife, including references to texts that post-date 2001. The original appeared as Schneider 2001a. For commentary on that afterlife, and another 're-do' of the essay, see Schneider 2011.

2 The approach to performance as 'an ephemeral event' has been a cornerstone to Performance Studies and has been evident as basic to performance theory since the 1960s. Interestingly, ephemerality remains. Barbara Kirschenblatt-Gimblett, another longstanding mem-

ber of and influential thinker in the field, employed the term 'ephemeral' in 1998 claiming that: 'The ephemeral encompasses all forms of behavior — everyday activities, storytelling, ritual, dance, speech, performance of all kinds.' (Kirshenblatt-Gimblett 1998: 30). In 1993, Peggy Phelan, building on Herbert Blau and Richard Schechner, read ephemeral as disappearance. In an excellent 1996 essay, 'Ephemera as Evidence: Introductory Notes to Queer Acts,' Jose Esteban Muñoz turned the table on ephemerality to suggest that ephemera do not disappear, but are distinctly material. Munoz relies on Raymond William's 'structures of feeling' to argue that the ephemeral —'traces, glimmers, residues, and specks of things' — is a 'mode' of 'proofing' employed by necessity (and sometimes preference) by minoritarian culture and criticism makers (Muñoz 1996: 10).

3 Building explicitly on Phelan, Jane Blocker's *Where Is Ana Mendieta* provides an example of art history's application of the ephemerality of performance as informed through performance studies. Blocker employed the equation of performance with disappearance to suggest that performance is the antithesis of 'saving.' See Blocker's own important complication of this position in her subsequent book, *What the Body Cost* (Blocker 2004: 105–7).

4 See Thomas 1993. The articulation of Greek antiquity as fore-fathering history itself is mythic. The 'disremembering' of other lineages ultimately served Eurocentric, geopolitical, racializing agendas. See Bernal 1989.

5 In the late 1960s, reaching English readers in the early 1970s, Michel Foucault had expanded the notion of 'the archive' beyond a material, architectural housing of documents and objects to include, more broadly, structures of enunciability at all. Foucault articulated 'the archive' as essentially discursive – invested of an investment in preservation – determining not only the 'system of enunciability' (what can be said) but also the duration of any enunciation (what is given to remain becomes what can have been said). An excerpt from Foucault's *The Archaeology of Knowledge* bears repeating:

> The archive is first the law of what can be said, the system that governs the appearance of statements as unique events. But the archive is also that which determines that all these things said do not accumulate endlessly in an amorphous mass, nor are they inscribed in an unbroken linearity, nor do they disappear at the mercy of chance external accidents; but they are grouped together in distinct figures [...]. The archive is not that which, despite its immediate escape, safeguards the event of the statement, and preserves, for future memories, its status as an escapee; it is that which, at the very root of the statement-event, and in that which embodies it, defines at the outset the *system of its enunciability*. Nor is the archive that which collects the dust of statements that have become inert once more, and which may make possible the miracle of their resurrection; it is that which defines the mode of occurrence of the statement-thing; it is *the system of its functioning* (Foucault 1972: 129, original emphasis).

6 See Keith Piper's installation, *Relocating the Remains* (1997). The work of Suzan-Lori Parks is also exemplary. See also Elam and Rayner 1994: 447–61.

7 Comments made at the panel 'Documentation in the Absence of Text,' during the conference 'Performance and Text: Thinking and Doing,' sponsored by the Department of Theatre Arts, Columbia University, New York, 2–4 May 1997.

8 See Barish 1981 and Weber 2004. That a distrust of mimesis should develop simultaneously with the development of archives in ancient Greece deserves greater analysis, especially given the fact that the first Greek archives did not house originals but seconds. The first archives were used to store legal documents that were not originals but official copies of text inscribed on stone monuments placed around the city. The documents were copies of stone markers that were themselves 'mnemonic aids' – not, that is, the 'thing' preserved. See Thomas 1992: 86–7. Thus the first archived documents backed up a performance-oriented memory that was intended to be encountered live in the form of monuments, art, and architecture. On the classical art of memory as performance-oriented, see Yates 1966: 1–49.

9 On social power over memory, Derrida writes: 'The meaning of "archive," its only meaning, comes to it from the Greek *arkheion*: initially a house, a domicile, an address, the residence of the superior magistrates, the archons, those who commanded. The citizens who thus held and signified political power were considered to possess the right to make or to represent the law. On account of their publicly recognized authority, it is at their home, in that place which is their house (private house, family house, or employees' house), that official documents are filed' (Derrida 1995: 2). But ancient archival practice is more complicated than Derrida lets on. In ancient Greece the word 'archive' was not used to refer to the housing of original documents. See Sickinger 1999: 6. I have alluded to this briefly in fn 8, but to complicate matters, the first official (though not the only) storeroom for documents in Ancient Greece was the Metroon – the sanctuary of the Mother of the Gods. The Metroon was established in part to bring some order to official documents that had been scattered in the keeping of the archons.

10 See Stoller 2002: 87–109 and Stoller 2009. See also Thomas 1993.

11 Psychoanalysis certainly posits flesh as archive, but an inchoate and unknowing archive. Is it a given in all circumstances that body memory is 'unknowing' and 'blind'? See Schneider 2006.

12 In his influential book *Orality and Literacy: The Technologizing of the Word*, Walter Ong makes the claim that because they are performance-based, oral traditions do not leave 'residue,' make no 'deposit,' do not remain. Arguably, this claim is debunked by his own insistence that many habits from oral culture persist (Ong 1982: 11). On the issue of body memory in general see Connerton 1989. Connerton surprisingly situates bodily memory as extremely fixed and unchanging. This aspect is critiqued by Neil Jarman in *Material Conflicts: Parades and Visual Displays in Northern Ireland* (Jarman

1997: 11). See also the work of Susan Leigh Foster, Mark Franko, Fred Moten.

13 Le Goff's work provides an example of the troubled leap from oral history to ritual to ethnicity and from ethnicity to 'peoples without writing' (Le Goff 1991: 55).

14 Cultural historians now accept popular and aesthetic representation generally as social modes of historicization, often under Maurice Halbwachs's rubric 'collective memory.' See Halbwachs 1992. Still, the process of approaching aesthetic production as valid historiography involves careful (and debated) delineation between 'memory,' 'myth,' 'ritual,' and 'tradition' on the one hand and the implicitly more legitimate (or supposedly non-mythic) 'history' on the other. See Kammen 1993: 25–32.

15 See also Horwitz 1999: 7–8.

16 See Vanessa Agnew on the myriad problems that arise for historians who attempt to credit live reenactment as any kind of access to history or any kind of complement to the historical record. Agnew accuses reenactment of 'theatre.' She rather reductively associates theatre with one of its historical modes – romantic sentimentalism – rather than, say, associating theatre with Brechtian alienated historicization. Agnew's primary critique of living history and reenactment is that the focus on reenactors' experiences sentimentalizes and subjectivizes history. See Agnew 2004: 335. But the case of the corpse is problematic. For, at least as described by Horwitz (1999: 7–8), Hodge is not naïve enough to think that he fully experiences what it means to be a corpse, even if it is true that his (mock) fallen body may (mock) alarm other (mock) soldiers who come upon it on the (mock) battlefield.

17 See Moten and Rowell 2004: 954–66.

18 See Nyong'o 2009: 152–3, for engagement with oral history and 'official' history in the example of Jefferson's descendents and the 'hidden in plain sight' theory of quilting patterns. Nyong'o, reminding us fulsomely throughout his book of the race politics always sedimented in debates about history and memory, writes that 'at issue was less a choice between the archive and memory and more a context over black representative space in memory [...] less a competition between 'élite' and 'folk' knowledge and more of a competition between academic and mass culture over the pedagogic stakes of remembrance' (Nyong'o 2009 153). Nyong'o's comments of the generative aspects of 'myth,' 'error,' and 'mistake,' and the palimpsest of racial politics that inform the stakes in mistake, are extremely useful as well.

19 See the chapter on Spiderwoman in Schneider 1997.

Chapter 5

Tension/release and the production of time in performance

Jon Erickson

In the first volume of *Time and Narrative* Paul Ricoeur draws upon a theory of time proposed by Augustine in Chapter XI of his *Confessions*. It is the idea that our only possible relation to time is a psychological one attached to temporality's three domains. Thus the past is constituted by our memory, the present is constituted by our attention, and the future is constituted by our expectation (Ricoeur 1984: 5–30)[1]. This tripartite form that our consciousness takes is our sole relation to time. But Ricoeur points out a paradox about the tripartite division: while each psychological element relates to past, present, or future, they are all only experienced in the present – but *as* the past, present, or future. In a comparable sense, Edmund Husserl refers to the fundamental intentionality of consciousness, with 'protention' and 'retention' as the immediately past and future components. Maurice Merleau-Ponty also speaks to this in a more radical sense when he says, 'We must understand time as the subject and the subject as time. What is perfectly clear is that this primordial temporality is not a juxtaposition of external events, since it is the power which holds them together while keeping them apart' (Merleau-Ponty 1962: 422). Making our relation to time solely related to our psychological state doesn't mean that the development of 'clock time' as a form of measurement cannot refer to something outside that state. That is, atomic clocks can be accurate down to nanoseconds in relation to the division of equal segments of the temporal framework of the completed rotation of the earth and the completed revolution of the earth around the sun. It is just that this exactitude has little to do with the actual experience of time by human beings. Kant made clear his position on this: 'Time is therefore merely a subjective condition of our (human) intuition (which is always sensuous, that is, so far as we are affected by objects), and in itself, independently of the mind or subject, is nothing,' and 'Time is nothing but the form of our internal intuition. If we take away from it the special condition of our sensibility, the conception of time also vanishes; and it inheres not in the objects themselves, but solely in the subject (or mind) which intuits them' (Kant 1990: 31–2).

There are times when we find ourselves in situations when time seems to drag on, or other times when it flies by, and we don't know where it went. At those moments we find ourselves saying things like: 'that seemed to have lasted a lot longer than the actual amount of time that passed,' or 'the time seemed to go by much faster than it really did.' I showed Jean-Luc Godard's *Weekend* in a film class, and after watching the excruciatingly extended tracking shot of a traffic jam on a country road, filled from beginning to end with the sound of honking horns, my students were all convinced the scene lasted between ten and fifteen minutes, and were surprised when I said it was only six minutes. While we take our standard clock-time, and recognize its passing, as the objective measure of everything else, what we fail to realize is that even our experiential relation to clock-time is not itself objective. That is, when we say that time passed slower than it actually did, we are really saying time passed more slowly than it usually does for us. While our bodies contain circadian rhythms that help us to wake up at regular times, for instance, even without clocks, they are also related to other natural cycles, such as sunlight, and so are not simply internal, with their accuracy depending upon that. But what our bodies experience and what our conscious minds experience in terms of the passing of time may not be exactly the same thing.

It is possible to get a sense of what a certain passage of time 'feels like,' but it is usually in relation to something else that constitutes an activity, even an apparently passive activity like thinking. Making three-minute eggs for myself every other morning for breakfast gave me an indication, for instance, of how much text of a book I could read while waiting, but even that depends on the type or difficulty of the book being read. We have no objective sense of what a 'real' five minutes by clock time means to measure against what seems in certain situations as a 'slow' or 'fast' five minutes. Our measures of time are that which we share with others who lead the same kinds of lives as we do. The lives of farmers or country folk (at least in the not too distant past) who have no problem sitting on porches for hours, making small talk or no talk at all has a quite different sense of 'objective' time than urban teenagers who feel themselves going crazy with boredom if they don't have something to constantly distract them. Buddhist monks who can sit for hours just breathing do not have the same sense of time as businessmen perpetually trying to close deals before different clients change their minds or go somewhere else. Even academics that teach in quarter systems do not have the same sense of time as academics teaching in semester systems. Nonetheless there are forces that work to homogenize separate senses of time: television is one of them. First in terms of the scheduled times in which shows come on that people watch; secondly, how many shows people watch; and thirdly, in the nature of the pace of editing of segments, of both commercials and shows alike. The gradually increasing speed of such things over the years must to some extent affect all that watch, no matter where they are in the scheme of things.

There have been experiments in the theater and in film with producing the action in real time. One thinks of the film *High Noon*, for instance, or Marsha Norman's play set in a laundromat, *Third and Oak*. Unlike the clock in *High Noon*, which the film occasionally refers back to in order to indicate Gary Cooper's time running out, the clock in Norman's play is on the wall for the audience to constantly refer to as the play progresses. But again, as I've indicated in what I've said about the relativity of the experience of time, what is our sense of 'real time' anyway? We think we should know what five minutes feels like, but if we were to actually sit and attentively watch a clock's minute-hand move over five minutes, would we know what that space felt like, would we be able to retain it objectively against all other event situations presumably lasting five minutes? One need only remember time spent in classrooms where a clock is clearly visible on the front wall, or I can recall my former wife going through labor in a hospital room while a clock is staring at her from the opposite wall. It's always interesting when a script calls for a minute of silence between utterances, and someone always says 'a minute is a long time in the theater.' How long? Compared to what? Compared to my desire to keep moving and to keep talking? Compared to what an audience can bear? Which audience?

It is my contention that time is actually produced in the theater for the spectators by the performance; it is produced for (and by) the performers as well, but that is a slightly different story, which I will come to later. Throughout, the experience of time arises out of the creation of instances of tension and release, at multiple levels, which produces rhythms that either carry along the spectator, or produces resistances. There is something basically coercive about this, but the coercion is typically felt only when one is resistant to what is presented, as opposed to being caught up within its force. The Russian filmmaker Andrey Tarkovsky put it this way:

> the director's sense of time always amounts to a kind of coercion of the audience, as does his imposition of his inner world. The person watching either falls into your rhythm (your world), and becomes your ally, or else he does not, in which case no contact is made. And so some people become your 'own,' and others remain strangers; and I think this is not only perfectly natural, but, alas, inevitable.
>
> (Tarkovsky 1987: 120)

Tarkovsky further notes that the individuality of the filmmaker is to be found in his or her sense of time: 'It is above all through sense of time, through rhythm, that the director reveals his individuality. [...]. Feeling the rhythmicality of a shot is rather like feeling a truthful word in literature. An inexact word in writing, like an inexact rhythm in film, destroys the veracity of the work' (Tarkovsky 1987: 120).

There is, in effect, an implicit contract in which the spectator agrees to give herself over to the temporality created by the theater artist or film director. The time created will nonetheless be experienced differently by those who are engaged or those who find themselves resisting, signifying the emergence of what Tarkovsky calls the 'allies' and 'strangers' of the artist's work. The development of tension in long slow takes (as in Tarkovsky's films), or in slowly emerging actions on stage may produce a kind of fascination with the beauty of its unfolding, or when inelegantly done produce what film critics call *longeurs*, which are more or less put up with for the benefit of the pay off of release. And while tension-release can involve, for the spectator at the simplest level, a wondering at where a particular movement, gesture, is going, creating a vision of bodily transformation, it is also inextricably tied in with a larger narrative desire, where the signs of the movement may also be read within the unfolding of meanings through dialogue.

Tension/release and the will to know

For the audience member, actions on stage that one attempts to recognize as elements of a particular narrative, or elements of a sequence of a larger narrative that nonetheless has a *telos* – which includes an intention (or cause) and carrying-out (or effect) to produce an end (meaning) – play a large role in establishing a sense of tension out of a desire to understand the 'point' of the actions. The tension is a pleasurable one when the process of behavior begins explaining itself, given that the real initial tension is incomprehensibility. But a different kind of tension can take place when the action is patently obvious but its consequence delayed. What happens, then, when the consequence is unexpected? What effect does the nature of this kind of release portend or reflect?

Dance may be a form that makes us question the requirement of a relation of narrative to tension and release. We may be interested in seeing how long someone can sustain a movement or what preparatory movement is going to lead us to expect a fantastic leap (the same in ice-skating). And in music the same is true in terms of crescendo, diminuendo, or bolero-like structures of modulation (every Roy Orbison song: will he make those high notes?). The idea of dance or music that develops in certain ways, but doesn't create a narrative can get us to ask about the relation of narrative to cause and effect. Narrative is necessarily causal in its structure, but causality is not necessarily narrative. And yet, do we not feel a compulsion to translate all causal experience into a meaningful narrative for ourselves, even if only at the level of reasoning about our shift of mood?

Min Tanaka

In August 1997, I witnessed a performance that struck me as being the closest I've seen to a realization of Artaud's ideal theatre of cruelty. It was at Jacob's Pillow, in the Berkshires, where I witnessed a work by the Butoh dancer Min Tanaka, working with a company of young American dancers. Called *The Poe Project (Stormy Membrane)*, it was billed as having a 'libretto' by Susan Sontag – a strange designation, as there was not one word uttered in the entire piece. What was rendered as 'libretto,' was in fact a sequence of themes that Sontag had extracted from the stories of Edgar Allan Poe: shipwreck, premature burial, guilt, the double, the plague, necrophilia, and so on. Min Tanaka either wore a raincoat with a beat-up fedora, or else a large white diaper. The attitudes displayed by the dancers seemed to be those of the inmates of an insane asylum, their movements tending toward obsessive-compulsive and hysterical behavior. There were cries that rent the air, coming from various inmates, male and female, with uncanny and contagious reproductions of behavior along with a strange rhythmic music of screams. There were moments of great beauty and strangeness, as when Tanaka appeared to ascend a ladder of light, and backlit figures partially obscured by scrims combined tiny figures with monstrous giants. But the grotesque and obsessive nature of the behavior was extremely difficult to tolerate: at points it seemed to me we really were watching the mad inflicting pain on themselves. One young woman kept audibly slapping her left forearm with her right hand for what seemed an extremely long period of time, so that I thought for sure a welt would be raised by the performance's end. Mad pawings and screamings went on for what seemed like an unbearable length of time (perhaps an hour), and about half the audience left before it was over. I felt my hands start to tensely grip the armrests of my seat. But the last scene created an incredible shift from everything that went on before. Suddenly all was calm, the lighting was soft, and we saw a tableau of several couples in various poses of sitting, lying, and standing, reaching longingly and lovingly toward each other. Music swelled: the adagio from Mahler's Fifth Symphony (notably the theme music from Visconti's film *Death in Venice*). Suddenly I was perplexed and a bit dismayed because it all seemed to become very saccharine and sentimental, almost parodically so, the looks exchanged rendering the lovers utterly ridiculous and camp. Tanaka suddenly stumbled onto the stage in his diaper, moving among them, but then as the lovers froze into their final tableau, turning and walking that peculiar Butoh pigeon-toed walk toward the back of the stage, his arms outstretched. As he approached the back wall, it opened, revealing another wall. When he got to that wall it too opened for him. As he walked through these walls it became progressively dark around him, until a wall opened and it was completely black, but with bright spotlights backlighting him. As he walked it appeared that smoke was rising from his body, but then I realized that the last wall had actually opened into the woods behind the theater and the smoke was really steam. He disappeared between the lights and into the dark woods as the music faded.

After, I felt as if this performance was an amazing lesson in performative behaviorism, in its elicitation through almost purely formal means, of a tremendous emotional reaction. I can only speak to my own reaction, and not to those of others, and I would have to say that those who left early unfortunately had no experience of this reaction, of this release. That is, while the tension kept building for what seemed an eternity, accompanied by a sense of strong aversion mingled with a riveted fascination, in fact a kind of real fear for the performers' safety or sanity, and an embarrassed self-consciousness about watching this process of self-inflicted wounding, the release, the sheer contrast of the last scene that I couldn't intellectually connect with what had gone before and which reeked of a garish sweetness, suddenly produced in me a violent and uncontrollable sobbing and shedding of tears. This was happening at the very same moment I was critically and intellectually repulsed by the overly campy nature of the last scene. I was split in two, an emotional reacting body and an utterly perplexed and skeptical mind. But then suddenly it occurred to me that it didn't matter how this last scene was constructed, as long as it presented the greatest possible contrast to all that had come before. In this sense I had the strange sensation of no longer caring about the nature of the scene, but caring only for the release it brought me. It was true, nonetheless, that the image of Min Tanaka walking into the spotlights in the midst of the dark woods was truly stunning.

I was reminded of the principle of tension and release a few years later when I saw the Butoh group Dai Rakudakan at the Wexner Center in Columbus, Ohio. It is a very large ensemble and I was somewhat disappointed by the showiness and presentational aspect which seemed uncharacteristic of the more intensely inward forms of Butoh I had seen before, like Min Tanaka, Sankai Juku, or Eiko and Koma. Nonetheless the characteristic of maintaining one kind of repetitive action and sound for an almost unbearable length of time was always followed by a sudden shift into its seeming opposite; a deeply primeval scene of yogically centered animal nature that resonated rhythmically over and over in a mantric trance until one was almost falling asleep suddenly reversed itself into utterly silly and ridiculous kewpie-doll figures doing cutesy dances, breaking the audience into peals of laughter.

It seemed to me that for Butoh this principle of repetitively winding up tension as far as it can go until the audience is nearly in a trance and then suddenly shifting into its extreme opposite stylistically was just the most overt exemplification of what performance's material employment of time is in *any* kind of work performed before an audience, whether it is music, dance, or theater. It occurred to me that to refer to theater as a 'time-based art' seems a misnomer, simply because it is not the case that performance is somehow based or grounded 'in' time: rather performance actually *produces* time (or, if you will, a sense of time – but what's the difference?) for the audience through the principle of tension and release. If Ricoeur is right, and time for human beings is *only* to be understood or experienced as a psychological formation produced by varying relations of memory, attention, and expectation toward the world, then any performative structure that influences those relations in a particular way actually produces a particular experience of time for the spectator. But if what Ricoeur says is true, then one can ask if producing an experience of time for the spectator and producing time for the spectator aren't in fact the same thing.

Dance performance and boredom

We should take note here that 'Butoh' is generally not included in theories or histories of theater, but of dance, even though it can represent that hybrid called 'dance-theatre.' This may be partially why I think dance and music can offer us almost purely formal examples of the experience of tension and release that produce a distinctly clear sense of time and timing. The repetition of particular movements, with all their variations, a dance's vocabulary combining and recombining in different syntactical senses, but building from simplicity to complexity whose release culminates in our recognition of the relation of the two at once: in Trisha Brown's 'Accumulations,' for instance. In music, clearly, there are myriad ways to produce the effects of tension and release, found both in crescendos and in modulations, in development and return.

Consider the time differential between performer and audience. Again, I think in some ways the test in terms of tension and release, between expectation and boredom can be more acutely read through dance. That is, instead of a conventional storyline or plot, we may be given sequences that work into a particular development or culmination based upon theme and variations. That is, we are given a sequence of movements in dance designated as a particular *vocabulary* of movements that are then varied and combined and extended in complicated ways over the course of the performance, generally moving (although not always) from simple introduction to complicated construction. Now the question for the audience is recognizing difference in these combinations so that it doesn't end up seeming to them as merely monotonous repetition. Here it could be the case that what the *dancer* is experiencing is a large variety of subtle variations while what the audience member – especially one not experienced in watching dance – may see is simply repetitiveness. But it nonetheless may be the case that what even a seasoned dance audience may see as a piece that is 'too long' may not seem too long for the dancer who loses herself to enjoying subtleties lost to the onlooker (this may also raise the question of 'self-indulgence,' which is always relative even to audience members). Thus I could designate a spectrum of response from an audience member not attuned to dance to one more attuned to reading it to a connoisseur of dance (including dancers, of course) – all the 'in' audience – to the dancer herself onstage engaged in the performance. (What is left out here is the relation of dancers to each other, whose sense of the dance as a whole may vary). In each case the degree of psychic investment, or relation of expectation to boredom, alters the temporal experience of the work. It also changes for the audience member who sees it more than once: knowing what is coming can improve attention to detail that can in fact make shorter what seemed long to begin with. It may be possible that it could work the other way, especially if there are sections that are not pleasing to the expectations of the audience. Knowing a work in fact increases the tension in attention paid to its realization, making critical narrative or formal shifts the points of distinction between what the audience desires to see and how the performer disappoints, meets, or surpasses that desire crucial for the quality of the release from the tension. So the way in which that realization of the 'already known' releases the tension can nonetheless provide a surprise of interpretation.

Levels of tension/release

Tension and release operates on a variety of levels starting with the microlevel: in dance it is found in every movement, in the muscles contracting and releasing; in theater it is in each gesture and speech-act. The power of the performer can be found in the quality of the tension in his or her body. In fact this power is most evident when it is held back, or in reserve. Zeami advises the Noh actor to only give at most 7/10ths of the energy of what could be expended. Eugenio Barba suggests that the power of the performer can be enhanced by creating oppositions of movement, or negating the intended movement by moving back, retracting the gesture slightly (Barba and Savarese, 1991: 176–85).

At a higher level, tension and release operate in the rhythm of scenes, established in the tempo and timing of response in dialogue, or the juxtaposition of pauses and speech, faster and slower rhythms in monologue. I think here of Strindberg's directions for the rhythm of Miss Julie's monologue about escape to Lake Como: its initial speed that seems a false enthusiasm designed to delay reflection about her reality, and when that reflection comes, slowing to a despairing end. (In this sense, 'release' is not necessarily to be read as the attainment of a satisfaction).

At an even higher level is the relation between scenes, where one scene may increase tension to a manic level, while another release it to some extent, only perhaps to prepare a greater tension for the next scene, gradually building step-wise toward the climactic end. One play where this rhythm seems most significant is Albee's *Who's Afraid of Virginia Woolf?* What's more, the degree of tension and degree of release is located in the number of characters interacting. The most manic tensions are created when all four characters – George, Martha, Nick and Honey – are present and acting out for one another, while the momentary respites that are both a release of tension and a preparation for further tension are found in scenes between only two characters: George and Nick, Nick and Martha, George and Honey, and sometimes even George and Martha.

The most crucial moments in a performance are the ones that require the greatest focus, and the tension that directs that focus occurs both in the shrinking of the space of attention to small areas between characters and also in slowing down the tempo of the action. One need only think of the expected kiss that may happen or may be interrupted or averted at the last moment. An example for me that indicates this issue is my response to *Angels in America*, after having seen two different productions of it. While reading it somewhat allowed the pathos of the individual relationships to sink in, seeing a production didn't allow this to happen. The sheer speed with which the play has to be performed in order to fit all the information into the allotted performance time undermined any possibility of my empathy for the characters, since they weren't given any time to actually slow down and feel anything, or allow me to feel anything for them[2].

The temporality of acting

There is a curious problem involved in the traditional acting of a role that depends on both the completeness of a foresight that determines all action in the present, a foresight that knows the final outcome of such action – which in Stanislavskyan terms is the 'through-line' – and the impression that must be given to the audience that one's character is operating completely in the moment with no such knowledge. Or at least that the knowledge is one that any of us have, a speculative possibility that emerges from an understanding of past circumstances. Thus a convincing performance that has presence to it has to be able, in its own actions, to disavow the complete knowledge of its outcome in order to demonstrate the fixed position of the character's consciousness in the present – which is everyone's condition. Of course one could make the case for the greater or less *speculative* ability of characters, which at the most extreme end would be the supernatural capability of the prophet (for example, Cassandra, Tiresias). But within any 'realist' scenario this is tempered by the idea that even prophets tend not to know or understand all the details of the outcome they foresee (unlike the actor who knows the full outcome of the script). But how often are we confronted by a cast of prophets, all who foresee the same outcome?

The problem, then, is fairly clear: the actor, to invest the most in the believability of his role, has to know the outcome, in the sense conveyed by the basic hermeneutical proposition that the meaning of any part of a text (or event) depends upon its relation to the whole (and vice versa) and so the fullest meaning given to any action in the present depends upon this sense of the whole. At the same time one should not allow this foreknowledge to distance one from the full exigencies of the present situation whose pressures are no sure basis for future knowledge for the character. And it is, of course, this *lack* of knowledge that determines the character's actions as much as any speculative possibility – it is *uncertainty* that figures in the focusing of the spectator's attention on the character's actions and endows these actions, through the mediation of the actor's skill, with presence. This uncertainty may be linked in some ways with that other uncertainty always possible in the theater – the actor will forget his lines or make mistakes in speech. But there's also the other uncertainty that is related to the disavowed future by *both* the spectator and the actor – the possibility that the actor may anticipate in reaction what hasn't happened yet: the timing involved at being startled at a gunshot, for instance, but also in pre-reacting to another's words.

So what is the audience's relation to this problem of foreknowledge and its disavowal for the sake of presence? On the one hand, it would appear to be less of a problem if the audience had never read or seen the play before, or having had it summarized to them (that is, having no foreknowledge of it themselves). At the same time, it is clear to any audience, whatever their own expectations, that the actors will have the entirety of this information, and so the concentration is on the unfolding of the content by the action, pretending, in a way, along *with* the actors, that the characters do not have this knowledge of their future. And such pretense seems easier if the audience *doesn't* have any foreknowledge.

On the other hand, if the audience *knows* a play, it puts them in a similar, if not the same, position as the actors themselves in terms of the dependency upon, yet disavowal of, any foreknowledge of the outcome of actions in the present. And any evaluation of an actor's performance becomes more critically focused the more a spectator knows a play or can compare one actor's performance of a role with another's. In such a case the disavowal of foreknowledge is weaker than in a play one is not familiar with or in the first experience of a play being performed that one knows. (All of this brings up the alternative conceptions of the results of greater or lesser experience in play-going: does it result in a greater power of discrimination in enjoyment or a kind of blasé attitude or jadedness that emerges with the loss of an 'innocent eye'?)

Now the nature of attention in the present is such that the danger of the presence of the performance at any moment being evacuated by the actor's (or the spectator's) foreknowledge is less likely than we think, given that the performance is the outcome of a practice that has become quasi-automatic in speech and act (the 'quasi' is what leaves a space for necessary or possible improvisation). Thus the entirety of outcomes is not conscious to the actor, which would make performing in the present impossible, but each outcome is played out sequentially through this practice.

The future becomes unconsciously embedded through practice in the body and on the tongue, emerging only when necessary, so that the acting operates in a semi-unconscious state. It is, for instance, akin to the relation between thinking and speaking in general – if I thought completely about everything I said before I said it, it is unlikely I would ever speak. And yet we do often think before we speak, but seldom – unless we prepare remarks in writing, have a full script to follow when we do speak. At the same time we do think *as* we speak, improvising and often clarifying our thoughts in the process – even as this thinking/speaking is in some sense 'emotively pre-shaped' by a general conceptual intention (which in dialogue is continually reconfigured through testing and feedback). The actor's job is to make this kind of act appear naturally out of a foreknowledge that is completely and already linguistically, if not also gesturally, predetermined.

Incomplete knowledge, memory and pain

The relations between Ricoeur's Augustinian tripartite division (memory, attention, expectation) clearly function in relation to cognition and objects of knowledge, between the already known and what is perceived in the present, the tension between the already given and new information that produces speculation about past reality or future possibility. One time-producing rhythm of tension that exists *between* the stage and the audience concerns what characters know or could know and what the audience knows or could know given the narrative evidence allowed so far. Hitchcock tells us that suspense is based on the knowledge audience members have that the characters in the film don't have, producing the desire in us to inform them and so save them from possible disaster or grief. In this our knowledge might be shared with none of the characters, or it could be with one for whom such knowledge is a source of pain and fear insofar as it isn't or can't be shared. In fact, Aristotle's identificatory acts of pity and fear rely upon this difference in knowledge, or at least fear for the character does. This is most evident in the tension inherent in the revelation of a secret, whether gradually or suddenly at the most propitious (or disastrous) moment, after possible delays, for instance. A traumatic memory is itself a secret of past pain, and to be effective its utilization requires a *rate* of revelation, or remembering, that seems plausible for the affected character's nature and circumstance.

This is obvious, for instance, in *Oedipus Rex*, even while we might also be saying to ourselves, why can't he see the truth, for god's sake, it seems so obvious! While the nature of the secret may be clear to us and less so to the affected character or characters, it may also be clearer to them than to us, but nonetheless provides a source of suspense insofar as we seem privy to the desire of characters to maintain a secret; then our desire to find the reason for this secrecy focuses our attention and piques our speculative imagination. Again, in *Who's Afraid of Virginia Woolf?* we are informed straight off about 'the kid,' who is supposed to be kept a secret from the guests. We don't know why. But gradually, of course, we come to realize that there is no kid. But here again, presumably we begin to realize this before the guests do so that we can savor their reactions.

For Aristotle the release of catharsis from the building tension of dread comes with recognition, with remembering. This is why some commentators refer to 'catharsis' as 'clarification of incident,' giving it a secure cognitive basis. The question may vary, however, as to whether the recognition that produces catharsis is recognition only for the character, one that brings the character's knowledge and the audience's knowledge to the same level, or whether it might be the case that the catharsis could result from recognition for the audience, and not the character. In any case, the tension between what is known and what is not known must be maintained at every moment in order to maintain the spectator's attention. What is not known must not be so predominant as to lose the spectator's attention in confusion, where what is given needs an extended amount of time to compare its relation to what has transpired before (although a space may be given to allow for this). But what is known should not swamp the mystery of what is as yet unknown as well.

To stay with Aristotle for a moment, 'pity and fear' obviously refer to the spectator's identification with, or dread of, a character's pain. Following Ricoeur's tripartite psychology of time, pain relates to trauma in the past, infliction or affliction in the present, and fear or anxiety about either infliction or worsening of affliction in the future. And yet either the threat of, or actual infliction of, pain produces greater tension than the mere expression of affliction, especially if it is primarily physical. Thus, in contrast to *The Poe Project*, which was a case of ongoing infliction, was a production I saw of Seamus Heaney's *The Cure at Troy*, his version of Sophocles'

Philoctetes. The title character is afflicted with a wounded foot that is painfully infected and refuses to heal. Philoctetes accents the course of the play with his painful cries and complaints about his foot. I don't know whether it was the acting, Heaney's version, or Sophocles's play itself, but this kind of expressed pain elicited no sense of pity or fear from me, but rather a strange kind of bemusement at a case of overacting. But can I say the same about the ongoing psychic pain experienced and expressed by Beckett's characters? It is sometimes less in what they say than how they say it, in the fact that there is nothing else for them to say.

We might also inquire about the temporal structure of pleasure, rather than pain. Here it can be read as nostalgia (past) – enjoyment/fulfillment (present) – and desire (future – which in terms of expectation can be read not only in terms of possible fulfillment or hope for continuation of pleasure, but fear of disappointment or cessation). The tension/release in comedy is well known in terms of blocking agents and happy endings, for instance. But the tension can be maintained in serial romances often by the question of whether a man and woman will go beyond being friends to being lovers, for instance.

Everything on stage carries with it, to begin with, an aura of futurity, and the action of a performance can either sustain the tension of this futurity founded in the well-tended curiosity of the audience or it can dissipate it in irrelevance. All such rhythms that produce a satisfying temporal experience for the audience work in relation to a continuing tension and release between the known and the unknown, the already recognized and new discoveries. This is locatable within the pragmatic semiotics of sequential gestures and acts as well as in verbal expression. With speech, rhythms can vary according to: (1) relatively transparent words that rush forward looking toward or for a conclusion; (2) words that constitute conclusions, however momentary, and that we contemplate as keys to the nature of prior events; and (3) words that present the tension of a puzzle, a mystery, posing an unclear relation of past knowledge to an unknown possible future or past that could significantly affect the present.

Our relation to futurity is founded in our understanding of causality. But in terms of our knowledge base, tension is diffused for the spectator once the action becomes predictable, and therefore boring. And yet something of what happens must be at least partly predictable in terms of causation for suspense and retention of attention to occur. But what is the relation between predictability and inevitability? What is inevitable is not necessarily predictable: in this sense inevitability is found only in retrospect, while predictability is based in foreseeing obvious outcomes, usually predicated on the specific formula of a genre. And yet I'm not satisfied that there is no connection between them at all. Inevitability may sometimes be what in retrospect strikes us as what we should have been able to predict, but for some reason didn't. For instance, to be plausible in terms of their actions, characters have to be to some degree predictable, and if they change, the reasons must be compelling ones. But change of heart must be plausible in terms of the character's makeup, but must also be plausible in relation to the timing of events being brought to bear on the character. Thus for instance, Creon's change of heart in *Antigone* must bear with it the tragic irony of its belatedness; in many ways tragedies are cases of bad timing – but the timing is not merely arbitrary, but contingent upon the nature of a person's character in general for whom such bad-timing makes sense.

Attempts at the subversion of the tension/release model

In certain forms of modern performance, there is an attempt to either transcend the tension/release production of temporal experience, usually in order to draw the audience member more fully into the space of the present, and alternative forms of perception that may be available there. In the early minimalist music of Philip Glass and Steve Reich (for instance, Reich's *Music for 18 Musicians*), a completely even and repetitive music seemed designed to produce trances in its listeners. In such pieces, release from a sense of perpetual accumulation comes with the last note. (Much more can be said about the music than this, but it relates more to formal innovations that speaks more to musicians' knowledge than to the layperson). But we can go back further, to John Cage's silent piece for piano, *4'33"* performed in Woodstock, New York in 1951, which was later rationalized by Cage as providing the means for the audience to shift their attention from their expectation of sound from a silent piano and still pianist to the ambient sounds around them as constituting the music. Whether this shift actually took place, however, is unknown, especially since many at the original concert, still focused on David

Tudor's ritualized actions at the piano, associated the piece with a 'Dada provocation.' The dance couple of Eiko and Koma, whose hour-long performances consist of incredibly slow shifting movements of their naked bodies, together or apart, slows down time for the audience, and make us more aware of extremely subtle shifts in formation in ways that can often result in visual surprises when the strain of attention draws the spectator back into himself and then back to the scene. Robert Wilson's celebrated *Deafman Glance*, where it takes Sheryl Sutton half-an-hour to cross a stage before striking a child with a knife also seems an attempt to focus on a continuous present, even while drawn toward in inevitable future act. But are these all cases of a continuous present free of tension, or an even more heightened and sustained state of tension that effects a release of a kind of perceptual 'surrender' in the spectator after a time, without any actual shift toward release on stage? Or as Cage wanted to have it, suddenly the audience's ears would open. This is also perhaps related to the jouissance Barthes specifies as the reward of tackling great but boring texts. (Difficult not in the sense of comprehensibility, as in Joyce or Faulkner, but in sheer repetitive accretion, as in Robbe-Grillet).

Samuel Beckett raises another issue: that of endless tension without any apparent release, reflecting what I call the 'ongoingness' of modern tragedy, caught in the vicious circle of an eternal return. One can, of course, conceive of humor as relative release, but one that makes the ongoing tension worse. But can the endless repetitive behavior of Beckett's characters be considered a development of a state of tension? While dread may constitute tension, does ennui? Again, a knowledge differential comes into play between stage and house, for while we recognize a certain reflective intelligence at work in Beckett's characters, there is also a significant deficit of memory involved, which in a sense makes the endless repetition bearable. And if we consider that the tripartite psychological division of time – memory, attention, expectation – requires cooperation between the three states (attention requires memory as well as expectation, memory requires attention, expectation requires memory), a deficit in any one area affects all three: lack of memory, lack of interest, lack of hope of anything different, most apparent in Beckett's work. This affects the nature of temporal experience as we've always considered it in terms of tension and release, and seems to homogenize it, and every moment of spectator attention to the present seems to represent the nature of the whole in microcosm, in its repetitive endlessness, even if coupled with the most gradual degradation. The source of dread isn't death but endlessness. But oddly enough what comes with such amnesiac repetitiveness is the arbitrary nature of events, lacking the usual sense of plausible causality. One day Pozzo goes blind and Lucky goes dumb. Perhaps one can reverse the sense of causality and ask if it isn't the sheer repetitiveness of our lives that makes us forgetful of our state in time. But we can only come to recognize this through performance's shaping of time for us in the promise of its meaning.

Works cited

Barba, E. and Savarese, N. (eds) (1991) *A Dictionary of Theatre Anthropology: The Secret Art of the Performer*, London: Routledge.

Kant, I. (1990) *Critique of Pure Reason*, trans. J. M. d. Meiklejohn, Buffalo NY: Prometheus Books.

Merleau-Ponty, M. (1962) *Phenomenology of Perception*, translated by C. Smith, London: Routledge and Kegan Paul.

Ricoeur, P. (1984) *Time and Narrative, Volume 1*, translated by K. McLaughlin and D. Pellauer, Chicago IL: University of Chicago Press,

Tarkovsky, A. (1987) *Sculpting in Time: Reflections on the Cinema*, translated by K. Hunter-Blair, Austin TX: University of Texas Press.

Notes

1 Expectation is a neutral term that encompasses even contrasting emotions such as desire and dread.

2 It is well known that Kushner considers himself a Brechtian, so presumably my remarks about empathy would be inappropriate. And yet Brecht's alienation devices, his gestus, wouldn't work without the initial elicitation of empathy on some level.

Part II

Being before

Stage and gaze

Engaging with semiotics, philosophy, performance theory and performer training, the essays forming 'Being before' introduce processes of division and multiplication that occur in the encounter between the observer and the other. More specifically, 'Being before' scrutinizes how these processes become manifest in the spectator/audience performer relationship; analyses the training techniques and framing processes that define them; and speculates about the key theoretical standpoints that are produced through them. Whilst the previous section focussed on presence in terms of 'Being here,' *hic et nunc,* this section looks at how in the encounter with presence in and through relationship with the 'other' needs to operate as networks of relational signs that are critical to understand the relationship(s) between performers, the roles they inhabit, and their spectators. 'Being before' thus questions the different terms and methodologies involved in these processes, starting from what 'Being before' involves hermeneutically, ethically and phenomenologically; then analysing presencing through acts of appearing and disappearing, being here and before, or on the edge; and showing, finally, how presence represents a *conditio sine qua non* for such encounters to occur. In these various processes, the fundamental divisions and encounters that define the theatrical relationship – the sense of 'being before'; of *being seen* in the act of performance and witnessing – are interrogated as principle mechanisms for experiences of presence. In doing so, these essays associate presence with an opening to the other and with the politics of the performed encounter, with witnessing, and open the question of being present within theatrical discourse itself. Here, too 'presence' remains and persists in ephemerality, in change and modulation, to be realized or revealed in negotiations, readings, and in 'mis-readings,' of acts of performance.

Chapter 6

Appearing as embodied mind – defining a weak, a strong and a radical concept of presence

Erika Fischer-Lichte

In June 1995, Heiner Müller's last production premiered at the Berliner Ensemble – Brecht's *The Resistible Rise of Arturo Ui*. Fifteen years later, it continues to be part of the repertoire, selling out each and every evening. Having been performed worldwide more than three hundred times, the production is still celebrated by audiences and critics alike wherever it is shown. What makes it so successful? And this not only in Berlin and Germany, but on all five continents? Although the *Berliner Zeitung* critic could not have foreseen such unprecedented success, he gave a plausible answer after perusing the fifty most important reviews published in the wake of the première: 'When, the morning after, the critics wrote their reviews for Berlin and the world, his name blazed in fiery letters: Wuttke! Wuttke! Wuttke!' (Heine 1995). And in fact, there was no critic who, full of admiration and amazement, did not speculate on the extraordinary PRESENCE[1] displayed by actor Martin Wuttke, starring as Arturo Ui, which kept spectators spellbound throughout the performance.

The performance, as well as the fascination of the spectators and the spell Wuttke cast on them, reached its climax with Scene VI – Arturo Ui taking lessons from an actor in order to learn how to walk, stand, sit and speak in public. In all three performances I attended, the very moment Wuttke appeared on stage for the scene, spectators stopped talking, coughing or fidgeting and directed their undivided attention toward him. All of a sudden, a seemingly absolute silence filled the space. Standing front stage right, Ui/Wuttke addressed the actor, played by Bernhard Minetti, already 90 years old at the time of the première[2]. Minetti sat in a wheelchair front stage centre, unable to demonstrate how to walk and to stand. Mumbling and stammering, yet well to be understood, Ui/Wuttke said: 'Okay. Here's the problem. I've been given to understand that my pronunciation leaves something to be desired'[3]. Some spectators started laughing – maybe because the obvious discrepancy between Wuttke's professional skills as an actor and Ui's lack thereof seemed funny. Their laughter thus revealed that they were well aware of the difference between Wuttke the actor and Arturo Ui the dramatic figure. Wuttke, who over the course of the performance had visibly responded to any perceptible change in the audience's behaviour, turned around abruptly and stared straight at the audience. His face wore a puzzled look, as if he were surprised by the laughter or even by the very presence of spectators. This, in turn, provoked widespread laughter in the audience.

In the performance, Wuttke not only played with his fellow-actors. He also played with the spectators, inviting them to join in. The performance thus developed out of Wuttke's acting, the effects it triggered in the spectators, Wuttke's response to these effects and so on[4]. He established a special relationship with the spectators, a particular bond sensed physically as a kind of energy flowing back and forth between actor and spectators. This bond, in particular in this scene, proved so strong that the spectators were quite obviously unable to turn their attention away from Wuttke. One quick glance back at the auditorium assured me that the spectators sat bent forward, their eyes fixed upon Wuttke. They looked absolutely spellbound – obviously experiencing the intense presence of the actor as well as themselves as being intensely present.

In the further course of the scene, Ui/Wuttke, following the suggestions of the actor as laid down in Brecht's text, acquired a particular vocabulary of the art of acting – walking by touching the ground with his toes first, head bent back, hands held together over the genitals; standing, arms folded so that the back of the hands remained visible and the hands rested on the upper arms; sitting hands on thighs, parallel to the belly, elbows sticking out from the body. He learnt how to speak in public by declaiming Antony's speech over Caesar's corpse from Shakespeare's *Julius Caesar*, imitating and, at the same time, transforming the actor's/Minetti's special declamation technique.

During the process by which Ui acquired these new techniques, Wuttke exhibited two different kinds of corporeality. On the one hand, he continued to reproduce the posture characteristic of Ui so far – slightly bowed body, knees bent, fidgeting gestures. On the other hand, he employed new techniques. Alternating between the two, he gradually developed the posture, movements, gestures and speech typical of Hitler. The spectators followed this process of transformation with great fascination: while they responded with laughter to Ui's/Wuttke's initial attempts to follow the actor's suggestions – in particular when the actor/Minetti asked Ui/ Wuttke to check his new standing technique in the mirror, and he looked into the audience with a searching glance – the very moment Hitler suddenly seemed to appear in Ui/Wuttke, the laughter stopped abruptly. The audience, so far completely gripped by Wuttke's acting and his extraordinary PRESENCE, suddenly seemed to realize that somehow this might mean that they were also under the spell of the dramatic figure Ui=Hitler and its presence. Here, the aesthetic and the political merged in an uncanny way.

In the scene itself, the question of Ui's presence is raised when Ui says: 'When I walk I want people to know I'm walking'[5]. This is reaffirmed when Ui, contradicting Givola, who tells him with reference to an impressive way of standing: 'Have two big bruisers right behind you and you'll be standing pretty,' replies: 'That's bunk. When I stand I don't want people looking at the two bozos behind me. I want them looking at me'[6]. At that time, however, most of the spectators more or less clearly distinguished between Wuttke the actor, to whose spell they submitted, and Ui the dramatic figure, who was laughable and funny. Yet at the end of the scene, Wuttke, Ui and Hitler seemed to merge, so that being seduced by Wuttke's PRESENCE, in a way, meant submitting to Hitler's presence, too. It seemed that here, spectators became ashamed of their laughter.

In order to emphasize this merging, that very moment the music set in: a particular theme from Liszt's *Les Préludes* – not only Hitler's favourite piece, but also the melody announcing the radio reports of the *Wehrmacht*, or a so-called '*Reichssondermeldung*'. The curtain came down and Wuttke/Ui/Hitler found themselves in front of it, facing the audience. To the sound of the music, the merging, at least partly, was undone: Wuttke's play now oscillated between representations of Chaplin's dictator and of Hitler, to which the audience responded with frenetic applause – not only obviously relieved by such an acknowledgement of the different figures being portrayed, but first of all in order to spend the energy which had accumulated over the course of the scene.

In the above description, as given from my perspective as a spectator, two aspects are highlighted that are fundamental for the following reflections on presence.

First, the very moment Wuttke appeared on stage, he was perceived by the spectators as present in a very intense way. The stronger the bond between actor and spectators became over the further course of the scene, the more intensified the PRESENCE of the actor was as sensed by the spectators, as if energy was circulating around the space. Therefore, in the following, the phenomenon of presence will be discussed as appearing in the bodily co-presence of actors[7] and spectators. The presence of film actors or any other kind of mediatized presence effects will accordingly not be considered, for they are due to different conditions.

Secondly, the scene itself posed the question of whether presence is to be ascribed to the actor, to his phenomenal body, his bodily being in the world, or to the dramatic figure he is representing, and thus to his semiotic body[8]. As the philosopher Helmuth Plessner explained, the one cannot exist without the other. In his view, the tension between both marks the de-centered position of human beings, i.e. their capacity to distance themselves to themselves; that is to say, the actor symbolizes the very *conditio humana*. Humans *have* bodies, which they can manipulate, instrumentalize and employ as signs, just as any other object. At the same time, if not in the first place, they *are* their bodies, they are body-subjects[9].

That is to say that the body-subject, i.e. the phenomenal body, and the body-object, i.e. the semiotic body, the actor and the dramatic figure represented, are inextricably bound up with each other. Which of these two bodies, then, appears and is perceived as present?

In the following, by reconsidering these two aspects, I shall distinguish and define three different concepts of presence – the weak, the strong and the radical concept of presence.

Weak concept of presence

The weak concept of presence is defined as 'being here,' before the gaze of an other. That is to say, the concept describes the *conditio sine qua non* for a performance to happen – the bodily co-presence of actor(s) and spectators. Even here, the question arises as to who is present and perceived by others –the actor or the dramatic figure?

This is a question the Church Fathers in late antiquity and the warring parties of the *Querelle de la moralité du théâtre* fought in seventeenth century France[10] had already struggled with. Both parties of the *Querelle* acknowledged theatre's ability to exercise an immediate sensual effect on the spectator and to trigger strong, even overwhelming affects based on the bodily presence of the actors. The atmosphere inside a theatre has been described as highly infectious[11]. The actors perform passionate actions on stage, the spectators perceive and are infected by them: they, too, begin to feel passionate. Through the act of perception, the infection is transmitted from the actor's present body to the spectators' present bodies. Both enthusiasts and opponents of the theatre agree that this transmission is possible only through the presentness of actors and spectators.

However, they differ in their assessment of the infection made possible by it: they either see the excitement of passion as a healing catharsis or as a profoundly harmful, destructive and estranging (from oneself and from God) disturbance, as Rousseau still argued in the second half of the eighteenth century. In his *Letter to Monsieur d'Alembert* (1758) he writes: 'The constant outburst of different emotions to which we are subjected in the theatre disturb and weaken us, making us even less able to control our own passions [...]' (Rousseau 1987: 210). Defenders and opponents emphasize that it is the bodily presence of the actor that leads to a transformation of the spectator: it 'heals' the 'sickness' of passion, results in loss of self-control, or can alter one's identity. According to both parties of the *Querelle* as well as to Rousseau, it seems that this transformation is due to the represented passions of the dramatic figure, i.e. to the actor's semiotic body. However, opponents of the theatre in the *Querelle* also argued that the sheer physical attributes of an actor exercise an erotic attraction for spectators of the opposite sex and stir immoderate desires. It would seem that such seduction is caused rather by the phenomenal body of the actor.

In the second half of the eighteenth century, a new art of acting was demanded and theorized by Riccoboni, Diderot, Lessing, Engel, Lichtenberg and others, which was supposed to rule out the latter possibility. Actors had to become proficient at expressing physically the meanings that the poet had expressed in the text of his play – especially the emotions, mental states, thought processes and character traits of the *dramatis personae*. To assist actors in obliterating their bodily being-in-the-world on stage, this reconceived art of acting transformed their bodies into a 'text,' consisting of physical signs for the emotions and mental states that constitute the respective dramatic figure. The aim was to eliminate the tension between the actors' phenomenal bodies and their semiotic bodies – their portrayal of the dramatic figures – in favour of representation. It is not the actor that should be perceived as being present on stage, but the dramatic figure.

The philosopher, and later director of the Royal Theatre in Berlin, Johann Jakob Engel chides actors in his *Mimik* (1785/6) for drawing the audience's attention to their phenomenal body and disrupting the perception of the signs that constitute the dramatic figure. For in the performance, spectators were to exclusively perceive the presence of and empathize with the dramatic figure. If their attention was diverted to the actors' phenomenal bodies, this would 'invariably destroy the illusion' (Engel 1804: 58). The audience would be forced to leave the fictive world of the play as represented by the actors' semiotic bodies, and enter the world of the physically present actors. The new art of acting was thus meant to make the actor's phenomenal body disappear into his semiotic body. The 'infection' triggered by the semiotic body and the dramatic figure it portrayed was to be maintained but modified, while the performer's erotic physicality was to be subsumed by the dramatic figure. Hence, the spectators' desires were directed at the fictive character present in and through the actor's semiotic body instead of the actor himself or his phenomenal body, who should neither appear nor be perceived as present on stage.

Of course, this construction never really worked. The tension between the actor's phenomenal and his semiotic body remained. Within the framework provided by the weak concept of presence, this problem is not to be solved.

Strong concept of presence

The strong concept of presence as actualized by Wuttke is defined by the actor's ability to occupy and command space and to attract the spectators' undivided attention. Spectators sense a certain power emanating from the actor that forces them to focus their full consideration on him without feeling overwhelmed, perceiving it as a source of energy. The spectators sense that the actor is present in an unusually intense way, granting them, in turn, the intense sensation of themselves as present. To them, presence occurs as an intense experience of presentness.

This definition draws on the description of the scene from *Arturo Ui* given in the introduction; the concept of presence reflected upon in that scene is the 'strong' one. It applies not only to Martin Wuttke, but also to all the actors to whom we ascribe stage presence. There is ample evidence that this kind of presence was also sensed in performances at other times and in other cultures and that it was/is usually experienced as an extraordinary event.

If, for example, we look at performance reviews of the famous German actor Gustaf Gründgens, dating between 1922 and 1962, we are confronted time and again with expressions of admiration and amazement at his intense presence. In an early review of Gründgens' Marinelli in *Emilia Galotti* (Stadttheater Kiel 1922), one critic stated: 'How he commands the space – with an almost dancer-like freedom of movement! Yes, that was the most memorable. It was so stunning that one at first forgot what [role] he was playing' (Kienzl 1999: 29). The critic Gert Vielhaber wrote of Gründgens' portrayal of Oedipus in his own production of Sophocles' *King Oedipus* (Düsseldorfer Schauspielhaus 1947): 'How to explain the stream of magic that spreads over the audience as Gründgens all but appears? [...] [H]e crosses the space, shaping it [...]' (Vielhaber 1947). Despite the twenty-five-year gap between them, both reviews emphasize how Gründgens commanded the space as soon as he entered the stage and profoundly affected spectators even before they could form an image of his role portrayal. It seems that he displayed this ability in every role, irrespective of the particular dramatic figure.

Gründgens managed not only to command the stage but also the entire auditorium, i.e. the full theatre space. He commanded it by – 'magically' – affecting the spectators and claiming their undivided attention. This vice-like grip on their attention was the second striking quality with which Gründgens made himself present to the spectators. According to the critic Herbert Ihering, commenting on Gründgens' portrayal of Mephisto in Lothar Müthel's *Faust* production (Staatstheater, Schauspielhaus am Gendarmenmarkt, Berlin 1932), '[i]t is not easy to break through the reserved bearing of a *Staatstheater* audience. This audience has worn out quite a few of us. Gründgens shakes things up. He makes things happen. He is provocative. But he forces people to listen [...]

Breaking through the boredom is an unusual event in the *Staatstheater*' (Ihering 1932).

In all these reviews, it seems that presence – in the strong sense of the concept – is not an expressive quality, related to the representation of a dramatic figure, but a performative quality, brought forth by a particular usage made of the body. This quality was theorized rather extensively by Eugenio Barba.

Barba distinguished between the pre-expressive and expressive levels of artistic articulation. While expressive articulation represents something, Barba located presence solely on the pre-expressive level of artistic articulation. The 'stream of magic' mentioned by Vielhaber with respect to Gründgens communicated itself to Barba with particular intensity at performances of Indian and Far Eastern theatre forms, which he therefore studied closely. In his discussions with performers, he came to the conclusion that their techniques and practices serve the purpose of generating energy within themselves, which then transfers to the spectator.

Barba defines the techniques and practices that allow the masters of Indian and Far Eastern theatre to generate this specific type of energy, realising it for the audience as a play of opposing tensions. The basic postures of traditional oriental actors and dancers derive from an alteration of balance which characterizes the performer's extra-daily technique and create a new balance requiring more effort and utilizing new tensions to keep the body upright. Moreover, oriental actors often begin their action in the direction opposite to their intended goal: if one intends to walk left, one first takes a step to the right, only to suddenly spin around and go left. These represent body techniques that, as emphasized by Barba, break with ordinary physicality and cause a disruption of the audience's expectations[12].

Barba assumes universal laws to underlie these practices, developed and actualized by performers of diverse cultures in order to conjure up energy within themselves and let it circulate through space, so it can be transmitted to spectators, who in turn also generate energy. However, I believe we must first thoroughly investigate these practices before it can be legitimate to refer all of them back to the same 'universal laws'. Quite obviously, Gründgens developed and applied certain practices, as did and does Martin Wuttke, in order to appear and be perceived as present in the strong sense of the concept. What these practices may be and which principles and 'laws' underlie them, we still do not know.

According to the reviews of Gründgens' performances as well as Barba's theory, it seems that the strong concept of presence is realized by the actor's phenomenal body. However, returning to the end of the scene described in the introduction, there was a moment when the actor, the dramatic figure and the historic figure to which it referred, seemed to merge, when it was impossible to distinguish between the phenomenal and the semiotic body of the actor. In order to deal productively with such a moment, it seems promising to introduce another concept – the concept of embodiment.

I refer to the concept as it was redefined by the anthropologist Thomas Csórdas. As Csórdas explains, until very recently cultural anthropology mostly concerned itself with the body as a mere symbolic tool in various cultural discourses, such as religion or social structures. Accordingly, cultural anthropology was dominated by the explanatory metaphor of 'culture as text'. Csórdas contrasts this metaphor with the concept of embodiment. He defines the body as the 'existential ground of culture and self' (Csórdas 1994: 6) and confronts the concept of representation with that of 'lived experience' and 'experiencing'. Drawing on Merleau-Ponty's phenomenology, Csórdas laments that none of the definitions of culture proposed by the various disciplines of cultural studies 'have taken seriously the idea that culture is grounded in the human body' (Csórdas 1994: 6). Only this insight can provide the starting point for meaningfully discussing culture and the body.

As Plessner already stated, the human body is not a material like any other, to be shaped and controlled at will. It constitutes a living organism, constantly engaged in the process of becoming, of transformation. The human body knows no state of being, it exists only in a state of becoming. It recreates itself with every blink of the eye; every breath and every movement bring forth a new body. For that reason, the body is ultimately elusive. The bodily being-in-the-world, which cannot *be* but *becomes*, vehemently refuses to be declared a work of art, or to be made into one. The actor instead undergoes processes of embodiment that bring forth his body anew and, at the same time, a dramatic figure – Arturo Ui or King Oedipus.

It is thus in the processes of embodiment that the actor's phenomenal and his semiotic body are inextricably bound up with each other. Therefore, all attempts to ascribe presence exclusively either to the semiotic body (as in the eighteenth century) or to the phenomenal body (as in Barba's theory) fail. Presence is produced by particular processes of embodiment, which are able to bring forth anew the phenomenal body of the actor as an energetic body and, at the same time, his semiotic body as a representation of a dramatic figure. However, it is conceivable that processes of embodiment performed by the actor or performer re-create his phenomenal body as an energetic body and thus produce presence in the strong sense of the concept, *without* representing any figure or anything else. But even in this case, the spectator may attribute certain meanings to the same processes.

Radical concept of presence – *presence*

Since the 1960s, theatre, action and performance art have tried out ever new ways to relate the phenomenal and the semiotic body of the actor, dancer and performer. Jerzy Grotowski, for example, did this by fundamentally redefining the relationship between the performer and his role. In his view, the performer cannot serve the purpose of portraying a dramatic figure. He sees the role as created by the playwright as a tool: '[the actor] must learn to use his role as if it were a surgeon's scalpel, to dissect himself' (Grotowski 1968: 37). The role is thus not supposed to constitute the ultimate goal of the actor's work, as demanded by the theoreticians of a new psychological-realistic art of acting in the eighteenth century. Instead, the emphasis lies on the actor's phenomenal body, his being in the world. He is asked to let the semiotic body merge with the phenomenal body. In order to achieve this goal, in training the actor Grotowski avoided:

> teaching him something; we attempt to eliminate his organism's resistance to this psychic process. The result is freedom from the time-lapse between inner impulse and outer reaction in such a way that the impulse is already an outer reaction. Impulse and action are concurrent: the body vanishes, burns and the spectator sees only a series of visible impulses. Ours then is a *via negativa* – not a collection of skills but an eradication of blocks.
>
> (Grotowski 1968: 16)

For Grotowski, 'having a body' cannot be separated from 'being a body'. The body is not supposed to be used as a tool – neither as a means for expression nor as material for the creation of signs. Instead, its 'material' is 'burnt' and converted into energy through particular processes of embodiment. By performing these processes, the actor turns into a 'holy' actor: 'It is a serious and solemn act of revelation [...]. It is like a step towards the summit of the actor's organism in which consciousness and instinct are united' (Grotowski 1968: 210). Grotowski's notion of the 'holy' actor was perhaps best approximated by Ryszard Cieślak in *The Constant Prince*. Discussing and explaining Grotowski's religious terminology, the critic Józef Kelera writes in ODRA XI (1965):

> The essence [...] does not in reality reside in the fact that the actor makes amazing use of his voice, nor in the way that he uses his almost naked body to sculpt mobile forms that are striking in their expressiveness; nor is it in the way that the technique of the body and voice form a unity during the long and exhausting monologues which vocally and physically border on acrobatics. It is a question of something quite different. [...] Until now, I accepted with reserve the terms such as 'secular holiness,' 'act of humility,' 'purification' which Grotowski uses. Today I admit that they can be applied perfectly to the character of the Constant Prince. A sort of psychic illumination emanates from the actor. I cannot find any other definition. In the culminating moments of the role, everything that is technique is as though illuminated from within. [...] At any moment the actor will levitate. [...] He is in a state of grace. And all around him this 'cruel theatre' with its blasphemies and excesses is transformed into a theatre in a state of grace.
> (Kelera in Grotowski 1968: 109).

The religious terminology is not used arbitrarily. In Grotowski's utterance the 'holy' actor is implicitly linked to the resurrected Christ who, through his suffering, death and resurrection created and appeared in a body that was both flesh and spirit. In the figure of Christ, the distinction or even dualism between body and mind, so characteristic of the occidental tradition of thought, is abolished. Here, the mind is embodied and the body 'en-minded'. The critic's choice of words too, suggests that in the performance of *The Constant Prince* Ryszard Cieślak transcended the two-world theory by letting his body appear as embodied mind.

The parallels between Grotowski's theory and practice of theatre and Merleau-Ponty's late philosophy are striking. The latter's philosophy of the lived body (*chair*, 'flesh') represents the ambitious attempt to mediate between body and mind, sense and non-sense, by using a non-dualistic and non-transcendental approach. Merleau-Ponty conceives of the relationship between these two entities asymmetrically, that is, in favour of the phenomenal body. The body is always already connected to the world through its 'flesh'. Any human grasp on the world occurs through the body; it must be embodied. In this sense, the body transcends both its instrumental and semiotic functions through its fleshiness[13].

Merleau-Ponty thus cleared the path for the redefinition of the term 'embodiment' as operated by Csórdas. Merleau-Ponty's contribution to philosophy, in this regard, is comparable to Grotowski's to the theatre. In the person of Ryszard Cieślak, an actor appeared on stage who eliminated the dualism of body and mind, his body appearing 'illuminated,' as his mind appeared embodied.

By reversing the relationship of actor and role, Grotowski also created the conditions for a redefinition of the concept of embodiment. In the context of the two-world theory, the term 'embodiment' was defined as lending one's own body to something 'bodyless' – a meaning, a dramatic figure, a spirit – in order to let it appear and be perceived. The body was conceived of as a mere vessel, a 'medium,' which was supposed to vanish behind the mediated, the embodied, without leaving a trace. The phenomenal body of the actor was conceived of as such a medium and the actor's skill was supposed to let it completely vanish behind his semiotic body, representing the dramatic figure. According to Grotowski's theory and practice, however, embodying denotes the emergence of something that exists only as body. If the dramatic figure Prince Fernando appeared in and through the body of Ryszard Cieślak, then it was a unique event tied to that specific body and brought forth by specific acts of embodiment. The bodily being-in-the-world of the actor provides the dramatic figure with its existential ground and the condition for coming into being. The figure exists only as embodied, i.e. in the actor's physical performance alone, and is brought forth by the processes of embodiment he performs. In the case of Ryszard Cieślak, the actor, by performing such processes, appeared as embodied mind.

The discourse on the concept of presence undertaken by theatre, action and performance art and aesthetic theory since the performative turn in the 1960s touches upon the mind-body dualism prevalent in Western tradition. The aesthetic discourse on presence discusses how components of body and mind meet and interact in order to make presence happen. Presence is defined as not 'primarily a physical but a mental phenomenon' notwithstanding its physical effects on performers and audience. 'Presence is an "untimely" process of consciousness – located simultaneously within and without the passage of time' (Lehmann 1999: 13). I agree with the definition of presence as a process of consciousness – but only insofar as it is articulated through the body and sensed by the spectators through their bodies. For, in my view, presence is to be regarded as a phenomenon that cannot be grasped by such a dichotomy as body versus mind or consciousness. In fact, presence collapses such a dichotomy.

When the actor brings forth his body as an energetic body and thus generates presence, he appears and is perceived as embodied mind. The actor exemplifies that body and mind cannot be separated from each other. Each is always already implied in the other. This does not only apply to the oriental actors and dancers whom Eugenio Barba witnessed, or to the 'holy' actor Ryszard Cieślak. It also applies to Gustaf Gründgens and Martin Wuttke, and to any actor who displays presence in the strong sense of the concept. Through the performer's presence, the spectator experiences the performer and himself as embodied mind in a constant process of becoming – he perceives the circulating energy as a transformative and vital energy. This I call the radical concept of presence, written as PRESENCE: PRESENCE means appearing and being perceived as embodied mind; perceiving the PRESENCE of another means to also experience oneself as embodied mind.

Due to their cultural tradition, Western audiences are used to defining themselves within the framework of mind-body dualism. They project its abolishment to the distant future or see it as a rare boon granted only to a few chosen individuals, usually as the result of spiritual epiphanies. When spectators sense the performer's PRESENCE and simultaneously bring themselves forth as embodied minds, they experience a moment of happiness that cannot be recreated in daily life. The philosopher Martin Seel asserts that 'we yearn for a sense of the *presence* of our life' and 'want to experience the presences in which we exist as sensual presences' (Seel 2001: 53). This 'sense of the *presence* of our life' is given in experiencing the other – the performer – and oneself as embodied minds. To recreate such an experience would require another experience of PRESENCE. Consequently, spectators might become addicted to these rare moments of happiness that the performer's PRESENCE alone offers them at the theatre. This might explain the extraordinary success of Heiner Müller's production of *Arturo Ui*. Here, Wuttke appears as PRESENT in the radical sense of the concept.

However, it is to be emphasized that, although in itself an extraordinary phenomenon whose coming into being we are still unable to explain (even assuming it is due to certain artistic techniques and practices), PRESENCE does not make anything extraordinary appear. Instead, it marks the emergence of something very ordinary and turns it into an event: the nature of human beings as embodied minds. Thus, ordinary existence is experienced as extraordinary – as transformed and even transfigured. Such an act of transfiguration was described by Grotowski, as well as by Kelera, by taking refuge in religious terminology. The philosopher Arthur Danto explains art as the 'transfiguration of the commonplace' (Danto 1981). In PRESENCE, the human commonplace of being embodied mind is transfigured. In perceiving it, we experience ourselves as embodied mind. The actor who grants us such an experience, rare in everyday life, will quite understandably be celebrated.

Works cited

Barba, E. (1986) *Beyond the Floating Islands*, New York: PAJ Publications.
Barba, E. and Savarese, N. (eds) (1991) *A Dictionary of Theatre Anthropology: The Secret Art of the Performer*, London: Routledge.
Brecht, B. (1981) *The Resistible Rise of Arturo Ui*, in J. Willet and R. Manheim (eds) *Bertolt Brecht. Collected Plays, Vol. 6/II*, translated by R. Manheim, London: Eyre Methuen, 1–100.
Csórdas, T. (ed.) (1994) *Embodiment and Experience: The Existential Ground of Culture and Self*, Cambridge: Cambridge University Press.
Danto, A. C. (1981) *The Transfiguration of the Commonplace: A Philosophy of Art*, Cambridge MA: Harvard University Press.
Engel, J. J. (1804) '*Ideen zu einer Mimik*' *Schriften*, 12 vols., Berlin: Mylius.
Fischer-Lichte, E. (2004) '*Zuschauen als Ansteckung*', in M. Schaub and N. Suthor (eds) *Ansteckung: Zur Körperlichkeit eines ästhetischen Prinzips*, Munich: Fink, 35–50.
——(2008) *The Transformative Power of Performance: A New Aesthetics*, translated by S. Jain, London: Routledge.

Grotowski, J. (1968) *Towards a Poor Theatre*, New York: Simon and Schuster.

Heine, M. (1995) 'Martin Wuttke: *Der mit der Legende ringt*', *Berliner Zeitung*, 5 July 1995.

Ihering, H. (1932) Review of *Faust*, dir. Lothar Müthel. *Berliner Börsen-Courier*, 3 December 1932.

Kienzl, F. (1999) '*Gustaf mit "f."* Wie Gustaf Gründgens entdeckt wurde', in D. Walach (ed.) *Aber ich habe nicht mein Gesicht': Gustaf Gründgens – eine deutsche Karriere*, Berlin: Henschel, 1–35.

Lehmann, H.-T. (1999) '*Die Gegenwart des Theaters*' in E. Fischer-Lichte, D. Kolesch, C. Weiler (eds) *Transformationen: Theater der neunziger Jahre*, Berlin: Theater der Zeit, 23–6.

Merleau-Ponty, M. (1968) *The Visible and the Invisible*, translated by A. Lingis. Evanston IL: Northwestern University Press.

Nicole, P. (1998) *Traité de la comédie et autres pièces d'un procès du théâtre*, edited by L. Thirouen. Paris: Champion.

Plessner, H. (1970) *Laughing and Crying. A Study of the Limits of Human Behaviour*, translated by J. S. Churchill and M. Grene. Evanston IL: Northwestern University Press.

Rousseau, J. J. (1987) *Discours sur les sciences et les arts/Lettre à d'Alembert sur les spectacles*, edited by J. Varloot, Paris: Edition Gallimard.

Seel, M. (2001) '*Inszenieren als Erscheinen lassen. Thesen über die Reichweite eines Begriffs*', in J. Früchtl and J. Zimmermann (eds) *Ästhetik der Inszenierung*, Frankfurt am Main: Suhrkamp, 48–62.

Vielhaber, G. (1947) '*Ödipus Komplex auf der Bühne*', review of *König Oedipus*, directed by Gustaf Gründgens, *Die Zeit*, 2 October 1947.

Notes

1 Regarding the writing in capitals, see p. 115–16. The radical concept of 'presence'.
2 After Minetti had fallen ill, he was replaced by Marianne Hoppe, four years younger than him. Later, they took turns playing the part. Meanwhile, both have passed away and have been replaced by Michael Gwisdek. Minetti and Hoppe had been great stars in the 1930s at the Staatstheater, the Schauspielhaus am Gendarmenmarkt Berlin (headed by Gustaf Gründgens) and in UFA films. There was still a certain 'flavour' to their acting that even in the 1990s recalled the 1930s.
3 '*So hören Sie. Man hat mir zu verstehen gegeben, daß meine Aussprache zu wünschen übrig läßt*' (Brecht 1981: 43).
4 Regarding performance as such an autopoietic feedback loop, see Fischer-Lichte 2008.
5 '*Wenn ich gehe, wünsche ich, daß bemerkt wird, daß ich gehe*' (Brecht 1981: 44).

6 'Stell zwei kräftige Jungens dicht hinter dich, und du stehst ausgezeichnet'/'Das ist Unsinn. Wenn ich stehe, wünsche ich, daß man nicht auf zwei Leute hinter mir, sondern auf mich schaut' (Brecht 1981: 45).

7 For the sake of simplicity, male forms are used throughout the text; naturally, they also refer to the female forms.

8 Regarding the distinction between phenomenal and semiotic body see Fischer-Lichte 2008.

9 See Plessner 1970.

10 See Nicole 1998.

11 It is striking how frequently the metaphor of infection, which renders the aesthetic experience in theatre as a somatic process, is applied in these debates. The term is also experiencing a renaissance in current debates on aesthetics. See Fischer-Lichte 2004.

12 See Barba 1986 and 1991.

13 See Merleau-Ponty 1968.

Chapter 7

'... presence ...' as a question and emergent possibility

A case study from the performer's perspective[1]

Phillip Zarrilli

This essay interrogates 'presence' from the performer's perspective inside a performance event – *Told by the Wind*[2]. Co-created by Kaite O'Reilly, Jo Shapland, and Phillip Zarrilli, *Told by the Wind* premièred at Chapter Arts Centre (Cardiff) on 29 January 2010 for an initial two-week run, was performed at Tanzfabrik (Berlin) on 27 March, and continues to tour internationally[3]. As noted in the final paragraph of Elisabeth Mahoney's review for *The Guardian*, the performers' 'presence' was central to her experience, reception, and critical response to the première performance.

TOLD BY THE WIND

Chapter Arts Centre, Cardiff: 29 January to 6 February 2010

Elisabeth Mahoney, *The Guardian*, 2 February 2010

Stripped of most elements we associate with drama, this intense meditation in movement revels in stillness. It's so still at times, you worry that scratching your head or crossing your legs will be audible to all. Performers Jo Shapland and Phillip Zarrilli, with writer Kaite O'Reilly, draw on Asian aesthetics, string theory and the Japanese theatre of quietude to present something that is beyond linear narrative, character and gripping plot twists.

    Instead, they offer fragments of memory, speech and gestures, composed in moments that have a haunting, painterly beauty to them. A man and a woman are on stage together at all times but, never connect; he speaks a little, tugged at by the past, she remains silent, trying to form words but expressing herself physically as she shuffles, runs and dances in bare soil.

With no dialogue or fathomable action to follow, you try to make connections even though everything resists them. Is she in the memory he speaks of? Is she a character in the music he is writing, or the dance he appears to choreograph? What happens, slowly, is that those nagging questions subside and a calmer understanding emerges. It's all very hypnotic, with repeated small movements and shards of sentences, and it has the astringent purity of a haiku poem, though haiku seems positively wordy in comparison.

The performers have a remarkable presence, even when their movement is barely perceptible. This is a challenging production, but oddly affecting and – quietly cleansing. On the opening night, the audience lingered at the end, as if not wanting to head back out into the noisy, demanding world.

Although Mahoney is the only of three reviewers to specifically use the term 'presence' with regard to the performers, all used a variety of cognate terms to describe an intensity, valence, and quality of the actors' work which attracted and kept their attention: 'hypnotic' (Vale 2010; Mahoney 2010), 'compelling' (Vale 2010), 'meditation' (Mahoney 2010), 'dreamlike' (Kelligen 2010), and 'mesmerized' (Kelligen 2010).

If some of the audience found the performance 'compelling,' 'hypnotic,' 'dreamlike' and/or 'mesmerizing' and if some perceived the performers as having 'remarkable presence,' I argue that 'it' emerged in the spatio-temporal realm of experience, embodiment, and perception shared between the performer(s), the performance score and its dramaturgy, and the audience. From the performer's perspective inside the performance 'presence' *should* only exist for the actor *as a question* – is it possible on *this* night with *this* audience to attain an optimal mode of engagement of awareness, deployment of energy, and embodied consciousness appropriate to the aesthetic and dramaturgy of *this* performance score?[4]

'Presence' is not some-'thing' I, as a performer either 'have' or should strive for; rather, I argue that the performer's relationship to 'presence' is paradoxical in that the spectator is most likely to perceive 'presence' as emergent when the performer begins from a dispositional state of bodymind readiness where enactment takes place 'on the edge of the absent' (Zarrilli 2002: 164). For the performer 'presence' can only ever be a question – an emergent state of possibility.

'Presence' as a problem

'Presence' is a highly contested and vexed term. Post-structuralist critiques of presence have rightfully debunked any notion of presence as an essence[5]. I argued long ago that:

> A reified subjectivist notion of 'presence' is as complicit in a dualist metaphysics as is the Cartesian 'mind'. Neither provides an adequate account of the 'body' in the mind, the 'mind in the body, or of the process by which the signs read as 'presence' are a discursive construct.
>
> (Zarrilli 1995: 15).

Given the public visibility of 'presence' and its central place in the phenomenon of performance, a number of scholars (Roach 2004; 2007; Dolan 2005; Fischer Lichte, 2008; Goodall 2008; and Power 2008) have begun a more nuanced discussion of the complex set of issues marked by the phenomenon of 'presence,' especially the pleasures afforded when one attends a performance where 'presence' emerges (Dolan 2005; Power 2008: 7). Cormac Power provides a useful account of three main 'modes of presence' in theatre – 'the making-present, the having present and the being-present' (Power 2008: 11) in order to demonstrate that 'presence in theatre is not a singular, monolithic entity' but a complex phenomenon (Power 2008: 13). Goodall writes a history of 'the poetics of presence – the rhetorics and imagistic language in which presence is evoked in different cultural and historical contexts, and across diverse forms of theatre and performance' (Goodall 2008: 7). Roach studies 'It' – as 'It' appears in 'common usage ... as *charm, charisma,* and *presence*' (Roach 2004: 556, original emphasis; Roach 2007), i.e., the association of the personal power of 'It' involved in creating stars and stardom. Dolan takes a different perspective. While warning that we should not 'mystify the notion of presence,' she is interested in attempts to understand its 'influence' (Dolan 2005: 52). She therefore examines how

'... presence ... talent and magnetism, can be used as a means to progressive, rather than conservative, goals' in and through performance (Dolan 2005: 30–1).

Following my earlier book-length study of psychophysical acting (Zarrilli 2009), I approach the question of 'presence' phenomenologically[6], assuming an 'enactive approach' to acting in which the actor as a gestalt optimally engages her bodymind fully in each moment of performance as she creates, encounters, and responds to the performance environment (Zarrilli 2009: 41–60). At all performance events in which actors appear at least momentarily in the same space as the audience, the performers may be said to be literally or phenomenally present[7], i.e., the audience and performers together constitute a performance event by their phenomenal co-presence (Fischer-Lichte 2008: 32–3; see Zarrilli 2009: 222). How they inhabit and experience the performance together constitutes a full phenomenology of the performance event. Fischer-Lichte labels the simple presence of the actor's phenomenal body on stage as 'the *weak concept of presence*' (Fischer-Lichte 2008: 94). In contrast to the '*weak concept of presence*' Fischer-Lichte defines the 'actor's ability of commanding space and holding attention' as 'the *strong concept of presence*' (2008: 96, original emphasis)[8]. I argue that 'the strong concept of presence' is not singular, but rather multiple – the quality, valence, and intensity of the actor's ability to generate an inner 'energy,' to engage one's entire embodied consciousness in each performance task, to command space and hold attention is always shaped by one's training/experience, as well as the dramaturgy and aesthetic of a specific performance.

From the stage actor's perspective, the 'strong concept of presence' is the territory marked by psychophysical processes of embodiment, attunement, awareness, and perception in which the actor's bodymind relationship to the enactment of a score makes available a certain degree, quality, or heightened intensity of relationship that is 'energetic' and attracts and sustains the spectators' attention[9]. This territory is the material basis of the actor's work and therefore is common to many systems of actor training and performance such as Beijing Opera where a good actor must 'radiate presence' (*faqi*) (Riley 1997: 206); the raising and circulation of *prana-vayu* in the embodiment of states of being/doing (*bhava*) in *kathakali* dance-drama (Zarrilli 2000: 65–97); the central role that the circulation of the vital energy (*ki*) plays in Zeami's articulation of 'vibratory theory' at the heart of the artistry of the Japanese *noh* actor (Nearman 1984; see Hare's translation of Zeami's acting texts, 2008); or contemporary psychophysical approaches to training the contemporary actor – whether my own approach or those of Grotowski, Barba, Stanislavski, Michael Chekhov, Lecoq, Mnouchkine, or others (Zarrilli 2009, Chapters 1–2)[10].

Although the territory marked by an audience's perception of 'presence' is central to the material basis of the performer's work, there are a number of problems with 'presence'. As observed by Roach of Stanislavski, 'presence' is often associated with and/or reduced to the notion of personal charisma – a reductive conflation of the actor's work with the actor's personality, leading to the 'disruptive effects' of 'Stage Charm' for the work of the stage actor (Roach 2004: 557). Similarly, 'it' can produce the 'cult of the individual' (Goodall 2008: 12) – and thereby produce a narcissistic subjectivity. And finally, what is marked by 'presence' is problematically reified by some as a kind of 'mysterious,' 'magical' or 'secret' power of the actor's art.

Given these problems, as a practitioner I have deliberately chosen not to use the term 'presence' when training or directing actors, when discussing acting as a phenomenon in the studio, or when describing my own process or relationship to acting. What for the audience may be experienced as remarkable – 'presence' – from the stage actor's perspective should remain *un*remarkable. The actor's job is to stay focused while deploying one's energy and awareness to the specific work she has to do in each moment of performance. I argue that the actor should not strive to attain 'presence'; rather, *if* 'presence' is perceived by the audience, 'it' emerges in the vortex of the performative moment. Therefore, in this essay I use the term 'presence' guardedly and with quotation marks to signal my reluctance to use the term in the studio[11].

Told by the wind: development

To provide sufficient contextual information for an analysis of the appearance of 'presence' in performances of *Told by the Wind*, I begin with an overview of the production's development and a brief outline of the performance structure and performance score. I then address issues between production and reception. I first address the issue of 'presence' in relation to the structure and dramaturgy of

Told by the Wind. I then examine 'the strong concept of presence' as marked and remarked upon by audiences for *Told by the Wind*[12.] I do so by providing a detailed phenomenological account of several sections of the performance score, articulating from inside that score how the performers shaped and deployed energy, awareness, and perception in enacting specific tasks/actions that constituted the score, and simultaneously addressing the question of how audiences experienced and responded to our psychophysical engagement of that score. I conclude with a brief summary of how the approach to psychophysical training I have developed through Asian martial arts and yoga supports the development and deployment of the type, quality, and intensity of 'energetic' attentiveness, awareness, perception, and attunement utilized when performing *Told by the Wind* and from which 'presence' emerged in performances as a question.

Developing *Told by the Wind*

Told by the Wind was co-created over an 18-month process as an experiment in intercultural theatre process and practice[13]. The process included several initial short, focused periods of research and development, devising, and writing; two longer intensive periods of devising, writing, and rehearsing that resulted in four work-in-progress preview performances in 2009 – three at Tyn-y-parc Studio, Wales, and the fourth at the Escrita na Paisagem – Festival de Performance e Artes de Terra in Evora, Portugal; and a final period of rehearsals culminating in initial performances at Chapter Arts Centre (Cardiff) and Tanzfabrik (Berlin). At various points in the development/devising process, each of the three co-creators took the lead, generating approximately one-third of the final performance score[14].

Zarrilli led the initial research and development phase of the project in which the three collaborators encountered and responded to a variety of intercultural and/or 'post-dramatic' (see Lehmann 2006) dramaturgies and aesthetics, both on their feet in the studio and around the table. These included:

- the dramaturgy of *noh* plays, especially 'phantasmal' dramas with female transformation scenes;
- key aesthetic principles that inform Japanese *noh*, especially *yugen*;

- the principles and qualities of 'quiet theatre' as exemplified in Ōta Shōgo's (1939–2006) body of work and his dramas of 'living silence' such as *The Water Station* which Zarrilli directed in 2004 (Zarrilli 2009: 144–73) and *The Tale of Komachi*, as analyzed by Mari Boyd in *The Aesthetics of Quietude* (2006);
- contemporary *noh*-inspired dramas including *Sotoba Komachi* (1952) and *Aoi no Ue* (1956) by Yukio Mishima (1925–70); William Butler Yeats' (1869–1935) plays for dancers including *At the Hawks Well* and *The Only Jealousy of Emer*; and more recent UK translations (Benjamin Yeho's *Nakamitsu* at The Gate in 2007) and experiments such as the collaborations between Hideki Noda and Colin Teevan (*The Diver* 2008; *The Bee* 2006 [Soho Theatre (London) and Setagayu Public Theatre]);
- Beckett's 'quiet plays' and prose works that evoke and address loss and otherness (see Zarrilli 2009: 115–43);
- Japanese *butoh*'s exploration of inner-states and images;
- Korean shaman (*mudang*) performances (see Hogarth 1999: 47); and
- the conventions, aesthetic concerns, and alternative ways of structuring 'post-dramatic' theatre found in the work of Gertrude Stein, Kantor's 'theatre of memory' and Heiner Müller's body of work[15].

To this initial list of sources should be added O'Reilly's dramaturgical interest in exploring shifts between first and third person voice central to *noh* dramas; the creation of 'internal monologues' – text and/or image-based scores which remain un-voiced but are the basis for the actor's internal psychophysical score; and 'voicing' some of the fragments of text that Zarrilli uses when side-coaching actors while teaching and when devising a psychophysical score through images and shifts in awareness. Shapland contributed much to considerations and explorations of our use of space, the relationship between the two figures within the space, issues of tempo-rhythm, choreography/movement composition, and attention to the material textures and sounds which helped create the *mise-en-scene*. Elements and principles of Zarrilli's approach to psychophysical training (Zarrilli 2009) remained central throughout the process, providing the basis for each performer's generation and deployment of an energetic awareness applied to each task and structure as it developed.

I will briefly discuss our three initial points of departure – phantasmal *noh,* the aesthetic principle of *yugen,* and 'quietude'. Although our initial point of departure was phantasmal *noh,* we explored dramaturgically and performatively how to suggestively touch, but not attempt to reproduce this source; therefore, our approach to phantasmal *noh* might be described as indirect. We did *not* want *Told by the Wind* to 'look' Japanese in some way, nor did we want to attempt to stylistically reproduce *noh.* We did not wish to literally reproduce the characteristic features of the relationship between the two central figures of phantasmal *noh* – the *shite* (doer/central performer) and *waki* (sideman/secondary performer, usually a wandering priest). In phantasmal *noh,* the *shite* often appears as a 'restless' female spirit who remembers a past event through a dream or unsettling memory, encounters the *waki*-priest-type figure who reveals what is troubling her, and is pacified and/or transformed in some way. Shelly Quinn describes phantasmal *noh* as like 'an echo chamber of allusions' (Quinn 2005: 14). While keeping female and male figures, in *Told by the Wind* we wanted both figures as well as their relationship to remain 'restless,' unsettled in some way like 'an echo chamber of allusions'; however, there is no sense of pacification at the conclusion of *Told by the Wind.*

Our indirect approach to phantasmal *noh* – touching but not attempting to reproduce *noh* – reflects the underlying aesthetic concept of *yugen.* As Tom Hare explains, *yugen* 'cannot be translated. It has been profitably described in various places as 'mystery and depth' and as 'what lies beneath the surface'; the subtle, as opposed to the obvious; the hint, as opposed to the statement' (Hare 2008: 472). In our creative process we constantly addressed 'the hint,' i.e., the question of 'what lies beneath the surface' for these two figures. Dramaturgically, could the two onstage figures be constantly present to one another, yet could the presence of each to the other remain, somehow, a question mark? At a certain point in our rehearsal process, O'Reilly framed and articulated this 'question mark' as follows: who is 'dreaming' whom? We interpreted 'dreaming' as the active task of constantly 'imagining' or 'conjuring' an-Other. Is She 'the dreamer of the dream of He?' And is He 'the dreamer of the dream of She?' Once O'Reilly articulated this active question mark so clearly, it became central to the final development of the dramaturgy for *Told by the Wind,* as well as the primary activator for the two performers.

Complimenting and informing our approach to *noh* were elements and principles of 'quiet theatre' associated with the work of contemporary Japanese playwright/director, Ōta Shōgo (1939–2006), as identified by Mari Boyd in *The Aesthetics of Quietude* (2006), and as developed in my previous productions of Ōta's signature non-verbal psychophysical score, *The Water Station* (see Zarrilli 2009: 144–73). Ōta created dramas of 'living silence' in which everyday action is slowed down and in which there is a divestiture of all unnecessary words. 'Quiet theatre' does not attempt to 'aggressively transmit meaning to the audience' (Boyd 2006: 3). Rather, it turns down the often busy volume of theatre's multiple modes of communication, paring away and divesting performance of anything non-essential.

> The underlying principle of quietude is what Ota Shogo terms the power of passivity. Passivity in art refers to the making of aesthetic distance. Instead of trying to aggressively transmit meaning to an audience, passivity exercises a spirit of 'self-reliance' that compels the audience to attend, focus, and participate imaginatively in the pursuit of signification, meaning, and pleasure. Passivity thus paradoxically engages the audience in a dynamic exchange of energy.
>
> (Boyd 2006: 3).

Working with that which lies 'beneath the surface,' in *Told by the Wind,* each element operates at a subtle, suggestive level.

During the development phase of our work we psychophysically explored the suggestive and minimal in the following ways: (1) slowing down everyday movement; (2) working with slight and/or sudden variations in tempo-rhythm with psychophysical actions to create juxtaposition, emphasis, or surprise; (3) using fragments of text to create possible narratives; (4) experimenting with multiple layers/strands of voicing/speaking/sounding such as switches from first to third person voice, description, directions, commands, etc.; (5) integrating and juxtaposing task-based actions, semi-improvised tasks/movement sequences; (6) sustaining embodiment of active images for lengthy periods; and (7) experimenting with repetition and synchronicity so that time and narrative are rendered more contemplative as each loops back on itself, but is never the same.

Figure 7.1 The Llanarth Group, *Told by the Wind* (2010).
Structure 5: Male Figure has stepped into the earthen square.
Photo courtesy Kirsten McTernan.

Told by the Wind: the performance score

By the conclusion of the process of developing/devising *Told by the Wind* we had developed the final performance score around ten sections or structures. This score is an interweaving of two templates or maps. The first template consists of the imaginative possibilities made available to the audience with regard to the relationship between the two figures inhabiting the *mise-en-scene* together, i.e., this is the dramaturgical or 'fictional world' – the possible 'narratives' made available by the performance score. The second template is the very precise, and often subtle map of how each performer deploys his embodied consciousness, awareness and perception to embody, enact and inhabit each specific task/action that constitutes their specific psychophysical score, and from which the 'fictional world' or 'narratives' are generated[16]. Both of these templates/maps are discussed and analyzed in detail below.

Immediate Performance Context: When the audience enters the black box studio theatre at Chapter Arts Centre (Cardiff), they

Figure 7.2 The Llanarth Group, *Told by the Wind* (2010).
Structure 5: Male and Figures move/counterpoint.
Photo courtesy of Ace McCarron.

hear the sound of water-chime music playing at a low level, and look down toward the dimly lit but visible playing space – a rectangular area approximately six by nine metres set off by a thin earth frame[17]. Toward the upstage right corner of the playing space (see Figs 7.1 and 7.2) are a small, off-white, weathered writing bureau, a spindle-backed wooden chair, and window frame suspended in the air. Just downstage centre and stage left is a different style of weathered, off-white wooden chair with a cloth-patterned seat, in front of which is a wooden box on the floor. On a diagonal between the two chairs, branches of evergreen are laid on the floor to demarcate and contain a square of earth of approximately two by two metres. At the middle of each face of the earthen square, smaller branches of evergreen demarcate four passageways into or out of the earth. The programme provides no information about the setting, location, or time of the performance. It lists the names of the co-creators, artistic consultants, and the two performers.

As soon as the audience is seated two performers – both barefoot – enter, walking slowly from the far upstage right corner of the theatre. The female (Jo Shapland) wears a dark brown, knee-length skirt and tightly fitting white v-neck top, while the male (Phillip Zarrilli) wears brown trousers with a loose-fitting white shirt. The female traverses the upstage edge of the playing space, and at the USL corner of the rectangle turns to cross downstage left while the male enters and crosses downstage right. Both figures stop and pause – the female just upstage of the stage left chair/box, and male just downstage of the stage right window/writing bureau. They turn to face the playing area, pausing at the threshold. As the pre-set lights begin to fade and as the water-chime music fades to silence, the two figures step into darkness.

Transitions between each of the ten structures are marked by shifts in lighting; however, there is never a complete blackout in these transitions with at least minimal lighting always present on the earth square and therefore on the performers. Throughout the 50–53-minute performance the Female Figure and the Male Figure are both onstage except for the penultimate structure when the Male Figure steps outside the rectangular playing space and into darkness offstage until he returns for the final structure. The two figures never make direct visual contact with one another. There is no dialogue per se, but Male Figure delivers fragments of suggestive text during 4 of the 10 structures (3, 7, 8 and 10). Female Figure occasionally mouths words that either remain unsaid or are barely whispered and remain inaudible. Male Figure's intermittent spoken text is delivered during approximately 11 minutes of the total running time. Except for the barely audible 'white noise' in the background throughout the performance, there are lengthy periods in which no overt and little inadvertent sound is made by the actors.

Told by the Wind: brief outline of ten structures

Since the analysis below focuses primarily on Structures 1, 2, 3 and 10, for these structures more detail and the full text are provided in the summary.

Structure 1: The two actors are discovered onstage: Female Figure is seated in the centre stage left chair, and Male Figure is seated in the upstage right chair. Their backs are to each other. In silence, for approximately three minutes the two figures only make subtle, slight physical adjustments to their positions as they listen in the silence. As the light fades out on Female Figure, Jo Shapland moves down-centre stage where she assumes a crouching position.

Structure 2:   While Male Figure remains seated at the desk upstage right, Female Figure is discovered downstage centre of the earth square with a withered evergreen branch casting a distinctive shadow on the floor in her right hand. She purposefully moves the branch ... slowly ... intently ... to an inner score. Pausing ... she drops the branch and her gaze slowly rises. The light on Female Figures fades to black.

Structure 3:   In relative darkness, Female Figure facing upstage at the periphery of the playing area, she begins a very slow sliding 'walk' – her bare feet sounding the surface of the floor. Continuing to gaze through the window frame Male Figure eventually speaks fragments of text, authored by Kaite O'Reilly:

> The desolation of Autumn.
> The 7th day of the 9th month.
>
> Returning.
> Night dew on feet.
> Wet.
> Stops.
> Looks to dew and to past...behind.
> Dew ... on feet.
>
> Takes three steps. Stops.
> Arriving.
> (*Sound of steps stops. Silence.*)
> (*Whispered*) A bird...
> Are you present?
>
> (*A beat. Suddenly Female Figure crosses, running from USL to DSR.*)
> (*Silence. MF listens, intent.*)
> That old compulsion.
> Some thing ... drawing you back ...
> ... here ... now ...

To stand and pause – take three steps…stop.
To look to the dew and the past, behind.

(*Pauses…observing*)
The end of Autumn … .
(*As a question*) What follows?

(*To the distance…observing…*) The dew on your feet.

Dew … wet … on feet.
(*Two beats. FF crosses from USL to DSR a second time.*)
(*To the space behind*) Are you here?

Structure 4: Female Figure is discovered in the same crouching position as in Structure 2 downstage centre of the earth square. She now holds in her right hand a large green evergreen branch which casts a shadow on the floor. In a moment of synchronicity Male Figure draws his right hand outward toward the desk as Female Figure executes a sweeping motion with the evergreen. Female Figure performs a detailed and precise psychophysical score, occasionally appearing to mouth words as she does so.

Structure 5: Lights brighten on Male Figure seated at the desk. With his eyes closed and a pencil in his right hand, Male Figure slowly rises as he 'conducts' a musical score moving around the chair. Unexpectedly he stops, looks to the paper on the desk, and bends to write. He stops, slowly lengthens his back. Taking several backward, halting steps he stops at the threshold of the earth square. Suddenly he is propelled backward into the earth square. For the first and only time in the performance, distant (recorded) sounds of 'spring' are audible – a wind chime, birds. He responds to the environment. Closing his eyes again, he resumes 'conducting' (Fig 7.1) as Female Figure simultaneously begins a 'dance' moving into, across, out of, and/or within the earthen square. Never looking to one another, at times they seem to be moving in response to one another or even together with one another (Fig 7.2). By the end of this 'dance' the sound has faded out. In the silence Female Figure resumes her seat CSL, and Male Figure is seated at the desk. Silence…an echo of the first structure. They both mouth words … whispered fragments, and listen in silence.

Figure 7.3 The Llanarth Group, *Told by the Wind* (2010).
Structure 7: Male Figure in the downstage centre left chair delivers text as Female Figure 'dances' a slowed-down version of her earlier dance from Structure 5. Photo courtesy of Ace McCarron.

Structure 6: Dancing an 'inner dance,' Female Figure is animated in her chair, levitates, and unexpectedly turns and rushes to the upstage centre entry to the earthen square where she stops unexpectedly at the threshold as Male Figure suddenly stands, looking out the window. Silence … a few beats …

Structure 7: Female Figure slowly lifts a foot, stepping across the threshold into the earthen square. As she begins a slowed down version of her earlier dance, without seeing her, Male Figure slowly crosses upstage of the earth square, and then downstage to the CSL chair in which Female Figure had been sitting. Placing his left hand on 'her' chair, he tells fragments of stories as she continues to 'dance' (Fig 7.3).

Structure 8: Female Figure is discovered downstage centre lying with her back on the floor, eyes closed, and Male Figure is discovered

Figure 7.4 The Llanarth Group, *Told by the Wind* (2010).
Structure 10: In the final structure, Male and Female Figures next
to one another, but each remains in their own parallel world.
Photo courtesy of Ace McCarron.

seated at the desk reading a text/score. At first he silently mouths
the words. He stands and marks the rhythm of the text with the
pencil in his right hand, simultaneously 'dancing' patterns of steps
in response to the text as he moves on a horizontal line upstage of
the earthen square from USR to USL, and back again toward the
desk. He begins to voice the text:

One foot in front of the other, another foot before the other,
step,
step, lightly step plod [...]

As text is voiced, Female Figure opens her eyes, sits, and comes to standing. When Male Figure completes the text, he gazes out the window, as Female Figure turns upstage and steps into darkness. Again, the sound of Female Figure's sliding feet. Listening, Male Figure repeats two lines:

> The seventh day of the ninth month...
> Returning ... .

Structure 9:   At the threshold, Female Figure steps into the earthen square and executes a subtle psychophysical score in response to the environment. Eventually she senses and is slowly drawn down toward the earth and repelled by the impulse to touch and reach into the earth. She eventually reaches into the earth, grasping what is there. She extracts a white cloth object ... slowly. The earth falls off parts of the object. It is revealed as a long-sleeved white shirt covered with fragments of earth. Placing her right hand/arm into the shirt, she inhabits the shirt and begins a slow stepping 'dance' as the lights fade.

Structure 10:   Lying on her back with her eyes closed near the chair CSL where Male Figure sits, they are revealed. As Male Figure delivers the text below, Female Figure opens her eyes, sits upright, comes to her knees so she is parallel to Male Figure (Fig 7.4), and goes through her inner physical score.

> Crouching ... she sweeps ... stops ...looks to leaves...drops brush...the Memory of leaves...right hand to chin...left follows...the weight of the chin in the hand...the smell of burning leaves...takes in the smell with the breath...close eyes...the memory in the leaves...watches smoke rise... surprised... memories in flames...takes in the smoke with the smell...takes in the past with the smell...senses the leaves down right...looks...senses left hand...skeleton of leaf...opens palm, looks to it...leaf crumbles...fragments of ash...catches ash in right hand...lets the ash drop...

Male and Female Figures simultaneously raise their gazes to a distant point on the horizon. Lights fade to black. The performance concludes.

Between production and reception:[18] a phenomenological account of 'presence' as emergent in told by the wind

Dramaturgy, structure and 'presence'

If 'presence' was observed as arising in *Told by the Wind*, 'it' did not arise in a vacuum. 'Presence' is always generated by the dynamic quality of the actor's embodied relationship to a specific performance score and its dramaturgy. As noted above, the performance score structures each of the actor's performance tasks/actions while the dramaturgy of the score sets the overall aesthetic and narrative parameters within which the performer psychophysically shapes and deploys her energy, awareness and perception as she attends to and embodies that score, and as she perceives and responds to each stimulus offered by the score within the performance environment. I begin this analysis with a phenomenological account of the dramaturgy-at-work in performances of *Told by the Wind*.

From the audience's perspective, the series of structures that constitute *Told by the Wind* provide stimuli that throw up possible relationships between the Male and Female Figures on stage; however, these narrative possibilities are never absolutely determined. Under the guidance of dramaturg/playwright, Kaite O'Reilly, we intentionally constructed a dramaturgy which refused complete narrative closure.

As each structure presents itself in turn, there is no absolute certainty that the associations that may have arisen for a spectator in response to a structure necessarily 'fit' where one might at first think they 'fit.' While it is clear that there *is* a relationship of some sort between the two Figures in the stage environment, precisely who they are and what their relationship had been, is now, or might be, is never finally resolved. Mahoney describes how a series of 'nagging questions' presented themselves to her as the performance developed:

> With no dialogue or fathomable action to follow, you try to make connections even though everything resists them. Is she in the memory he speaks of? Is she a character in the music he is writing, or the dance he appears to choreograph?
>
> (Mahoney 2010)

Michael Kelligen describes the possibilities and questions thrown up for him about the two Figures:

> A man, not young, in crumbled clothes sits at an old white bureau. He is looking out through a window [...] He turns his head inwards, he may be looking for the younger woman who is sitting at the other side of the stage. She turns her head, she may be looking for him [...] They never meet. Did they know each other once? Are they yearning for each other? Are they just figures passing by in the evening light?
>
> (Kelligan 2010)

The possibilities posed as questions by the reviewers mark the ever-shifting engagement of the audience's imagination as they responded to the possible narratives put into play by the two figures within the *mise-en-scene*.

Some of our choices for the *mise-en-scene* – weathered off-white wooden furniture/window-frame suspended in space, and costumes (brown skirt/pants; white tops) – invited specific associations tied to certain places/spaces and period, while not allowing others. However, the evergreen-bound earth square between the furniture USR and CDSL complicated and unsettled these possibilities. The playing space could *not* simply be read as 'a' single settled place. For Erika Fischer-Lichte, the juxtaposition of the naturalistic element of the furniture with the use of real soil meant 'what was out was in' and this turned everything 'inside out' (Fischer-Lichte 2010). Maria da Paz observed that:

> ... the earth square in the middle of the space ... gave me the awareness of belonging and at the same time of distance; [the Male Figure] and [the Female Figure] were ... separated by it, but at the same time it was what [the two] had in common somehow keeping [them] together.
>
> (da Paz 2009)

For some, such as Duarte da Silva, this 'dis'location of space/place was paralleled by a sense the performance 'takes the spectator to another time and place' (da Silva 2009). Eleaonora Marzani explained how for her in *Told by the Wind*:

there is no time. The connection between the two figures may suggest some flashback, getting back to a time of memories, or again it can be a future vision, or a story created by imagination, or maybe a wish out of a man's mind. There are all the times and there is no time at all; what is (not) going on is out of time or is in a constant present of some other dimension ...

(Marzani 2009)

Without a settled narrative, with everything 'inside out,' with no direct eye-to-eye contact between the two Figures, with only fragments of text and no dialogue per se, one way of explaining the 'relationship' between the figures is as a shifting set of possibilities. Mahoney's observation that 'everything [in the performance] resists' the making of 'connections' reflects the audience's process of re-constructing narratives that, by the end of the performance, were often not completely settled. This openness to multiple, suggestive possibilities is reflected in Mahoney's comparison of *Told by the Wind* to 'the astringent purity of a haiku poem, though haiku seems positively wordy in comparison' (Mahoney 2010).

Another way of describing the performance score and its dramaturgy phenomenologically is that it presents itself to the audience's experience and consciousness as something like either an 'echo chamber of allusions' (Quinn 2005: 14) or a jigsaw puzzle. 'Solving' jigsaw puzzles engages one in seeing/sensing solutions to the possibilities each piece of a puzzle presents as it is encountered. The first structure presents one piece of the puzzle – Male Figure seated at the writing desk looking out the window, and Female Figure seated on a diagonal opposite with a framed earthen square between them. They do not speak or look to one another. The second structure presents another piece of the puzzle with the Female Figure squatting downstage centre, focused on the slow 'sweeping' action with the delicate, weathered, fragile, brown evergreen in her hand while the Male Figure remains at the desk upstage. How does Structure 1 'fit' in relation to Structure 2?

In Structure 3, the fragmentary, poetic text delivered by Male Figure reveals 'the desolation of Autumn.' Looking out the window, he observes a figure moving in a landscape, arriving ... somewhere. Although some contextual information is provided, no absolute 'answers' are forthcoming; rather, further questions are posed or additional pieces of a puzzle are suggested, such as Male Figure's contemplative, 'The end of Autumn. What follows?' By the end of the performance all the pieces of the puzzle are present, but they do not fit together in an absolute way that constitutes a framed and finished whole. Erika Fischer-Lichte explained how:

> What the story was did not have to be pinned down [...] The performance was not vague, but there was a certain kind of indeterminacy so you were free to have associations [...] It was open and invited the spectator in as a whole person [...].
>
> (Fischer-Lichte 2010)

From Tony Brown's perspective, narrative in *Told by the Wind*:

> became a much more amorphous thing. It was almost as though, because of the deep interaction between what was happening between the lit space and the observers in the darkness, that we audience members were creating the action in a web of space, time, movement and sound. Causality was suspended but was in a strange way important. It was very clear that the 'characters' (if that's what they were) had a hugely deep effect on each other but the why, where, when and how of it could only be grasped like the effect of a breeze – invisible but tangible.
>
> (Brown 2010)

Initial responses to Told by the Wind

Reviewers and spectators alike commented on the unusual and difficult demands made by *Told by the Wind* on spectators. Tony Brown explained how 'this was a different experience for an audience [...]' where 'one was made to work hard as an observer' (Brown 2010). Allison Vale of *The British Theatre Guide* opened her review with an admission of her scepticism about what she might experience at *Told by the Wind*:

> I'll be honest. I'm a fan of traditional, narrative theatre. I like being part of a passive audience, soaking up a damn fine plot, executed by fully developed characters. I enjoy the security of the alternative reality they create [...] I wasn't at all sure I wanted to be compelled to find my own meaning and

significance in 'embodied silences, splintered interactions and slowed-down motion.'

(Vale 2010)

The 'hard work' began when the audience entered the theatre and first encountered quietude. Taken together, the first two non-verbal, psychophysical structures of *Told by the Wind* last approximately five minutes. The performers make no overt sounds. There is only the ambient 'noise' of the live performance environment and the hardly audible 'white noise' that fills the silence. It is only at the beginning of the third structure when Female Figure begins to slide her bare feet on the floor that a 'sound' emanates directly from one of the performers.

The Guardian's Elisabeth Mahoney explained how it was 'so still at times, you worry that scratching your head or crossing your legs will be audible' (Mahoney 2010). Responding to an online post on *The Guardian's* website by AJHampton [sic], Mahoney further explained how during the first part of the performance she 'was quite cross in fact [...] I struggled a bit to begin with and felt the day's thoughts whirring round my head (as I always do with yoga, fighting the calm) [...]' (Mahoney 2010a).

Although at first disconcerted by the initial quietude, a shift in perception and reception eventually occurred for many in the audience. Mahoney explained how she eventually 'settled, and got the richness of it [...]' (Mahoney 6 February 2010). For the initially skeptical Allison Vale the 'rigorous' demands the performance made on her as a spectator ultimately made the performance 'all the more affecting for that' (Vale 2010). At least for Vale, an alternative mode of spectating to the usual emerged in her response to *Told by the Wind*: '[...It] is easily the most hypnotic piece of theatre I have experienced. The extraordinary poise and perfection in the movement, texting and staging of this piece makes for a beautifully contemplative sixty minutes' (Vale 2010).

What elements of the performance were sufficiently 'rich' to attract the attention and eventually 'settle' initially restive spectators such as Mahoney and skeptics such as Vale? What precisely was it that made the performance 'hypnotic,' 'compelling,' and 'mesmerizing'? To answer these questions I turn to an analysis of the second dimension of the performance score for *Told by the Wind*, focusing on the dynamic quality of the actor's embodied consciousness, awareness, and perception deployed in enacting some of the specific tasks/actions that constitute the total performance score.

A phenomenological account of the actor's performance score

At the beginning of *Told by the Wind*, when Jo Shapland and I step into the playing space and are seated to begin Structure 1, our initial performance task is to open and engage our peripheral awareness to the possible presence of an-'other' in the environment. Phenomenologically, from my perspective inside the performance, the act of 'opening' my peripheral awareness means using indirect visual focus, i.e., my eyes do not attempt to focus specifically on anything/anyone/anywhere. Since my visual focus is secondary and indirect, my energy and awareness open to and attend to the spatial environment surrounding me – to my right, my left, and/or behind me. The 'other' to whom I am opening my awareness is *not* a specific individual, but rather a possibility or a question. This 'other' is constituted by a series of embodied questions, such as:

> 'Is someone/something there?'
> 'Is 'she' present?'
> 'Is 'she' there?' 'Where?'
> 'There...there...or there?'

I do not literally *ask* myself these questions in my mind, nor is this 'other' or this 'she' given a specific name, identity, or history[19]. Rather, I psychophysically engage my embodied consciousness in subtly responding to the impulse of a 'question' or 'possible presence' if/when/as each question/possibility emerges in the moment of performance. It is important that this embodied process of questioning/probing remains indeterminate. My focus/attention should not 'land' or resolve itself. It is a constant process of active searching/questioning.

About half way through Structure 1, this initial embodied probing/questioning becomes much more specific – both Jo Shapland and I begin to attune our auditory awareness to our possible 'other'. We actively engage psychophysically in what may be described as 'attentive listening,' i.e., opening our ears to the sonority of the immediate environment. In his essay, *Listening*, philosopher Jean-Luc Nancy asks the question: 'What does it mean for a being to be immersed entirely in listening, formed by listening or in listening, listening with all his being?' (Nancy 2007: 4). The psychophysical task here is to 'let go' and abandon oneself completely to this state of deep, profound 'listening' where all that exists is *a question*. Nancy asks, 'What secret is at stake when one truly *listens*' and thereby encounters 'sonority rather than the message?' (Nanacy 2007: 5). We are listening, but what is 'there' remains a 'secret' – unknown to each of us. There *is no 'message'*. No 'thing' and no 'one' emerges as an answer to the psychophysical 'questions' posed. Our embodied consciousness/awareness is always 'on the edge of meaning'; however, 'meaning' and understanding never emerge. As Nancy explains: 'To be listening is always to be on the edge of meaning, or in an edgy meaning of extremity, and as if the sound were precisely nothing else than this edge [...]' (Nancy 2007: 7). The kind of 'listening' I am attempting to describe here is not an isolated or passive act of the 'ears' hearing; rather, it is an act of absorption so complete and full that one's embodied consciousness is woven in the moment.

Optimally, this process of embodied attunement of the ear absorbs and then re-directs our energy and awareness in a process of taking in, searching, and questioning. The specificity and intensity of our engagement with these psychophysical tasks within the first structure means that, as performers, we are animated and energized 'inside' – not in a psychological or motivational sense – as we attune our embodied consciousness to what might be present in the environment. The result of this intense internal psychophysical engagement is subtle, slight adjustments in each of our physical positions within a field of possibilities. Although we are basically 'still,' we are *not* frozen; rather, each of us is animated from the inside-out by constantly being active and reactive. Phenomeno-logically our performative engagement with deep listening may be described as opening a space of possibility within us as performers/stage-figures.

If the first non-verbal structure of *Told by the Wind* engages the performers in a deep form of attentive listening, in Structure 2 there is a phenomenological shift. The Female Figure is revealed in a crouching position centre stage where she holds in her right hand a withered evergreen branch which casts a long shadow on the floor. For approximately two minutes, Female Figure is intently engaged in executing a slow, subtle psychophysical score as '...she sweeps ... stops ... looks to leaves ... drops brush ... the memory of leaves ...' Shapland's performance score is *not* literally known to the audience. What *is* available to the audience is the specificity, degree, quality, and intensity of psychophysical engagement that she as performer brings to each task within this structure's score, and the sensory and imaginative links she makes between actions/tasks within it, including:

- her sensory/tactile engagement with the touch/feel of the withered branch on the skin of her fingers/hand,
- the weight and rhythm of the branch as she executes the arc of each sweeping motion,
- her embodied relationship to the impulse to drop the branch or look down to 'leaves,'
- the appearance of a 'memory' in the (imagined) leaves, and
- the associations that may arise in relation to being present at the 'threshold' of the earthen square.

Upstage of Female Figure, as Male Figure I begin the structure gazing out the window, but eventually shift my sensory awareness from the auditory as primary to *between* the auditory and the visual. My ears remain 'open' to the environment, but the question of a possible presence engages me in both looking *and* listening. But again, these questions are again not answered and indeterminate.

In Structure 3, after approximately seven sliding steps Male Figure delivers the first line of text: 'The desolation of autumn.' Unlike dialogue in a realist production, delivering the fragmentary, suggestive, poetic text of *Told by the Wind* necessarily engages the performer in a mode of voicing/sounding which cannot be pedestrian. Phenomenologically, the performer's optimal relationship to the voicing of text in *Told by the Wind* is to engage one's entire embodied consciousness in hearing/sensing the 'saidness' of each line. At a technical level, this involves the performer in ensuring that the pitch of the text when delivered is 'hitting' and thereby 'vibrating' not only the throat resonator, but also the chest resonator. If and when the delivery of the text is 'on pitch' to resonate in the chest, the inner 'vibration' of the text as it is said creates a temporal 'residue'. From inside speaking the text, similar to the shifts of voice in *noh* dramatic texts which move between third and first person, so I attempt to keep a dialectic between the constant presence of third person observation and first person experience. For example, in delivering the following sequence:

Returning.
Night dew on feet.
Wet.
Stops.
Looks to dew and to past...behind.
Dew...on feet.

I interweave my sensory awareness between 'seeing' this possible other 'returning,' and sensing myself *as* this 'other' with the 'Dew ... on [my] feet.' I therefore engage the tactile awareness of the feet of my bare feet on the ground in the speaking 'Dew ... on feet.' The Male Figure's 'other' is therefore always available and at times present within my embodied awareness in the experienced 'saidness' of lines like 'Dew ... on feet.' This dialectical mode of 'saidness' moving between third person description and first person inhabitation keeps the text from 'landing.' It is not simply a narrative description. Delivering any of the text in *Told by the Wind* I maintained this dialectic between first and third person – between 'being' and 'witnessing'.

For both Male and Female Figures their 'other' always remains *both a question and a possibility* that is shaped and reshaped throughout the performance. Their 'other' is always present in some way in the *mise-en-scene*, and their traces are always available, but that 'other' is never directly seen and they never interact. The presence of the 'other' is indeterminate and keeps shifting.

In Structure 3, I not only sense this 'other' within me, but address this possible other outside me when I literally ask the question, 'Are you present?' There is silence ... a pause. And then a sudden and unexpected rush of action as Female Figure suddenly runs across the earthen square from USL to DSR – momentarily lit at the centre of the earthen square behind Male Figure. This 'other' has passed within five feet of me as Male Figure, but I *do not move*. Remaining externally still is essential to the dramaturgy and dynamic of the performance as a whole. By not looking/seeing 'her' pass and by not overtly responding to her passing, her possible 'presence' to Male Figure remains a question...a possibility. Where was 'she' in relation to 'he'? What is the earthen square in relation to the space Male Figure inhabits at this moment in the dramaturgy?

From inside playing Male Figure, my task is to allow the question I have just asked to *echo or resonate as a possibility* in the silence that follows its asking – 'Are you present?' My gaze is indirect. I am listening and open to a possible presence. 'Is there a presence, here, now?' Suddenly, something disturbs the still air of the environment. I feel/sense the disturbance of the air/wind on my left hand/arm as it grasps the back of the chair. As Jo Shapland passes within five feet of me, I literally feel/hear/sense her as she passes. But inside Male Figure's state of deep listening, I only absorb and take in disturbance of the air/wind as it passes *as a question, or possibility*. If 'she' is present, 'she' is still immaterial in some way ... indeterminate.

This sense of the simultaneous presence and absence of the 'other' to both Male and Female Figures was played out in different ways throughout the remainder of *Told by the Wind*. In the concluding, tenth Structure, even as we are literally side-by-side (see Fig 7.4), we still inhabit two 'worlds'. Our 'other' is present as a trace, a question, a possibility.

Given the dramaturgy and performance strategy of *Told by the Wind*, Jo Shapland and I constantly worked with the simple, phenomenal co-presence of the other actor, as well as within the possible presence of our (fictional) 'others' within the world of the performance. The dialectic between the presence and absence of our fictional 'other' was fundamental to the aesthetic, shape, quality, and dramaturgy of *Told by the Wind*. We had to work constantly on the edge of this 'other's' appearance at the same time s/he never materialized.

Acting as a 'question': 'presence' as emergent

I have provided a detailed phenomenological description of several sections of the actors' performance score for *Told by the Wind* and of the dramaturgy of the whole. Perhaps the most important aspect of these descriptions is the attention to precision and detail about both templates which together create each performance. I would argue that only when performers have confidence in and clarity about the precise nature of their performance score can they allow themselves the freedom to be 'surprised' in the moment-by-moment enactment of that work in performance. I therefore agree with Jane Goodall's astute observation that if/when 'presence' is experienced by the audience it is due in part to the performers' 'attention to detail, process and technique' (Goodall 2008: 33). With regard the emergence of 'presence' in *Told by the Wind*, Allison Vale reached a similar conclusion in her summary of how the performance worked on her:

> [...] Kaite O'Reilly's hauntingly poetic snatches of text ripple through the piece, adding texture without informing plot or character. The slow, silent grace of his play without dialogue, this ballet without music, make the experience of sitting in the audience a wholly introspective one. At times it feels more like a meditation than theatre [...]. It is precision in the crafting and execution of this piece which makes it so compelling.
>
> (Vale 2010)

Of course 'presence' does not emerge and a performance is not 'compelling' or 'mesmerizing' simply because an actor repeats with precision the details of their performance score. Precision and detail are necessary to the actor's work, but they are also potential traps. It is the quality and valence of embodied consciousness, awareness, and perception that are deployed in relation to each specific task/action *in the moment of each enactment* that determines whether 'presence' might or might not emerge at a particular performance.

In this essay I have described the inherent indeterminacy and lack of narrative closure that is central to both the dramaturgy of the whole and of the performance scores in *Told by the Wind*. Perhaps, as Jane Goodall also argues, the emergence of 'presence' in response to *Told by the Wind* was due in part to the fact that 'Presence is often bound up with paradox, a holding together of contraries, as if the one who embodies it is a convergence point for opposing forces.' (Goodall 2008: 188)

At this point in my argument, I want to consider the implications for the acting process more generally of the issues raised in this case study of *Told by the Wind*. Although indeterminacy, questioning, 'holding together contraries,' and a dialectical process between presence/absence are all specific to *Told by the Wind*, I would argue that they *all* describe and point to the optimal state actors *should* embody when performing – a state of being/doing where one's embodied consciousness is absolutely 'on the edge' of what is possible ... what might come ... what might happen ... what might be said ... in each moment of doing, whatever the dramaturgy.

Too often actors are looking for 'answers,' want closure, or simply try to repeat something that seems to 'work' and is successful[20]. Rather than closure, answers, or what seems to work, paradoxically acting should always be considered as a 'question'. Even though actors 'know' as a horizon of possibilities each task/action that constitutes a well-rehearsed performance score, phenomenologically actors should situate themselves in the indeterminate position of being 'on the edge' of *not knowing*. This place of 'not knowing' is a state of readiness – a dispositional state of possibility to which the actor can abandon herself in the moment. To inhabit this state of not knowing what is next or what might emerge is to inhabit a place where there is the potential to be 'surprised' in the moment of abandonment. Paradoxically, the 'knowing' actor must become innocent, and each task/action must always become a 'question' in the moment of enactment.

Inhabiting this place of 'not knowing' is not a comfortable or easy place because it requires one's unrelenting attention. To inhabit this location, and to achieve an optimal relationship of the actor to the psychophysical scores described here is only achieved through rigorous psychophysical training (see Zarrilli 2009, *passim*). As Goodall asserts, '… through the extreme rigors of performance technique, the body and the mind are torn from their comfortable lodgement in habit and circumstance' (Goodall 2008: 159). I would argue that only as rigorous training dislodges the practitioner from 'habit and circumstance' can the performer be 'alive' to the moment of abandonment and surprise. In this sense only a form of *radical* training that constantly moves the performer into a territory of constant discovery, surprise and 'questioning,' even in the repetition of exercises that might become habitual, can such training be effective in allowing the performance to become available to each moment as it appears in the now.

The process of embodied 'questioning' discussed here and utilized in *Told by the Wind* is a way of opening oneself in the moment to an unknown. When the actor opens into the unknown, this may also open an imaginative space for the audience in which they too enter a potentially compelling space of deep 'listening,' 'seeing,' or 'feeling'[21]. It is an unusual place because it only exists on the edge of possibility.

Works cited

Anonymous (2009) written responses to the Tyn-y-parc preview performances.

Barba, E. (1995) *The Paper Canoe*, London: Routledge.

Brook, P. (1979) *The Empty Space*, Harmondsworth: Penguin.

Brown, T. (2010) personal email communication to Phillip Zarrilli, Cardiff.

da Paz, M. (2009) personal email communication to Phillip Zarrilli, Lisbon.

Da Silva, D. (2009) personal email communication to Phillip Zarrilli, Lisbon.

Dolan, J. (2005) *Utopia in Performance*, Ann Arbor MI: University of Michigan Press.

Feral, J. (1982) 'Performance and Theatricality: The Subject Demystified', *Modern Drama*, 25, 17081.

Fischer-Lichte, E. (2010) personal interview/discussion, translated by S. Jain, Berlin 27 April.

——(2008) *The Transformative Power of Performance: a new aesthetics*, translated by S. Jain, London: Routledge.

Goodall, J. (2008) *Stage Presence*, London: Routledge.

Hare, T. (2008) *Zeami: Performance Notes*, New York: Columbia University Press.

Kelligan, M. (2010) '*Told by the Wind*', review Theatre Wales Website. Online. Available at: www.theatre-wales.co.uk/reviews/reviews_details. asp?reviewID=2260 (accessed 31 January, 2010).

Mahoney, E. (2010) '*Told by the Wind*', review *The Guardian*, 2 February, 2010.

——(2010a) '*Told by the Wind*', review Guardian.co.uk. Online. Available at: www.guardian.co.uk/stage/2010/feb/02/told-by-the-wind-review (accessed 28 July 2011).

Marzani, E. (2009) personal email communication to Phillip Zarrilli, Evora.

Nancy, J.-L. (2007) *Listening*. N.Y.: Fordham University Press.

Nearman, M. (1984) 'Feeling in Relation to Acting: An Outline of Zeami's Views', *Asian Theatre Journal*, 1:1, 40–51.

Pavis, P., Yarrow R. and Korklin, B. (1997) 'Underscore: The Shape of things to Come', *Contemporary Theatre Review*, 6/4, 37–61.

Power, C. (2008) *Presence in Play: A Critique of Theories of Presence in the Theatre*, Amsterdam: Rodopi.

Quinn, S. F. (2005) *Developing Zeami: the Noh Actor's Attunement in Practice*. Honolulu HI: University of Hawaii Press.

Riley, J. (1997) *Chinese Theatre and the Actor in Performance*, Cambridge: Cambridge University Press.

Roach, J. (2004) 'It', *Theatre Journal*, 56, 555–68.

——(2007) *It*. Ann Arbor: University of Michigan Press.

Segal, W. (2003) *A Voice at the Borders of Silence*, New York: Overlook Press.

Stanislavski, C. (1975) 'Direction and Acting', in Toby Cole (ed.) *Acting: A Handbook of the Stanislavski Method*, New York: Crown Publishers.

Vale, A. (2010) *'Told by the Wind'*, review British Theatre Guide. Online. Available at: www.britishtheatreguide.info/reviews/toldwind-rev.htm (accessed 5 February 2010).

Zarrili, P. (1995) *Acting (Re)considered: A Theoretical and Practical Guide*, London: Routledge.

——(2002) 'The Metaphysical Studio', *TDR: The Drama Review*, 46:2, 157–70.

——(2009) *Psychophysical Acting: an intercultural approach after Stanislavski*, London: Routledge.

Notes

1 I use 'actor' and 'performer' interchangeably throughout this essay.

2 *Told by the Wind* was produced by The Llanarth Group (Llanarth, Ceredigion, Wales, UK) – Artistic Director, Phillip Zarrilli. The Llanarth Group was formed in 2000. I acknowledge, with thanks, the following support: *Told by the Wind* was funded in part by the Arts Council of Wales and an AHRC practice-led grant. I also acknowledge, with thanks, the support for writing this essay provided by a residency as a Fellow at the International Research Center, 'Interweaving Performance Cultures,' Freie Universität (Berlin) directed by Prof. Dr Dr h. c. Erika Fischer-Lichte.

3 Scheduled performances included Exeter Phoenix (11–12 October 2010), The Grotowski Institute, Wroclaw, Poland (22–23 October 2010), and as part of the Chicago Theatre: Past, Present, Future Symposium (18–21 May 2011).

4 I use of the term 'score' to refer to both the visual/auditory/enacted/tactile elements made available by the actor(s) for the experience of the audience, as well as what Pavis calls the 'subscore,' i.e., that which lies *underneath* the actor's visible material score' (Pavis *et al* 1997: 29). The specific discussion of *Told by the Wind* which follows provides specific examples from the performance score in this larger/expanded sense of 'subscore'.

5 For example, see Power 2008: 117–148.

6 Given my phenomenological approach I address some of the issues examined in Erika Fischer-Lichte's *The Transformative Power of Performance* (Fischer-Lichte 2008).

7 In contrast to 'presence,' the simple, literal, phenomenal presence of the actor need not be set off by quotation marks.

8 Power devotes a chapter ('Having Presence') in his book to this 'strong' form of 'presence,' and coins the specific term 'auratic presence' (Power 2008: 47). For a much earlier critical discussion see Féral 1982.

9 This form of the actor's presence is most associated with the work of Jerzy Grotowski and Eugenio Barba. Barba provides the following

description of the how this type of 'presence' is derived from the operation of principles informing pre-expressive modes of training and embodiment: 'These principles, when applied to certain physiological factors – weight, balance, the use of the spinal column and the eyes – produce physical, pre-expressive tensions. These new tensions generate an extra-daily quality which renders the body theatrically 'decided,' 'alive,' 'believable,' thereby enabling the performer's 'presence' or scenic *bios* to attract the spectator's attention *before* any message is transmitted' (Barba 1995: 9). Goodall argues that this form of 'effective stage presence … begins with control of the performer's own bio-energetic fields' as the performer maintains 'a calmness at the centre of all the sound and fury that adds to the dramatic power while it is raging' (Goodall 2008: 48). The type of processes Barba describes, those I have described in *Psychophysical Acting* (2009) as well as in *Kathakali Dance-Drama* (2000), and those described later in this essay are grounded in the materiality of psychophysical processes and should not, therefore, be mystified. The actor's relationship to breath, focus, perception, attentiveness, etc. may be paradoxical and even non-ordinary; however, I would argue that this paradoxical/non-ordinary experience is anything *but* holy or transcendent. Grotowski's use of the term 'holy actor' should be understood and examined historically and contextually. Any language which mystifies the actor's work I find highly problematic and think has no place in the studio or rehearsal room.

10 As both Fischer-Lichte and Power argue in their own ways, a complete analysis of how presence works must extend beyond the processes of embodiment that create or manifest energy and explore additional issues and/or other modes through which 'presence' emerges (see Fischer-Lichte 2008: 96–100; Power 2008, *passim*). In this brief essay I remained focused on one 'mode of presence' – the performer's relationship to the generation and creation of what is perceived as ('the strong concept of') 'presence' in a specific performance, and the spectator's experience of such 'presence'.

11 Goodall makes the following helpful distinction between presence and charisma: 'charisma needs to be understood in a longitudinal sense, as a heightened life-force that animates a whole career and fuels the trajectory of a sustained mission in the world. Presence is an expression of life force in the moment, so that the moment itself is transformed in a way that has an impact on all who witness it' (Goodall 2008: 46).

12 In performances with different dramaturgies and a different aesthetic logic, the type and quality of 'strong presence' may be quite different from that in *Told by the Wind*. In some of Forced Entertainment's productions, such as their recent, '*And on the thousandth night …*' (Hau 1, Berlin, 2010) or in Spalding Gray's monologues such as *Swimming to Cambodia*, the performer's mode of presencing is quite different from 'strong … presence' and could be described as 'cooler' than that discussed in relation to *Told by the Wind*. The pleasures of such performances derive not so much from a heightened intensity of

the performer's 'energy' but an intelligent if 'everyday' investment in what is said. The performer's mode of being present to her work takes place in a different register and with a different intensity than that described here with regard to *Told by the Wind*.

13 A future essay will specifically address how *Told by the Wind* negotiated in an alternative way the complex issues of intercultural production.

14 Our process was enhanced by the presence, feedback, and suggestions of two artistic consultants – Mari Boyd (Tokyo), a specialist on Japanese theatre, especially the work of Ota Shogo and 'the 'aesthetics of quietude' (Boyd 2006), and Peader Kirk, Artistic Director of Mkultra (London) and a professional theatre director, performance maker/deviser, and teacher of devising process. They each provided targeted feedback separately and from their own perspectives for two days as *Told* was in development, just prior to the official première, and in response to our initial performances.

15 Among these seven sources, the first three played a central role in the development of *Told* dramaturgically and stylistically, the fourth and fifth contributed somewhat, while the final two sources remained in the background.

16 Both part of performance score are not present somewhere in the actor's brain or mind; rather, these maps exist within the perceptual experience of each performer as a horizon of possibilities. They have been gradually sedimented into one's embodied consciousness through experimentation and repetition and are available for (re)enactment. At each performance, in the present moment of doing the actor optimally does not think about either the dramaturgy as a whole (the 'fictional' world) or one's embodied relationship to specific tasks/actions; rather, the performer's embodied consciousness, awareness and perception are deployed in relation to each task/action in the moment in two ways: (1) the actor shapes and deploys his 'energy' as he attends to and embodies each task/action of the score within the dynamic and stylistic parameters of the performance aesthetic as rehearsed, and (2) the actor perceives and responds to each stimuli offered in the performance environment, adjusting as necessary to any new stimuli in the environment. In an enactive model of acting (Zarrilli 2009: 41–60), the actor operates with a subjectivity that is constantly shifting as one tactically improvises – making adjustments to and or from what presents itself in the moment. Any particular iteration will be both similar to, but different from previous enactments of the score. The longer the period of development/rehearsal or performance, the larger the field of experience that accumulates as an expanding field of possibilities.

17 I describe here the performance as realized for the premire run at Chapter Art Centre's theatre which seats approximately 100.

18 This section of the essay draws on a fifteen responses to nine performances: (1) six short anonymous written responses by audience members written immediately after the work-in-progress showings at the Tyn-y-parc Studio, Wales; (2) three detailed responses to the

Evora, Portugal performance (received via email); (3) three published reviews were written in response to the initial run at Chapter Arts Centre – two (*Guardian* and *Theatre Wales*) responsed to the opening night (29 January 2010), and the *British Theatre Guide* review was a response to the 4 February 2010 Chapter performance; (4) three unsolicited responses to the Cardiff performances – two received by email and one blog posted on the National Theatre Wales website. These responses constitute approximately 5% of the total audience for the nine initial preview and Chapter Art Centre performances. Four additional opportunities arose for public feedback: (1) a talk-back after the 5 February 2010 performance at Chapter Art Centre with approximately 60 audience members present; (2) a talk-back following the 27 March 2010 performance at Tanzfabrik in Berlin with approximately thirty-five audience members present; (3) a 90-minute discussion with nine Fellows/Staff at the Research Institute for 'Interweaving Performance Cultures' at Freie Universität (Berlin) on 10 April 2010, and (4) a discussion with Prof. Erika Fischer-Lichte on 27 April 2010.

19 The psychophysical process I am describing is counter to many approaches to constructing a character in realist character-based acting. Asking and answering questions about this 'other' or 'she' would settle the questioning. The questioning is a form of psychophysiological activation that should *not* be settled. This process activates the actor precisely because the questioning remains unsettled.

20 The process of 'not knowing' I am discussing has nothing to do with problematic notions of getting the actor 'out of her comfort zone' and manipulating the actor's 'emotions'. I have described the active state of readiness and one approach to training the actor toward this state in *Psychophysical Acting* (Zarrilli 2009: 81ff).

21 Fischer-Lichte's analysis calls our attention to the mutuality of embodied experience which collapses the absolute dichotomies between actor/spectator and body/mind. She observes how when spectators experience the 'strong presence' of the actors and are compelled by the intensity of the performance to become completely engaged in the act of spectating, they may have 'an intense sensation of themselves as present' and even 'experience themselves as energized' (Fischer-Lichte 2008: 96). Fischer-Lichte describes this process as potentially 'transformative' in that there is 'a constant process of becoming' – what she calls, 'the *radical concept of presence*' (Fischer-Lichte 2008: 99).

Chapter 8

Out-standing standing-within

Being alone together in the work of Bodies of Flight

Simon Jones

Since 1996 Bodies in Flight, co-directed by choreographer Sara Giddens and myself, has made a series of practice-as-research works exploring what performance can contribute to our understanding of the contemporary experience of identity and knowledge-production (see Jones 2009; 2009a). Inspired by Martin Heidegger's and Emmanuel Levinas' thoughts, I want to describe how performer–auditor–spectator participation in two of our performance-events has led me to move from the former's notion of 'preserving' an art-work *within* the co-presence of that work and its participants, to the latter's insistence that co-presence must be realized *quintessentially* as a face-to-face between persons. The one requires the active deconstruction of our making of ourselves – what in Bodies in Flight we have come to call *de-second-naturing* (see Giddens and Jones 2009; Jones 2007); the other permits its ethical reconstruction, experienced fundamentally as a together-aloneness. This leads me to question the limits of 'interactivity' as *the* current mode through which presence in performance is increasingly articulated.

In Bodies in Flight's 2002 performance, *skinworks*, commissioned by Arnolfini (Bristol) and Now Festival (Nottingham), we explored the participants' co-presence through *dislocating space* by rendering an online sex-chatroom actual. *Dream→work* (2009), commissioned by Singapore Arts Festival and Nottdance Festival, *desynchronized time* to produce its mood of co-presence by dwelling alongside whilst being-outside-of the morning rush-hour. The former asked what happens when a virtual place is physicalized in the space of the performance-event itself, specifically what happens to the desires that force that place into being, desires disembodied in the virtual realm. The latter required its participants to walk through both the space and time of commuting, whilst listening to the differing rhythms of an 'every-person's' stream of consciousness mixed live with happenchance street sounds.

Skinworks generated a welcoming and seating of each auditor-spectator individually, so that their introduction into the space was collectively noted, and the gathering of the chatroom made palpable. A seating arrangement emerged whereby each individual auditor–spectator was isolated in their own space, around which performers circulated. In this way, people arriving in couples and groups were separated and seated apart, the first seats being positioned apparently at some distance from each other, the precision and proximity of the overall seating plan not becoming clear until the majority were seated. By this means, individuals were both alone and together, both carrying the sense of joint arrival and now separated from loved ones. *Dream→work*'s auditor–walkers, however, were in the midst of the actual, mixed right into the present of its occurring, but nevertheless progressively stepping aside by both stepping inside the performer's head and stepping outside the current of events: *of* the middle of things, but not *in* the middle. Thus both works express a basic principle of Bodies in Flight – always to re-sensitize each individual audience-spectator to their own embodied experience of the performance-event (see Machon 2009); to re-express a fundamental drive in all performance: this gathering of the asocial (see Blau 1990).

For Bodies in Flight then, the performance-event is a privileged site for modelling the possibilities of bodies mixing: performer-auditor–spectator–participant. It is this middle that meddles: a mixing of fleshes, between and within bodies artificially delimited. I now realize that *skinworks*, in making the virtual place of the chatroom actual, was ex-posing the crucial difference between the so-called interactivity of that digital realm and the essential co-presence of performance. And even with *Dream→work* when eschewing the obvious disembodiedness of internet technologies and working within the very intensities of the everyday commute, passing close by others can often be alienating, as if one were not actually there. Both these works came to be about the difficulty with immediacy: that it is not immediate. Moreover, the particular co-presence of performance challenges our easy recourse to the technological solution for problems of engagement, participation and citizenship – interactivity.

Figure 8.1 Bodies in Flight, *skinworks* (2002). Photo: Edward Dimsdale.

Indeed, the seductive illusion of speed and dependence on last-minute-dot-com service industries both drive contemporary culture to pare down the instance of response: by closing up the space between call and answer, this apparently immediate disclosure lends to any exchange the force of a *presence*. This instant gratification reinforces not only 'the need for speed,' but the sense of belonging inherent in the response made to the call: I exist because I am interacting: to tweet or not to tweet, that is the question. The interactive appears to accelerate time and condense space: a self-fulfilling immediacy with all the force of touch, without a space between, without a channel or medium – *im-mediate*. However, this interactive force, despite its coupling of the cultures of advanced capital to the converging technologies of trans-national industries, with their apparently benign claims of greater personal choice and freedom, actually occludes all that will not yield itself *easily in an instant*. Within interactivity's eventness, the possibilities of a face-to-face encounter are degraded to an inter-*acting*. Even Nicolas Bourriaud, the champion of 'relational aesthetics,' recognizes this fundamental problem with interactive technologies. 'The "society of the spectacle" (see Debord 1992) is thus followed by the society of extras, where everyone finds the illusion of an interactive democracy in more or less truncated channels of communication' (Bourriaud 2002: 26). To inter-act with the other becomes a tasking, rather than a being-with, such that the other can be *re-placed* by a machine that does a passable impersonation of the other, that is, a machine that does the same tasks: the Turing test, the computer on the other end of the phone that 'speaks' in the first person. Space is not opened out so that one can see oneself in relation to the other: it is collapsed so that distance, which gives a place for difference to happen, cannot be felt. And time is filled with tasking, so that one cannot stop to think, since this kind of thinking – the recognizing the other – must have its *own* time to contemplate the scene, first *with* the other, then *of* the other.

Claire Bishop's critique of Bourriaud's description of relational aesthetics focuses on their often game-like structure, with de facto rules and predictable outcomes. As Bourriaud himself had noted – 'Artistic activity is a game, whose forms, patterns and functions develop and evolve according to periods and social contexts; it is not an immutable essence' (Bourriaud 2002: 11). To which she responds: 'One could argue that in this context, project-based works-in-progress and artists-in-residence begin to dovetail with an "experience economy", the marketing strategy which seeks to replace goods and services with scripted and staged personal experiences' (Bishop 2004: 52). Interactivity requires that one not only 'respond' to the next stimulus, but that the information exchanged be 'relevant,' appropriate, proper, thus ensuring the disappearance of difference, or more accurately, at best its non-appearance and at worse the suppression of its appearing. Communicating re-places communion; a commun-icating only possible because grounded on the previously agreed norms of a third party, of society. Indeed, Bishop is right to criticize Bourriaud's overemphasizing the audience-spectator's radical interest in the relational art-work 'as fundamentally harmonious, because they are addressed to a community of viewing subjects with *something in common*' (Bishop 2004: 68, original emphasis). She calls for participatory work which provokes the differences between individuals and troubles the very relations through which the work works: 'the presence of what is not me renders my identity precarious and vulnerable, and the threat that the other represents transforms my *own* sense of self into something questionable. When played out on a social level, antagonism can be viewed as the limits of society's ability to fully constitute itself' (Bishop 2004: 66–7, original emphasis).

This analysis echoes one of Heidegger's key definitions of the art-work:

> In setting up a world and setting forth the earth, the work is an instigating of [...] strife. This does not happen so that the work should at the same time settle and put an end to strife by an insipid argument, but so that the strife may remain a strife. [...] It is because the strife arrives at its high point in the simplicity of intimacy that the unity of the work comes about in the instigation of strife.
>
> (Heidegger 1978: 175)

Furthermore, for Heidegger this strife is where 'opponents raise each other into the self-assertion of their essential natures [...] each opponent carries the other beyond itself' (1978: 174).

Levinas' objection to simple physical proxemics also echoes Bishop's objections and can equally be applied to the participatory art-work: 'The idea of contact does not represent the primordial mode of the immediate. Contact is already a thematization and a reference to a horizon. The immediate is the face-to-face' (Levinas 1969: 52). In inter-'acting,' one is fully 'occupied' in this to-and-fro of exchanging: in effect, one acts or plays the 'part' of being inbetween – 'inter'. One is not dwelling in the space-time of the event as oneself, but explicitly as *not*-oneself, as *an-other* (any-other) who only appears to the extent that their qualities can be interactive, that is, expressed as turns taken in the exchange, moves made explicitly in order to sustain that exchange, the commun(e)-icating. This means that the an-other can only ever be normative: a part-other, an un-whole-other, ultimately an unreal other who cannot become as real as one is oneself, even in the intimacy of the exchange's turn-taking. This in turn effectively reduces the capacity of one's own self to become, as Heidegger pointed out in *Being and Time*:

> In these modes [of averageness] one's way of Being is that of inauthenticity and failure to stand by one's Self. [...] The Self of everyday Dasein is the *they-self*, which we distinguish from

the *authentic Self* – that is, from the Self which has been taken hold of in its own way. [...] *Proximally*, it is not 'I,' in the sense of my own Self, that 'am,' but rather the Others, whose way is that of 'they'. In terms of 'they,' and *as* the 'they,' I am 'given' proximally to 'myself'.

(Heidegger 1962: 167, original emphases)

Against this, performance's face-to-face of othernesses has no such beforehand under-standings or under-pinnings. This encounter goes beyond normative interaction, which requires of the self that its other be already like it-self, towards an altogether different becoming. I would argue that this radical potentiality of the face-to-face accounts for the so-called 'live' event's remarkable resistance to the seductiveness of interactive technologies. Against what has been repeatedly asserted in advance of each new wave of digital technology, the 'recorded' has not re-placed the 'live'. Whilst the latter has become ever more imbricated with the former's technologies, it resists a final, ironic (dis)appearance on to the screen: for example, the resurgence of bands playing gigs, whilst their music is downloaded for free from file-sharing sites, demonstrates not only the bands' refusal to disappear commercially, but also their listeners' desire to experience them in the flesh. Indeed, the Auslander–Phelan debate in Performance Studies has tended to describe the performance as a quasi-object, which can only be accessed by way of recorded media or doomed to a Pyrrhic vanishing before the forces of commodification. To this extent, it has continued Derrida's deconstruction of Artaud's valorization of 'pure presence,' without considering Derrida's telling admission that theatre is 'neither a book nor a work, but an energy, and in this sense it is the only art of life' (Derrida 1978: 247). If we think of performance less in terms of its textuality or its thingness, we are left with what remains – its eventness. And here the experiential, phenomenological approach, laid out by Heidegger in his definition of the art-work and developed by Levinas, will help us to understand more clearly performance's unique contribution to (human) life.

The artist performs a crucial function in Heidegger's ontology: 'In the being of the artist we encounter the most perspicuous and most familiar mode of will to power. Since it is a matter of illuminating the Being of beings, meditation on art has in this regard decisive priority' (Heidegger 1981: 70). And yet it is the inter-relationship between art-work and auditor–spectator where the work happens: for Heidegger, it is only truly made in its *preserving*, that is, in the work that those who did not author the work contribute to its making.

> Preserving the work means standing within the openness of beings that happens in the work. This 'standing-within' of preservation, however, is a knowing. [...] He who truly knows beings knows what he wills to do in the midst of them. [...] [T]he essence of *Existenz* is out-standing standing-within the essential sunderance of the clearing of beings.
>
> (Heidegger 1978: 192)

The art-work only exists through the complicit and inclusive encountering of communal attending, of spending time together: 'A work, by being a work, makes space for that spaciousness. [...] The work as work sets up a world. The work holds open the open region of the world' (Heidegger 1978: 170). Furthermore, the precise definition of 'knowing' is also one of difference, of standing out in the crowd, of recognizing that this very inbetween, across which we come together, is also a gap that divides us, an incomplete medium, or rather, a bundling of media (middles) each with their very own kind of incompleteness, *a cleft cleaving* both unto and asunder at one and the same time and one and the same point in space. Or as Stephen Mulhall writing on Heidegger puts it:

> [W]orking out an ontological characterization of Dasein is not just an essential preliminary to, but forms the central core of, fundamental ontology. [...] First, and most importantly then, Dasein is said to be distinctive amongst entities in that it does not just occur; rather, its Being is an issue for it.
>
> (Mulhall 1996: 14).

So, this 'knowing' jointly sustains an attending to not-knowing or the issue of knowing, that is, performance's quintessential work – *the problem of the person*. The art-work becomes that which is jointly preserved as a problem of knowing what it is to be a person: the art-work remains in its asociability, its extra-ordinariness, only for as long as the citizen, that is, the social form of the person, has not yet incorporated what differentiates it from the person, which is precisely the person's problem of becoming, *out-standing standing-within*. This is also why performance as a way of knowing the world is always a re-turning to or re-using: as child's play returns to what fascinates, as in delights or perturbs, that which is not yet understood, so artists and audiences return to performance texts or reviving plays or sustaining performance traditions. This is performance's way of preserving the working through of the problem of being human, that licenses us, as in the sense of – gives us a space-time, a where-when to dwell in these unknowables.

> [Poetry as] language, by naming beings for the first time, first brings beings to word and to appearance. Only this naming nominates beings *to* their Being and *from out* of their Being. Such saying is a projecting of clearing, in which announcement is made of what it is that beings come into the open *as*. [...] Projective saying is saying which, in preparing the sayable, simultaneously brings the unsayable as such into a world.
> (Heidegger 1978: 198–9, original emphases)

In *skinworks*, the performers take each auditor–spectator by the hand and lead them individually to their seat. This sweaty touch is the only physical contact between any persons in the entire work. By the uncertain, sometimes smiling looks on their faces, it was an intimacy both felt and to be endured which forced open the impossible dimensionality of the chatroom, *by way of* each person's re-sensing of their own embodiedness in the space, their own participating in the event.

> Ontically, of course, Dasein is not only close to us – even that which is closest: we *are* it, each of us, we ourselves. In spite of this, or rather for just this reason, it is ontologically that which is farthest.
> (Heidegger 1962: 36, original emphasis)

In crossing underneath a large, suspended screen, upon which webcam video-clips were being manipulated by the performers, each auditor–spectator not only crossed from their everyday, normalized space into the extra-ordinary fictional space, but transformed from a *they* into an *own-self*. And since for Heidegger, the 'subject' is not *in* space, but *of* it: this could only have been felt spatially as a moving across and between, as *a being towards*: '[B]ecause Dasein is "spiritual", *and only because of this*, it can be spatial in a way which remains essentially impossible for any extended corporeal Thing. Dasein's making room for itself is constituted by directionality and de-severance' (Heidegger 1962: 419, original emphasis).

So, although 'essentially impossible,' the re-sensing of the performance space as virtual chatroom was made palpable through the moving across and the unexpected intimacy of being touched. And this coming out of the anonymity of the crowd, who had up until then been *watching* the event from the other side of the projection screen, was experienced as a hyper awareness of the bodily self, an appearing as one's own-self amongst a host of others, who were now *listening* to the 'chat' of that impossible place – a co-presence of being alone together. This crossing of media, from the predominantly visual to the predominantly aural, forcing each participant to transform from spectator to auditor, further re-in-forced the re-appearing of each one's own-self, as looking around or at each other or at the performers became patently undoable for many. The very intimacy of this re-sensitizing not only reinforced this paradoxical co-presence of being alone together, but expressed it as a problem of becoming a person, as Being at issue with its own Being (see Jones 2008 for further discussion of this work).

> *this body feels so strange tonight*
> *ill-fitting*
> *like I'm performing it rather than living it*
> *a quasi-thing hardly crediting this quasi-real*
> *look*
> *somebody, look at this*
> *halfway through a riff that's suddenly playing itself*
> *makes you kind of queasy cos you know you're in for the ride*
> *but high so high*
> *cos it can't be you that's doing these things*
> *you can't be held responsible*
> *sex without secretions, ha*
> *a world of blame and not a single guilty soul.*

Skinworks concludes with the physical body exhausted as the still desiring mind runs out of imaginings, confronting both the endless, inhuman space of the internet and the infinite possibilities of desire without bodies: in facing this void, it confronts the central crisis of Heideggerian ontology. However necessary to the art-work the co-presence of its auditor–spectators, and however decisive the artist's work to the problem of Being, for Heidegger all this is fundamentally stymied by death: 'Death is the possibility of the absolute impossibility of Dasein. Thus death reveals itself as that *possibility which is one's ownmost, which is non-relational, and which is not to be outstripped'* (Heidegger 1962: 294, original emphasis). Not only is the individual's death theirs and no one else's, this unique and impenetrable relation is what most defines the individual's life: in Heidegger's terms, it offers them the way to live *authentically*: 'Dasein is the possibility of Being-free *for* its ownmost potentiality-for-Being' (Heidegger 1962: 183). If, as an art-work, performance's defining relation is the co-presence, not of thing–work–auditor–spectator, but of performer–auditor–spectator, then the ontological isolation of each person, defined by their own death, renders this relation unworkable: this co-presence can preserve nothing but the impossibility of its own becoming. It is now-here, outstanding the everyday and standing within the performance-event, that I want to introduce Levinas' crucial amendment to Heidegger's ontology which, I believe, gives performance as an art-form its particular potential: the participation of the other in this problem of the person.

For Levinas this embodied encounter between two persons is actually the unspeakable and indeterminable point when-where we experience both the concreteness and the possibility of our humanity, what he terms its totality (the ideologies and practices within which we conduct our daily lives) and its infinity (the absolute possibilities of the universe within which we live which automatically and necessarily challenge us both in fear of death and in hope of justice): 'The thou is posited in front of a we' (Levinas 1969: 213). Performance puts an individual before another before a host of others: it actualizes Levinas' idea – '*The individual and the personal are necessary for Infinity to be able to be produced as infinite*' (Levinas 1969: 218, original emphasis). In doing so, performance draws attention to the very possibilities of this encounter: its deconstructive work actually enacts them *within* the event: it produces them, as in *forces them to appear* [*pro-ducare*: to lead forth], within this relation *of face-to-face*, not necessarily literally, but always the putting somehow of some one before some other. And this very action both grounds performance and allows its essential co-presence to overcome death.

The approach, inasmuch as it is a sacrifice, confers a sense on death. In it the absolute singularity of the responsible one encompasses the generality or generalization of death. [...] But we can have responsibilities and attachments through which death takes on a meaning. That is because, from the start, the other affects us despite ourselves.

(Levinas 1998: 129)

Levinas is careful to insist that the face-to-face should not be limited to a literal encounter, although it can only happen *by way of* that concrete singularity: the very embodied and experiential specificity provokes the potentiality of the human confronting the possibilities of infinity.

The way in which the other presents himself, exceeding *the idea of the other in me*, we here name face. This *mode* does not consist in figuring as a theme under my gaze, in spreading itself forth as a set of qualities forming an image. The face of the Other at each moment destroys and overflows the plastic image it leaves me, the idea existing to my own measure and to the measure of its *ideatum* – the adequate idea. [...] *It expresses itself.*

(Levinas 1969: 50-1, original emphases)

Furthermore, that facing goes beyond Heidegger's *solicitude* of one Being to another: the approach requires an answer; and the response always entails a responsibility impossible to fulfil.

[I]n vulnerability lies a *relation to the other* that is not exhausted by causality, a relation prior to all affection by the stimulus. The identity of the self does not set limits to submission, not even the last resistance that matter 'in potential' opposes to the form that invests it. Vulnerability is obsession by others or approach to others. [...] An approach reduced neither to representation of others nor to consciousness of proximity.

(Levinas 2006: 64, original emphasis)

In a recent article, Simon Bayly builds on Bruce Wilshire's earlier insight that 'The intimate relationship between actor and auditor is not a face-to-face encounter, but a presence in a "mask" indwelling a presence "without a face"' (Wilshire 1982: 96). Bayly asserts that performance's contribution to an understanding of Levinas' *facing* is to make the difference between presentation of self and the self itselves problematic.

> What a theatrical thinking offers in response [to Levinas' notion of vulnerability and self-effacement] is that the function of a mask is not to hide the face as site of pure revelation of the individual soul but rather to reveal it as complicated and complicating figure of appearance. [...] In erasing the distinction between mask and face, the graphic symbol of the personae announces the impossibility of a pure appearing or a simple revelation of selfhood.
>
> (Bayly 2008: 29)

Levinas would argue that the appearance is always already the mask of an image, which the approach of a face undoes formally and ethically in requiring infinite responsibility: 'Proximity appears as the relationship with the other, who cannot be resolved into "images" or be exposed in a theme' (Levinas 1998: 100). This is vulnerability without bounds in the concrete-*ness* of the specific encounter. In using the metaphor of the same approaching the other, Levinas precisely describes a process of appearing, dis-appearing and re-appearing, inherent in the movement towards, thence away from, and re-turning back towards, the other. This movement – variously described in theatrical terms as 'an entry' or 'visitation,' fundamental to appearance, appearing before the other, even appearing on stage, necessitates instability, un-doing and re-doing in its insistence on the dynamics of approaching the other, a touching without ever reaching, always underway and never undergone, always in action and never done. This is the sensing of the matter materializing, rather than the ostensible appearance of matter materialized, the (quasi-)thing that can only be pointed to. This approaching is thus *a pre-position-ing*, before either the performer takes a stand or the auditor–spectator under-stands, before the place is occupied, the point is made, when-where 'we' 'know' 'where' 'we' 'are'. Thence-then the possibility of true communion, on the outside of inter-acting, without rules, disclosing in infinite depth what it means to be human: a clearing always underway as clearing: immediacy as infinite un-doing of itself: an infinite self-un-doing.

The absolute experience [of the Other] *is not disclosure but revelation*: a coinciding of the expressed with him who expresses, which is the privileged manifestation of the Other, the manifestation of a face over and beyond form. [...] The life of expression consists in undoing the form in which the existent, exposed as a theme, is thereby dissimulated. [...] He who manifests himself [...] at each instant undoes the form he presents.

(Levinas 1969: 62, original emphasis)

Dream→work attempts to place both Heidegger's being alone-togetherness and Levinas' call of the Other into the very everyday from which the art-work essentially flees. A group of twelve auditor-walkers follow two performers through the streets of a city (to date – Bristol, Nottingham and Singapore) during the morning rush-hour, listening through earpieces to the internal monologue of an every-person in the daily process of re-constructing their publicly facing self, moving from dreamtime to realtime. The literal face-to-face and touch of *skinworks* is re-placed by a more complex encounter: the performers disappear into the crowd only to re-appear indirectly by way of the gathered gazes of the auditor–walkers. The very sharing of public space, the middle-ground of the everyday, re-in-forces the complex co-presence of auditor–performer–crowd, who 'perform' Levinas' third party and force out of the immediate now-here of the performance-walk a confronting of what it is possible to become, that is, for Levinas, the problem of justice.

You will have seen him on the tram ... and he will have been the one who got away ... like the others. It's so hard to see the someone else as whole. You will have glimpsed them on the tram, cutting across your path, cutting you up, whatever ... in your road or in your face ... and then how hard to think of them as a whole person just like you. Yes, you will have known they have their human rights, are equal under the law ... supposedly ... in an ideal world. But ... how hard to think and feel him wholly there ... her wholly there ... whole in this world ... before you ... you as me. Before an us that will have made perfect sense of you and me, of all the possible yous and mes, will have admitted all-comers to the completeness of this you and this me, an absolute open only us.

(heard at Broadmarsh Shopping Centre, Nottingham whilst looking at commuters using the escalators)

Figure 8.2 Bodies in Flight, *Dream→work,* Nottingham (2009).
Photo: Tony Judge.

Unlike *skinworks*' re-spatializing, this co-presencing amongst the everyday is not essentially experienced spatially, but temporally, as a de-synchronizing of times. The ever-increasing tempo of living, as Paul Virilio has described, is articulated through technologies which effectively repress all other times to clock-time: the efficiency requirements of the rail network and the factory production-line dominate the chronologies of bodies, weather systems and the earth. Whereas for Heidegger, our experiencing of time passing is further evidence of our Being's ontological isolation – '*Temporality is the primordial "out-side-of-itself" in and for itself.* We therefore call the phenomenon of the future, the character of having been, and the Present, the *"ecstasies"* of temporality' (Heidegger 1962: 377, original emphases) – for Levinas, the jointed times of encountering the other articulates this primary couple with all the other others:

> [T]he contemporaneousness of the multiple is tied about the *diachrony* of two: justice remains justice only, in a society where there is no distinction between those close and those far off, but in which there also remains the impossibility of passing

by the closest. [...] The other as other, as a neighbour, is in his presence never equal to his proximity. [...] Between the one I am and the other for whom I am responsible there gapes open a difference, without a basis in community. [...] Proximity is a difference, a non-coinciding, an *arrhythmia in time*.

(Levinas 1998: 159 and 166, emphases added)

In this sense of proximity and temporal dissociation, *Dream→work* steps over the middle ground (space) *where* we all necessarily live with our commonsense and our ideologies: it jumps over the gerund (time) of living *whilst* still remaining in the midst, in the middle of things, as the work happens on the streets. It oscillates between *immediates* (that which happens there and then before the participants) and *profounds* (that which is at the deepest reach or furthest throw of the mind and so cannot be there and then). In this sense, *Dream→work* invites its auditor–walkers to enter into a communion in the midst of the (technological) corporate, each in their own way, to see the corporate as if from the outside of the everyday problems of agency and attachment for what each thinks it is, and yet from the point of view of the communion of the performance's contingent, temporary host. Thus in Singapore the background synchronization of financing and trading is interpellated by each walkers' heightened sensory awareness of their own nows of being there then in the streets of that particular Central Business District. This is provoked by opening up sonically the various gaps in each one's embodied mode of walking those very streets through feeding back live sound-grabs, re-presenting the present aural environment. The other of time is set forth diachronically through texts which open up the possibilities of other times (with their places), of children and death, provoking memories and hopes through jointly listening to and having to consider these possibles in the face-to-face with the performer – *the* other as distinct from everyday capital's *an* other, any other, quasi-other.

Paradoxically, in order to clear a space for these possible times to be produced – the instances of immediates and the reveries of profounds, *Dream→work* steps over its own locality. Since we necessarily must be in the midst of things somewhere, to dwell *in the temporality of* the cultural specific with its ideological constraints would simply be to re-produce them in a reductive Marxist sense. In stepping over the middle-ground, we still leave the auditor–walkers as the carriers of that middle, in fact the actual

Figure 8.3 Bodies in Flight, *Dream→work*, Singapore (2009).
Courtesy of spell#7 performance. Photographer: Yuen Chee Wai.

possibles of that middle. They work the middle, which we step over; they respond from that middle to our producing of the immediates and profounds. And this answering the call of what is there and could be there, from within the there, places them both within the middle of things and outside it. They become aware of their together aloneness: they are the necessary middle; or rather, the necessary being in the middle of things, amongst the host amidst things. The rhythms of the work force them to step aside in two opposing directions simultaneously: towards the immediate, what is passed over and no longer noticed; and towards the profound, what cannot normally be borne in the rush of the everyday and so is passed under, since there is not *normally* time to disclose it and open it out.

So, as the work is peopled by a host of such ideological enactments, it is relieved of doing that work itself. Furthermore, *Dream→work*'s refusal to dwell in that middle, the absence of the specifics of that cultural, ideological matrix calls forth the presence of the auditor–walkers' own ideologies: space *without* ideology *admits* the possibilities not of a 'non-ideological' place, but of a reconfiguring and reconstituting of space-time *with* the ideological.

And that reconfiguring is *properly* the future work of the auditor-walkers themselves *after* our work in the work is done, since they must live in that space once we are gone.

> The act of consciousness is motivated by the presence of a third party alongside of the neighbour approached. A third party is also approached; and the relationship between the neighbour and the third party cannot be indifferent to me when I approach. There must be a justice among incomparable ones. There must be a comparison amongst incomparables and a synopsis, a togetherness and contemporaneousness; there must be thematization, thought, history and inscription.
>
> (Levinas 1998: 16)

Thus the clearing of *Dream→work* must be predicated, in our case – literally grounded, on its relation to the everyday, whence it emerges and *through which* every participant must have passed in order to reach this clearing and be involved in the work. For the work to be first recognized as a work, in order for its preserving to become possible, it must be different from that everyday: it must produce its very relation to the everyday *as its work*. This echoes what for Heidegger is the very definition of Being – that for Being its own being is an issue for it: art's relation with the everyday is hence *posed as a problem for the work* and its participants and their own relatings to the world whence they have jointly emerged in the preserving of the work. To see the world thence askance is to see it as if for the first time, and so to see what it is possible to do with that world. And not incidentally, that seeing of the Heideggerian 'earth' must be by way of the Levinasian 'element' and from the point of view of Merleau-Ponty's 'flesh,' that which is normally occluded and hidden by everyday technology and ideology and habitude, having the *occasion* to disclose itself fully. In this way, even those very lived technologies, ideologies and corporeal habits of movement and thought are turned against themselves to *ex-pose* what they normally *en-close*: to set the earth, the element, the flesh forth before the preserving participants. Thence performance cannot be interactive: its participatory aesthetics must be by way of and about presence: to be in the co-presence of is to appear before the other, performer–auditor–spectator, a face-to-face, as Levinas described it, of absolute alterity. Performance poses, as in positions or places, the problem of the other, which is as much as to say the problem of oneself, of becoming a person: poses this problem of the other before each other: two others mutually recognizing the other othering.

> The idea of Infinity is transcendence itself, the overflowing of an adequate idea. If totality cannot be constituted it is because Infinity does not permit itself to be integrated. It is not the insufficiency of the I that prevents totalization, but the Infinity of the Other.
>
> (Levinas 1969: 80)

Works cited

Bayly, S. (2008) 'Figuring the Face', *Performance Research*, 13:4, 25–37.

Bishop, C. (2004) 'Antagonism and Relational Aesthetics', *October*, 110, 51–79.

Blau, H. (1990) *The Audience*, Baltimore, MD: John Hopkins University Press.

Bourriaud, N. (2002 [1998]) *Relational Aesthetics*, translated by S. Pleasance and F. Woods, Dijon: Les Presses du Réel.

Debord, G. (1992) *The Society of Spectacle*, London: Rebel Press.

Derrida, J. (1978 [1967]) *Writing and Difference*, translated by A. Bass, London: Routledge and Kegan Paul.

Giddens, S. and Jones, S. (2009) 'De-second Naturing: Word Unbecoming Flesh in the Work of Bodies in Flight', in S. Broadhurst and J. Machon (eds) *Sensualities/ Textualities and Technologies: Writings of the Body in 21st Century Performance*, Basingstoke: Palgrave Macmillan, 38–50.

Heidegger, M. (1962 [1927]) *Being and Time*, translated by J. Macquarrie and E. Robinson, London: Camelot Press.

——(1978) 'The Origin of the Work of Art' in M. Heidegger *Basic Writings*, edited by D. F. Krell, London: Routledge, 143–89.

——(1981) *Nietzsche – Volume 1: 'The Will to Power as Art'*, translated by D. F. Krell, London: Routledge and Kegan Paul.

Jones, S. (2007) *Imag[in]ing the Void*. Online. Available at: http://presence.standford.edu:3455/Collaboratory/1173 (accessed 27 July 2011).

——(2008) 'Places Inbetween: I do not have to be there with you tonight, A Case Study of Bodies In Flight's Performance *skinworks*', in D. Cecchetto, N. Cuthbert, J. Lassonde and D. Robinson (eds) *Collision: Interarts Practice and Research*, Cambridge: Cambridge Scholars Press, 245–60.

——(2009) 'The Courage of Complementarity', in L. Allegue, S. Jones, B. Kershaw and A. Piccini (eds) *Practice as Research in Performance and Screen*, Basingstoke: Palgrave MacMillan, 19–32.

——(2009a) 'Working on the Middle Ground: a Case study of Institutional Inter-action about Practice-as-Research', in L. Hunter and S. R. Riley (eds) *Mapping Landscapes for Peformance: Scholarly Acts and Creative Cartographies*, Basingstoke: Palgrave MacMillan, 14–25.

Levinas, E. (1969 [1961]) *Totality and Infinity – an essay on exteriority*, translated by A. Lingis, Pittsburgh: Duquesne University Press.

——(1998 [1974]) *Otherwise than Being*, translated by A. Lingis, Pittsburgh: Duquesne University Press.

——(2006 [1972]) *Humanism of the Other*, translated by N. Poller, Urbana: University of Illinois Press.

Machon, J. (2009) *(Syn)aesthetics? Towards a Definition of Visceral Performance*, Basingstoke: Palgrave Macmillan.

Mulhall, S. (1996) *Heidegger and Being and Time*, London: Routledge.

Virilio, P. (1986 [1977]) *Speed and Politics*, translated by M. Polizzotti, New York: Semiotext(e).

Wilshire, B. (1982) *Role Playing and Identity: the limits of theatre as metaphor*, Bloomington: University of Indiana Press.

Chapter 9

Mis-spectatorship, or, 'redistributing the sensible'

Nicholas Ridout

'Who's there?' Herbert Blau has already established this opening question, uttered by Barnardo as the first words of *Hamlet*, as perhaps the key question for any study of the theatrical audience. As Blau himself observes, the study of the audience is beset with difficulties regarding the presence of its object. The problem often seems to be that there's no one there. Or that no one who attempts to respond to Barnardo ever turns out to have the right credentials, whether they offer themselves as sociological data or personal confession. These difficulties are particularly acute in the context of the widely held conviction, especially among those of us who practice 'spectator studies' (of which more in a moment), that it is the audience or spectator who produces meaning in and around the theatrical event. Blau writes:

> We can speak as we wish of the audience's producing meaning, as if that were somehow a solution to the complexities of power, but we are still left with the problem of evaluating the meaning which is produced and equilibrating it with the balance of power. While this is difficult enough with the individual spectator (or reader), what are we really to make of the continuing sentiments about collectivity that are, more than with other forms, still encouraged by the folk-lore and institutions of theatre?
>
> (Blau 1990: 280)

So this essay, which seeks to 'make' something – an argument, perhaps – out of the presence of the spectator, must confess from the very start that it has no answer to Barnardo's question, while attempting at least to 'make' something of the 'sentiments' by means of which we sustain our belief in the audience's capacity to 'make' meaning.

More recently, in the context of an ongoing investigation of the potential for the production of knowledge by attending to the work of expert-practitioners, Susan Melrose has suggested that much of what passes itself off today as performance studies might better be understood as 'spectator studies' (Melrose 2006: 120–2). In particular, Melrose is persuaded that the two activities – expert performance-making and expert spectatorship – are incommensurable. This only becomes a problem when one expert – the expert spectator – claims to produce knowledge that might stand for or above the knowledge produced by the other – the maker of performance. In this essay I want to make sure that spectator studies comes out of the closet in which Melrose suggests it usually takes refuge. I also want to trouble the notion of expertise that seems to underpin the knowledge produced by means of spectator studies. For a measure of inexpertise may be crucial to an interruption of the consensus around value to which experts, both performance makers and spectators, routinely contribute, a consensus in which we agree only to see and hear what we already know.

One name for that consensus (which is as political as it is aesthetic) is what Jacques Rancière calls 'the distribution of the sensible'. For Rancière 'the distribution of the sensible' refers to the entire system of social and cultural processes, codes, values and material realities through which we jointly understand the world, and according to which we make our judgements about what and who belongs where, who has the right to speak and be heard, who counts when it matters, and who gets to be recognized as an expert. Rancière's aesthetics thus involves a call for that consensus to be interrupted by politics:

> Politics occurs when those who 'have no' time take the time necessary to front up as inhabitants of a common space and demonstrate that their mouths really do emit speech capable of making pronouncements on the common which cannot be reduced to voices signalling pain. This distribution and redistribution of places and identities, this apportioning of spaces and times, of the visible and the invisible, and of noise and speech constitutes what I call the distribution of the sensible. Politics consists in reconfiguring the distribution of

the sensible which defines the common of a community, to
introduce into it new subjects and objects, to render visible
what had not been, and to make heard as speakers those who
had been perceived as mere noisy animals.

(Rancière 2009: 24–5)

It will therefore be the figure of the mis-spectator around whom
this attempt at reconfiguration will be organized. This inexpert
figure closely resembles Rancière's 'emancipated spectator,' who,
in his essay of that title (see Rancière 2009a), emerges as the
producer of meaning upon whom the theatre does not need to
exercise its powers of educational reform. Rancière departs in this
respect from the thinking of Bertolt Brecht, for whom the
production of the 'expert spectator' was a crucial element in the
reform of the theatre in the interests of politics (see, for example,
Brecht's notes on how to make 'a theatre full of experts' in Brecht
1964: 44). For Rancière, Brecht's error lies in the assumption that
the spectator begins as in-expert and un-emancipated, in need of
prosthetic support (see Rancière 2009a). I should therefore be
clear, right now, that as far as I am concerned, there is nothing
whatsoever wrong with the mis-spectator.

The mis-spectator is in his seat. At least he is where he is
supposed to be. Present and correct. He has accustomed himself to
the fact that there is only one stage for everyone, and he is happy
to find that the presence of other spectators does not impede his
view. This is 'because, thanks to an arrangement which is, as it
were, symbolical of all spectatorship, everyone feels himself to be
the centre of the theatre' (Proust 1989: 482). Centre stage, then, 'as
it were,' the mis-spectator now understands why Françoise had
said, on her return from a melodrama which she had watched from
the highest gallery, that she had had the best seat in the house.
Does the mis-spectator not mis-spectate spectatorship here? This
'arrangement' of which he speaks, or rather, writes, is normally
understood to be 'symbolical' of a certain social and spectatorial
hierarchy, in which, so the story goes, the best seat in the house is
assigned to the King, and in which servants such as Françoise make
do with the side-effects of an auditorium organized around the
gaze of their sovereign. This theatre, though, makes a King of
Françoise, or so the mis-spectator would give us to believe.

So the mis-spectator is in his seat, feeling, perhaps, a little like a
King himself. And he is experiencing pleasure, still. At least that is

what the author would give us to believe. For let us recall, here and now, that the mis-spectator is a boy named Marcel, and that his author is the novelist Marcel Proust, and that it is Proust, or perhaps even a narrator function designed by the same Proust, who holds Marcel's mis-spectatorship up for our attention. At this point in the novel – the beginning of volume three of twelve – we do not, strictly speaking, even know that the boy's name is Marcel, although we may have assumed as much from the autobiographical nature of the text, Proust's twelve-volume novel *A la recherche du temps perdu*.

So, the mis-spectator is enjoying himself, we give ourselves to understand. There he is, in his seat, the right seat, the best seat, the only seat he has. The curtain rises on a writing table and a fireplace, and still, his pleasure 'endures' (Proust 1989: 482). He has time to reflect that these ordinary objects mean that the actors who are about to present themselves will not be like actors come 'to recite,' but that they will, instead, be 'real people' upon whom he will be able to 'spy,' without being seen. His presence will not interfere with their presence to him. Strange that the very objects that might recall the homes and drawing rooms in which he had previously witnessed actors reciting at evening parties should here convince him that this time he will see 'real people, just living their lives at home.' The representation of a home by means of a writing table and a fireplace seems to present to the mis-spectator a far more convincing representation of home than home itself.

His pleasure, remember, still 'endures'. But now it is broken by 'a momentary uneasiness'. Two angry men appear on stage, arguing with one another. To the astonishment of the mis-spectator the thousand-strong audience looks on and listens in silence at this intrusion. Amid his astonishment the mis-spectator now realizes, as waves of laughter start to erupt among the other spectators, that this is a 'curtain raiser'. But for a moment – a moment of uneasiness – the mis-spectator had seen two 'insolent fellows' invade the stage and appropriate the space and the attention of the public. For this moment of uneasiness, some people had made themselves present where they shouldn't. The charge of insolence levelled against them by the momentarily uneasy mis-spectator suggests that this misappearance might be a matter of class. Not quite the reversal of places implied by Françoise's assumption of the place of the King, of course, but, by the looks of things, the way Marcel Proust seems to want us to see Marcel seeing things, that is, a little seizure of power, a fit of insubordination, a behaviour of those who do not know how to behave.

The mis-spectator's unease is about to turn to terror. The curtain-raiser is followed by an interval. The audience, back in their seats, start to become impatient for the resumption of the action. The action in question is what the mis-spectator has come for. This is his first time in the theatre, and he has come specifically to see the great tragedienne of the age, Berma, in the role of Phèdre in Racine's play. The build-up has been somewhat excruciating. The mis-spectator is not the healthiest of boys and his mother has been very anxious about the consequences of his becoming over-excited. The doctor had advised his parents not to allow him to go to the theatre, for fear that he might be ill afterwards, perhaps for weeks. When finally his mother relents – 'we don't want to make you unhappy,' she says – the situation is still not resolved, since the mis-spectator now fears for the distress that the risk to his health will induce in his parents: 'I would rather not go, if it distresses you,' he says. The mis-spectator now experiences the prospect of the performance merely as the event which will bring to an end the suffering of his hesitation. He fears that his pleasure will be marred by the weight of obligation – the obligation to experience pleasure – that the risk, to his own health and to his parents' happiness, will entail.

The impatient audience is stamping its feet. The mis-spectator is terrified. This is yet more 'bad behaviour'. The other spectators are clearly 'ill-bred'. What a hideous scenario. He has come to the theatre, to worship for the first time at the throne of the goddess of beauty, to receive intellectual benediction at the Holy of Holies. And the riff-raff are threatening to spoil everything. Do they not know how to spectate? The 'stamping brutes' with their 'insensate rage' are going to upset the star of the show, who will respond, in her vexation at their behaviour and her disdain for their evident unsuitability even to be here, by acting badly. The mis-spectator alone knows how to conduct himself, in the presence of the star presence, and now, because there is only one stage for everyone, he is going to be punished for the misdemeanours of the rest. He will be deprived of the 'rare and fragile impression' he has come here to seek. Despite, or rather, precisely because of the arrangement that ensures that he has the best seat in the house, his pleasure is going to be stolen from him by the nine hundred and ninety nine occupants of all the other best seats in the house. There is something fundamentally wrong with the whole set-up, in which 'solar myth' and 'delphic symbol' are made to appear before 'stamping brutes'. If only the mis-spectator had stayed at home, after all, nursing his fevered fantasies of a one-to-one encounter with the 'Mycenean drama,' everything would have been all right. But he had to come here, the idiot, and have everything spoiled for him by the theatre. The theatre, he realizes, is other people. And other people just don't know how to behave.

The opening scenes of the play afford him his last moments of pleasure, although they also bring further confusion. There seems to have been a cast change. He knows that Phaedra herself does not appear in these scenes, and yet, the first actress to emerge onto the stage has 'the face and voice, which, I had been told, were those of Berma.' Soon he realizes that he is mistaken. This is not Berma, because a second actress, responding to the opening speech of the first, 'resembled her even more closely.' What is going on here? First, how has he been told, and by whom, what Berma's face and voice are like? The mis-spectator has been relying on hearsay, and even though it contradicts his knowledge of the play itself, it persuades him that Berma has switched roles, and is playing, not the princess, but one of her servants. Even as he realizes that he is mistaken, he mis-takes again. Yes, this is really her, this second actress. Or, at least, she resembles her (more closely). There's a slippage here, from the first actress, who, or so he has been told, somehow, has the face and voice of Berma, to the second, who, he observes, resembles her more closely than the one who has her face and voice. To have Berma's face and voice is thus not to be Berma, but rather to resemble her less closely than another actress. And to whom does this second actress bear a closer resemblance than the first, who, after all, has the very face and voice of Berma? The first actress possesses the actual attributes of the great tragedienne, while the second merely resembles her more closely. Resembles the first actress more closely than the first actress resembles herself, then? This is hopeless. Actresses appear to be indistinguishable from one another, at least in the theatre. They seem to lack all presence, or, to think of it another way, both are equally present, but neither can be distinguished by her presence alone, as he had anticipated Berma could.

Yet he is still experiencing his last moments of pleasure: these actresses, whoever they are, offer noble gestures and skilful changes of tone. He understands the significance of lines from the play to which he had not, in his solitary reading at home, paid sufficient attention. For a few minutes everything seems to be going all right. Then, 'in the cleft of the red curtain' a third woman appears and the mis-spectator recognizes his mistake: 'the two actresses whom I had been admiring for some minutes bore not the least resemblance to her whom I had come to hear' (Proust 1989: 484). For it is this third woman who is Berma herself. The mis-spectator had established resemblance where there was none. He had confused two ordinary professionals with the transcendent celebrity. And he had allowed himself to take pleasure in the labour of these professionals, to find meaning where his own reading had found none, to admire that which was not, in fact, that which he had come here to admire. Just as in the earlier confusions between Françoise and the King, between the insolent fellows and the actors of the curtain-raiser, and in the struggle over spectatorial behaviour between the stamping brutes and Marcel the mis-spectator, there has been a redistribution of roles or a change of cast (just as the mis-spectator had momentarily suspected). And in each change of cast there has been a confusion of class: between servant and sovereign in the cases both of Françoise and the King, and Phaedra and Oenone, and between those who know how to behave and those who do not (the subtle and vicious demarcations of a self-stratifying bourgeoisie), between spectators and mis-spectators. In this last case, of course, it is the mis-spectator who knows how to behave, and the spectators who are misbehaving, or, to be more precise, who are mis-spectating.

So now the star is on stage, and pleasure is at an end. In vain does the mis-spectator strain every sense to glean from her performance any reason to admire her. It's all happening too fast, it seems. 'Scarcely had a sound been received by my ear than it was displaced by another.' (Proust 1989: 484) She is barely present, she cannot arrest time. He is observing intently, preparing in his mind each line from the text he has read and memorised so avidly at home. There is a discrepancy between the time of reading and the time of performance, for which the mis-spectator is utterly unprepared. He is unable to identify what Berma is bringing to the role. He hears her speech as though he were reading, or as though Phaedra herself were speaking. There is no Berma here: no talent, no intelligence, no beautiful gestures: she is not, after all, a presence. He tells his grandmother, who has accompanied him to the theatre, that he can't see very well. She lends him her opera glasses. Through the glasses he sees not Berma, but her image. He puts the glasses aside, and now feels that the figure on the distant stage is no more the real and present Berma than the magnified image in the glasses had been. First the star appears three times – in the two actresses who preceded her onto the stage and in her own person – and now she is doubled out of existence somewhere between the distant figure on the stage and the magnified image in the glasses. This event – the encounter between transcendent theatrical genius and aspirant young aesthete – is simply not taking place. All around him the event appears to be in full swing. A moment of stillness in which Berma raises her arm in a glow of greenish light brings rapturous applause from the 'whole house'. They seem to know how to see and hear Berma: it is only the mis-spectator who labours in agonies of disappointment. Phaedra's declaration of her illicit love for Hyppolitus fails to deliver the imagined effect. Berma delivers the speech in a 'uniform chant,' no more likely to gain its effect than the efforts of 'the least intelligent of actresses' (Proust 1989: 485) or students at an academy. In the eyes and ears of the mis-spectator, once again, all the workers of the stage have become equal and an appalling age of cultural indistinction has dawned.

In this new age of cultural indistinction it will become very difficult, if not impossible, to detect certain forms of irony. Consider this passage, which precedes the scenes of mis-spectatorship which I have just discussed, and which describes the labour of the family cook, Françoise, as she prepares for the evening that is to follow the disappointing matinée. The mis-spectator's father is bringing M. de Norpois home for dinner. It is M. de Norpois who has been encouraging the mis-spectator in his aesthetic ambitions. A suitably artistic effort is required:

> Françoise, rejoicing in the opportunity to devote herself to the art of cooking in which she was so gifted, stimulated, moreover, by the prospect of a new guest, and knowing that she would have to compose, by methods known to her alone, a dish of *boeuf à la gelée*, had been living in the effervescence of creation; since she attached the utmost importance to the intrinsic qualities of the materials which were to enter into the fabric of her work, she had gone herself to the Halles to procure the best cuts of rump-steak, shin of beef, calves'-feet, just as

Michelangelo spent eight months in the mountains of Carrara choosing the most perfect blocks of marble for the monument of Julius II.

(Proust 1989: 480)

At first sight it seems that someone is taking the piss. To describe Françoise's culinary efforts in the language of aesthetic judgement (just as one might, for example, describe the work of the great actress) would appear to be a form of mockery, directed from a position of social and cultural privilege towards the servant classes. Françoise is no Michelangelo, however sumptuous her *boeuf à la gelée*. However, there is nothing in this passage to suggest that Françoise herself conceives of her labour in such terms. She is going about her business, choosing the best ingredients for her dish: someone else is offering the comparison with Michelangelo. And since the narrator of this passage seems to show nothing but genuine admiration for the quality of Françoise's cooking, are we then to assume that the conventional terms of this usually ironic comparison, are to be reversed? Or at least that the labour of the cook and the artist are to be considered as being of equal value?

Shortly after this passage, there is a brief account of how Françoise has come to mis-speak York ham:

Believing the language to be less rich in words than it is, and her own ears untrustworthy, the first time she heard someone mention York ham she had thought, no doubt – feeling it to be hardly conceivable that the dictionary should be so prodigal as to include at once a 'York' and a 'New York'– that she had misheard, and that the ham was really called by the name already familiar to her. And so, ever since, the word York was preceded in her ears, or before her eyes when she read it in an advertisement, by the affix 'New' which she pronounced 'Nev'.

(Proust 1989: 480–81)

This looks, again, like a standard trope of class condescension towards those less adept in the languages of the world, and particularly those aspects of those languages that serve as marks of class privilege by way of cosmopolitan sophistication. It might give us pause, then, to reconsider the preliminary conclusion we had drawn about the equal value ascribed to cooks and to artists. However, as we read on, and enter the theatre of mis-spectatorship in which Marcel is unable to tell one actress from another, even when one of them is the transcendent genius that is Berma, not to mention his inability to distinguish actors from non-actors, and his confusion over who is real and who just has someone else's face and voice, we might conclude that Françoise's seeing and hearing of the word New (or Nev) before each appearance of the name York, is an act of mis-spectatorship equivalent to that performed in the theatre by Marcel, and that whatever irony might be attempted in the comparison between her cooking and the sculpture of Michelangelo is to be mis-read as a sincere statement of comparative value. Mis-spectatorship, then, is a revelation of equality.

Françoise is the equal of Michelangelo; any actress the equal of any other. It is only by means of the consensus of expert spectatorship and in the perceptions of those who are habituated to the theatre that such equality gives way to distinctions of class and taste. As the account of the applause with which Berma's performance is greeted suggests, its quality or value is entirely a matter of opinion, a question of who buys it and who doesn't. Effective regimes of value tend to reinforce themselves reflexively, in the absence of any external yardstick by which something as imponderable as good acting might be measured. The imaginary yardstick by which the audience here measures Berma is nothing other than Berma herself, conceived as the yardstick against which all acting must be measured. The mis-spectator, then, fails to recognise a yardstick when he sees one, revealing the pure performativity of theatrical value: good acting is good acting, and it is by conforming oneself to this process that the spectator becomes habituated to expertise, and gradually ceases to be the mis-spectator. The habitué or expert spectator, of course, is the narrator of Marcel's spectatorial encounters, who, in revealing the foundations upon which his own distinctions (of class and taste) are constructed, inadvertently exposes to the spectatorial eyes of the reader of his text, an alternative way of accounting for what gets made visible here.

Of course this effect depends upon the fact that the mis-spectator in question here is a kind of invention. He might be quite unable to respond to Barnardo with even the barest call of 'Present!' Whatever the extent to which this episode may recall an episode from the actual life of its author, the central figure of the narration has been written in order to generate a specific, and ironic perspective. He has been sent out, into an imaginary theatre, in order precisely to perform those acts of mis-spectatorship that will permit the reader of the text to see what is at stake in theatrical spectatorship itself. As a presence in the text, then, the mis-spectator interrupts the machinery of the theatre, by making present to himself, and thus, to the reader (but perhaps not to the narrator, who retains his condescension), some of those things that the machinery of theatre normally works to obscure, or rather which the machinery, in collaboration with 'expert spectatorship' colludes in rendering absent. What the mis-spectator performs, then, is the re-presentation of that which had been rendered absent, the assignment of parts to those who have no part (or smaller parts than the main part), the counting of those who do not count alongside the Bermas and the Michelangelos who always do. If the mis-spectator makes any meaning it is by disrupting the consensus which masquerades as collectivity in the folklore of the institution of the theatre.

Works cited

Blau, H. (1990) *The Audience*, Baltimore MD: Johns Hopkins University Press.

Brecht, B. (1964) *Brecht on Theatre: The Development of an Aesthetic*, edited and translated by John Willett, New York: Hill and Wang.

Melrose, S. (2006) 'Constitutive Ambiguities: Writing Professional or Expert Performance Practices and the Théâtre du Soleil, Paris', in J. Kelleher and N. Ridout (eds) *Contemporary Theatres in Europe: A Critical Companion*, London: Routledge, 120–35.

Proust, M. (1989) *Remembrance of Things Past, Volume One*, translated by C. K. Scott Moncrieff and T. Kilmartin, Harmondsworth: Penguin Books.

Rancière, J. (2009) *Aesthetics and Its Discontents*, translated by S. Corcoran, Cambridge: Polity Press.

——(2009a), *The Emancipated Spectator*, translated by G. Elliott, London: Verso Books.

Chapter 10

Looking back

A conversation about presence, 2006

Tim Etchells, Gabriella Giannachi and Nick Kaye

Figure 10.1 Forced Entertainment, *Bloody Mess* (2004).
Photo: Hugo Glendinning.

GABRIELLA GIANNACHI: *Do you approach the presence of the performer and the 'character' or 'role' in a specific way or with a particular attitude?*

TIM ETCHELLS: In Forced Entertainment's process, we tend to think about a kind of base line – about the performers being present, in a certain way, more or less as themselves – or as kind of slightly exaggerated or extended versions of themselves. And from there, there is a kind of process of stepping into either task, or character, or role, or into some kind of enactment. I think that often in the pieces you will see both. Certainly, the performers are present, let's say, 'as themselves,' doing the job – and then, in a layer above that, you will see them enacting or stepping up into something that's slightly more artificial or staged, if you like, or that maybe is not exaggerated. A nice way to think about this, for me, is a quotation from Elizabeth LeCompte, the Wooster Group director. She says at one point – I read somewhere – that their *Three Sisters* piece, *Brace Up!* (1993), is two stories: it's the story of the *Three Sisters* and it's the story of the actors making their way through the *Three Sisters*. You see these two stories in parallel – and although we don't work with dramatic texts such as Chekhov, we do – in a way – often think about the pieces in this 'parallel track' kind of a way.

NICK KAYE: *You seem to be implicitly talking about a kind of doubleness in performance. Do you think this doubleness is specifically linked to presence?*

TE: I think, for me, watching performance, I am aware of people on a number of levels, like I'm seeing past one layer of what they are doing to another layer and then maybe to another. Perhaps there's something important about this experience that we have, of seeing layers of information, the feeling that we are seeing through, from one layer to another to another. As watchers, we aggregate all of that information and we make a kind of map that allows us to say: there's somebody there. None of those layers is quite enough on its own – presence has to do with the combination. I suppose another way to think about that would be to say: I don't know if there is such a thing as simply 'being there,' just being present. Being present is always a kind of construction. Perhaps we could think of presence as something that happens when one attempts to do something, and whilst attempting to do that thing you become visible; visible in 'not quite succeeding' in doing it, visible through the cracks or the gaps.

As human beings we are always present or perceived through something – through a particular aperture or through a particular grid or through a particular frame. I'm talking about social structures, frames of behaviour, social space and expectation. In fact, it's these layers or frames or constrictions that make you visible – that make you there. Some people might harbour the fantasy that there is an easy or absolute 'here I am'. But I don't know if this can exist in society. Perhaps it can exist for some group of guru-like beings who exist in some abstract place, but in the real world we are already all performing too much. There are already too many frames, codes, limits and needs that we are performing in relation to and appearing through.

GG: *In* Certain Fragments *(Etchells 1999) you write that 'presence now is always complicated and layered, a thing of degrees, and in these strange times one can feel closer to a person, sometimes, when they are further away than when they are fully and simply before us' (Etchells 1999: 97). I was interested in the relationship between this statement and the idea of framing and shielding.*

TE: For me, presence is perhaps related to something that, on the one hand, as subjects, we deploy in the form of certain signs in order to appear, but actually presence is so much about reception too. It's about reading. And reading is a complicated act. One of the things we do as readers of signs and situations – and as readers of all things – is respond to absences – and we tend to fill absence. So, you know, the way the telephone makes us imagine the whole person, or the way that in texting or instant messaging, in writing to someone, you sort of spend time with other people but you are not in the same room as them. Because the 'presence' of these other people is purely in language, there is a huge job for you in mentally unpacking what's written or, in the phone conversation, unpacking what's being said – to "create" or summon people. Of course, it's good to spend time with actual people in actual places, but there is this extraordinary thing that when there's distance involved, when your presence to other people is mediated via the phone or via text or other means – because these things involve an investment on the part of the reader or participant – you can, in a strange way, be extraordinarily close and connected as well, despite or even because of, the distance. Fundamentally this is again about frames, which are apparently quite restrictive, but which can be extraordinarily productive in terms of letting people appear. The constriction can become a kind of gift inside which people operate as agents, but also can be read with an extraordinary level of profundity. Something like this might be true of a workshop exercise where the performers are asked to behave inside extremely restrictive sets of behavioural instructions: to sit or to stand behind a table and so on. Here, in spite of – or let's say because of the kind of cruelty of these impositions – they manage to be present in an extraordinarily vivid way. So I think restriction, absence, distance, blankness – all these things which, in a way, have a negative connotation if we want to talk about presence – can actually all be extraordinarily positive. The fantasy of pure or unmediated presence can be quite disturbing in fact – I can only think of it as a horrible gushing forth! – because we can only ever construct ourselves through all kinds of filters, frames, barriers and social frameworks.

NK: *In discussing presence in performance you tend to emphasize interruption, failure and blankness, almost as if presence is best brought into play by staging its antithesis.*

TE: This may be my taste, but I think it's generally true that as watchers we enjoy reaching through something to find something. We don't necessarily enjoy the train driving right at us. We like to find things and, in a way, interruption and the failure – and blankness – are all ways of inserting some noise, some disturbance or some 'anti' signal between you and what's being said. Again, these glitches are the things that make it possible for us to see what's happening and to invest in it. Spaces are very productive – they demand to be filled. An example that I have used is a particular performance I made with Forced Entertainment where one of the performers had an extraordinary long text, which was quite hard to take in. I realized at a certain point that when two of the performers were messing around in the space, causing a lot of disturbance during this text, I found myself, as a watcher, suddenly pulled to this text in an extraordinary way, because – I think – somebody was making it very difficult for me to get to it. There's nothing purposely perverse about that – I think we are always looking for these slightly circuitous routes. Socially, and as audiences, there's a pleasure in that.

Figure 10.2 Forced Entertainment, *Exquisite Pain* (2005).
Photo: Hugo Glendinning.

GG: *In relation to this, in* Certain Fragments *you also write that 'the theatre must take account of how technology [...] has rewritten and is rewriting bodies, changing our understanding of narratives and places, changing our relationships to culture, changing our understandings of presence' (Etchells 1999: 97). Could you expand on that? In what ways does technology change our understandings of these things?*

TE: We are in an era where there's a fairly large degree of technological change – to do with networking, especially, and communications – and I don't think we can understand, really, what that's doing to us as people or as a culture. It's quite hard to get your head round it when you are in the middle of it, but in a way, you do sense that these things, these changes are making a profound difference. A superficial response to this situation as performance-makers might be to think about reflecting those technological changes directly on the stage – basically by answering the question: how can we put this kind of technology on the stage in different ways? How does this technology change the form of performance? To me, that is less interesting than the question, how do these technological changes affect us as human beings, in a deeper way, in the way that we think of – and feel – ourselves in the world? There are so many examples of this. My kids have no expectation when a photograph is taken that they should wait longer than two seconds to see it because they just want to look at the back of the camera. That's not how I grew up with images. We now expect to have the images immediately, as part of what's happening, and to be able to watch again. We have it even in performances. During school parties, or concerts, or whatever, people will be videoing while someone is performing and they're passing phones along to each other, sending the little clips to their friends, all while they are watching. It's not that we particularly encourage this in Forced Entertainment! but I am interested in the ways that this simultaneous watching and recording changes how we think of ourselves and how we think of our relationship to our own images. That is what interests me – those kinds of changes in the construction of the social sense of individuals. That's what's exciting to me. I don't care so much about how artists might put the technology on the stage – I'm more interested in how we get a fix on how these shifts affect what we are as human beings.

NK: *You have also talked about your interest in the 'texture' of authenticity, which seems in a way paradoxical, especially with regard to performer presence. I wondered how that related to these affects of technology?*

TE: To give slightly separate answers – in one sense, when you work in performance – as we have done for over twenty years – you start to notice that there are certain ways of being on stage or in public that maybe "guarantee" that you will be listened to. Things that ensure or suggest that what you are doing is felt as 'real' or as 'really happening'. There are also certain things you can do in a performance (unwittingly perhaps) which mean that what you say is not listened to – that it somehow doesn't quite seem to happen. All of these things aren't in your control, but you do get some sense of control perhaps. In different projects you learn certain strategies or tricks or textures of how the 'authentic' might be read or how it is constructed – and of course you get interested in being able to reproduce those things, or else to make a point of not being able to reproduce them.

It's particularly easy to talk about this in relation to language. In the beginning of the company's work – and this maps into the thing about technology – we worked with texts that were evidently written. There was an interest in writing with a capital 'W' – an interest in poetry, if you like. Increasingly we have come to work with improvised text and speech, so there's been a shift in the work from an interest in writing to an interest in spoken language. One of the things you notice as soon as you start working with a video camera on a daily basis – as we did may be 10, 12 years ago – is that when you transcribe actual speech it's quite extraordinary. I mean, the patterns of looping, self-qualification, unfinished sentences, ideas that flow off in particular directions. Often, now, we are effectively transcribing text off videotapes of rehearsals and using that as the basis for scripts. What I like about this process is that a performer will improvise a particular part of a show and, the first time they do it, it will have a really rich texture of dense qualification, using language in the most amazing, fluid ways. The second time they improvise it, it tends to be this intense over-simplification of what they did before. But when you go to the transcripts of the first one and you look at it as text, you can end up with stuff that sounds like you are really saying it now, for the first time – which is really interesting – if you are able as performers to reproduce that of course! We have become hugely interested in working from transcription – and that's only possible because of the ubiquity of technology. And maybe that gives you an understanding of a certain linguistic texture of authenticity.

GG: *What implications do words such as 'presence,' 'being there,' 'aura,' 'awareness,' 'or self-awareness' have for you in this process?*

TE: The thing we talk about the most, really, when we are working, is the idea of 'being there'. At one level I think we seek this probably impossible thing – a very simple, human-scale presence beneath the theatrical – a way of simply being in a space and with some people. The other thing that is relevant is an understanding of theatre, of performance – we often invoke that as performers we are people at one end of a room who are paid to do something for a bunch of other people in the same room. It's a deliberately rather levelling description of the form! But I think we want to stress this idea of 'some people in a room,' and just to feel – as it's very hard to articulate – to feel the absolute banality of that. That's something that we have focused on and, I think, you sense it in the group's work – that the performers tend to show or deploy a very relaxed, very human scale or version of themselves on stage. They don't look like they are in some other universe. There's a certain feeling of ordinariness, which I think is completely constructed – I am not under any illusions about that. I think that ordinariness, that human-scale presence, is a thing that we stage – and we work very hard on how we want it to appear. We attempt to create a kind of intimacy – an easy working day 'nowness' on the stage and with the audience.

What we have gone after in the work is to find a way that the performers look like they can just be there. I think you can get that by training and by working for twenty years, like we have done. To some people it comes more easily. I sometimes think my brother was more or less born that way. He was a postman – he works on a fish farm now – but we can put Mark in any of the pieces and he is immediately comfortable, just doing what he's doing in a very easy, measured sort of way. I think that's very interesting. I think there is an interesting thing about people who 'give time' to the thing that they are actually doing. There is a kind of democracy, a lack of judgement and hierarchy about their presence – as if to say 'whatever' they are doing, important or not, that's the thing they are doing. They are not anxiously anticipating something over there; they are not fretting about what they just did. They are just doing that thing – and that is so extraordinary to watch. I mean, in an era in which everything is fragmented and mediated, the live actor is the one who stands up and says 'I am here. You can look at me'. There's a huge simplicity to a lot of the live work that we have done – a sort of peeling away of things to the point where we are often standing in a line at the front looking back at the audience – and very much measuring this body on the stage and this bunch of people watching; measuring the distance between the two.

NK: *In the images of empty stages and empty theatres that you created with Hugo Glendinning, there seems to be a tremendous sense of potential – of suspense – as if the image captures or produces a very potent moment – or promise. Does this link in some way to what you are describing with the paring down of the performers' activity and 'being there'?*

TE: Yes. There's a very nice quote from Peter Handke. He says, basically, that the trick is to have other people – the audience – tell stories and then persuade them that you told them a story. What we have done often in the performance work is to create spaces of possibility – and these pictures of empty stages are just that – when you see an empty stage, of course, you have to imagine the performance that would take place there. You fill it. It's like you just rush in and start making meaning happen. And similarly, you know, all the very minimalist text performances that we've done with Forced Entertainment – a lot of the pieces where you have repetition or you have very blank images – are also very much about creating this kind of space. I work on the assumption that in art at least, nobody likes to be told anything. Instead we like to find things. So when art offers something blank or something that just slightly resists or frustrates my ability to 'get it clearly,' I go in there and imagine – I want to get my hands dirty. I think that's what people like to do. We have developed lots of tactics, I suppose, for creating different kinds of spaces or different kinds of experiences that invite the active participation of watchers and which give looking a kind of agency. Theatre on the whole thinks that it's a didactic medium – it thinks it's got to tell you something. We have always been much more of the kind of camp that says, what you are doing is creating space for other people to fill – and in that sense their watching is hugely active. I think when you get people investing like that, then things happen – and one of those things is presence. If you think about the greatest movie actors – my God, it's really a collection of people with faces like a brick wall, the camera goes to there and sees those eyes – Martin Sheen at his best in something like *Apocalypse Now* – there's nothing coming back. And when there's nothing coming back, the viewer does all the work – you are telling yourself stories because there's nothing actually there. I think of what Michael Haneke does in films like *Funny Games* or *Hidden (Caché)*, or other people working with very formal, slightly distant camera. That work is so amazing and it is very much about creating emotional, narrative and architectural spaces that are empty at a certain level – and because they are empty, you go in. Blankness is a huge magnet – people really, really rush into that; they fight it as well too of course, because at first they can get nervous in art or cinema or performance if they're 'not being told anything'.

Figure 10.3 Tim Etchells, Hugo Glendinning and Forced Entertainment, *Nightwalks* (1998). Photo: Hugo Glendinning.

GG: *This makes me think of Forced Entertainment's interactive CD-ROMs such as* Nightwalks *(1998). In exploring these still scenes, something has evidently happened in this space and yet it's still. And that stillness is provocative – it makes you look more frantically.*

TE: Yeah. I think the link for me is that often, when we have made theatre pieces, we've temporarily constructed a space in the rehearsal room and then there's a process for us, in a way, of figuring out what could or would or should happen there in that space we've built. And sometimes we can't figure out an answer – so we build something else – and sometimes we can figure out an answer and that becomes the performance. The process for us is, I suppose, understanding that the space, the architecture, 'is a kind of writing' – it makes things possible, it makes things happen, it suggests some things and denies others. A line of chairs at the front or a cluster of chairs at the back tells you different things about what might happen. You might be wrong in your guessing, but those are clues, architectural clues. That's always been part of how we've worked. So *Nightwalks* and *Frozen Palaces* (1997) and the model city installation *Ground Plans for Paradise* (1994), and even *Nights in this City* (1995) when we did it in Sheffield, were about seeing what happens when you create, in a sense, empty spaces, empty city streets, and empty model city streets, or photographed scenes that have figures in them, but where the figures are completely frozen, locked into a single moment in which they become a kind of scenery. What does a viewer or an audience do with that? How do you encounter that? What kinds of mental processes start to happen?

I suppose, for us, that's very much related to the kinds of explorations we have always made in the rehearsal studio, but here translated into a form where it can be somebody else that thinks, yeah, ok, what could go on here? It's the viewer's imagination that makes the link between this figure in the distance and this object in the landscape, or that doorway, or whatever. In the theatre you sit in the dark and normally you do all that work in your head. In the interactive digital work it's the same – you are making the meaning, you are joining things up – but via the computer interface/navigation you are also steering the gaze of the piece. A more explicitly active role is dramatized in a certain way. And the CD-ROMs of course are very solitary experiences. In the theatre pieces there is always a kind of social negotiation going on. As an audience member you might be absolutely captivated by looking at something on the stage, but another spectator may be bored to death or walking out. So in performance, one's encounter with the work always has a social dimension; there's always a negotiation of some kind, in the auditorium. On the other hand, sitting alone at your computer making your way through *Nightwalks* – it's a much more private space you are able to go into. It does not have the same kind of social question, which I think at the time we made these CD-ROMs was interesting for us to get away from. We are always trying to give ourselves a holiday from the constraints and the topics that live performance forces us back to!

GG: *At the same time, engaging with these works can produce the illusion or sensation of some kind of spatial and social negotiation – even in the absence of the performer – I found myself going through a series of emotions, of being trapped and trying to get back and being unable to do so.*

TE: I think the difference for me has to do with social negotiation. In the digital pieces you go from one photographed environment to another to another and in each of them you find the kinds of images and clues that we've put in there – a guy lying on a bed of old clothes, a pantomime horse outside some high-rise building, a yellow shirt discarded near a smashed-up phone booth… These things have a particular flavour and suggest certain things more readily than others. They're also linked in what is, without question, a limited set of ways – I mean your possible routes through the work are determined to a certain extent. That produces the sense of encounter, limit and frustration even that you describe. The difference though is that in encountering these things, you don't have to negotiate with any other real people – there aren't 200 other people sitting with you and giving their opinion (by reacting) as the work unfolds. So there's privacy to one's encounter with the digital work whereby one's relation to it is not negotiated socially. For me, that's probably the key difference – that in the theatre or performance everything is negotiated socially, whilst in *Nightwalks* or *Frozen Palaces* – or in a way in the photo works such as *Empty Stages* (2003-), which we mentioned – that doesn't really happen. Those works are just there – people look at them and they work on them in their own minds, quite privately. I guess it's more like novels – our experience reading a novel doesn't have that social dimension either – it's another form that operates more privately.

Works cited

Etchells, T. (1999) *Certain Fragments: contemporary performance and Forced Entertainment*, London: Routledge.

Part III

Traces

After presence

Written by researchers in performance studies and archaeology engaging with phenomenology, philosophy, archaeology, performance and documentation, and including an interview between archaeologist Michael Shanks and artist Lynn Hershman Leeson, 'Traces: After presence' interrogates readings of the performance of presence in the recollections, records, or documents that remain in the aftermath of the event. Here the question of presence is approached as a fulcrum of relationships between present and past: as a means of interrogating the persistence of ephemeral and performative acts in memory, trace and documentation; and as a conceptual framework for understanding performance and its documentation, memory and its affect on the present. Thus these essays address articulations of presence through mechanisms of trace and remainder invested in performance itself, where the ephemerality of the event, and its claim to the *present tense*, finds paradoxical relationships with signs of distance, absence, and the past. Within these contexts, the question of how presence may be curated, planned, or presented, and the impact of institutional re-stagings of ephemeral works, as well as the implication of re-animating and re-mediating the archive through new media, provides an arena for discussions of the extension, recovery and memory of past events. Here, too, the emergence or memory of presence is also addressed in perceptions of imminent absence and absence as immanent presence – and so in experiences and rhythms of appearance and disappearance that remain *in process*. In each of these cases, the sense of presence is read as occurring in the engagement with the trace, so producing complex relationships with the past events they may appear to inscribe into the present.

Chapter 11

Temporal anxiety/ 'Presence' *in Absentia*

Experiencing performance as documentation

Amelia Jones

Temporal anxiety, a 2010 preface to an essay written in 1996

In 2010 the activities of one institution alone crystallized the importance of continuing with the critique of assumptions about documenting and historicizing live art, which I introduced in my 1997–98 essay reprinted here. The Museum of Modern Art, New York, after 80 years of resolutely promoting and consolidating modernist conceptions limiting art to painting, sculpture, or possibly (in some forms) 'high art' photography or film, mounted a number of key shows foregrounding the importance of performance and the performative in post-1960s art[1]. The most notable was the provocatively entitled, and heavily promoted, *Marina Abramović: The Artist Is Present*, notoriously featuring the artist herself, seated in the gleaming white atrium of the Museum and soliciting encounters with visitors. This 'presence' of the artist complemented a large-scale retrospective of her performance works as recalled through vitrines of objects, photographs, video and film documentation, and re-enactments of several key pieces by young artists and dancers[2].

Also displayed at the formerly hidebound and performance-resistant MoMA were, at the same time, two other performance-related shows. First, part of the Gilbert and Lila Silverman Fluxus collection, newly acquired by the Museum, occupied a small gallery, filled with vitrines of oddly pristine Fluxus detritus including objects, boxes, and scripts. Secondly, there was also in spring of 2010 an installation at MoMA of the *Mirage* performance project by Joan Jonas, one of the most important artists active in producing hybrid work across performance and video since the early 1970s.

This energetic and cacophonous installation, which gave a sense of the unpredictable and uncontainable nature of performative installations at their best, was prefaced by a thoughtful text probably by the show's curator Barbara London, noting Jonas's strategic activations across media. This text suggested, importantly, the impossibility of recreating earlier performative events and installations in any but new forms[3].

While not discounting the wow-factor of sitting across from Abramović, the usefulness of having access in some form to her past works, and the fascination of seeing Fluxus materials cleaned up, aestheticized, and historically presented by the very kind of institution whose value systems Fluxus by and large sought to critique and overturn, I would argue that the Jonas installation was the only of the three renditions of performance histories that was in any way subtle or thoughtful. The other two events seemed poignant but failed attempts to recall complex performance histories – failed because, particularly in the case of 'The Artist Is Present,' hypocritical in their promise to deliver on the one hand precisely what, on the other, they claim to be unique to the momentary encounter of the live: 'presence' itself. As I have argued elsewhere, 'The Artist Is Present' exemplified the politically dangerous trend towards reifying precisely that which is still being claimed as 'authentic' in its supposed transfer of unmediated emotions and energy[4]. In short, 'The Artist Is Present' exemplifies what is lost when performance is institutionalized, objectified, and, by extension, commodified under the guise of somehow capturing the ephemeral. You can't 'curate,' plan in advance, or otherwise *present* 'presence'; it is something that *happens* of its own accord through interpersonal encounters.

These MoMA shows, however, did mark an epochal moment in the loosening of the grip of the more conservative aspects of modernism in the art world; it also simultaneously marked a watershed moment in the history of live art. What are we to do with the fact that, when the art world and its corollary discourses such as curating, art criticism, and art history scholarship (which are always already imbricated in the art market) embrace performance they seem inevitably to turn live acts into objects? What are we to do with the seemingly inexorable removal of the very energy and unpredictability of the body-to-body exchange potential to live performance when it is historicized and commodified, particularly through curatorial placement in museums such as MoMA?[5] For nothing could have been less spontaneous or natural (if by 'presence' we imply the possibility of unexpected relational sparks flying) than the spectacle of an artist sitting in a giant circus-ring like structure in the center of the institution at the center of the self-proclaimed urban center of the international art world.

We are at a turning point where claims of the special status of performance as authentically delivering 'presence' are in direct conflict with the simultaneous efforts to raise the status and economic value of performance events by displaying them in museums. These claims of the special status of the live were actively repeated by MoMA with their staging and promotion of the Abramović exhibition (through the very title 'The Artist Is Present,' among other aspects) even as the museum turned Abramović's 'live' body into a focus of spectacle and, with a phalanx of guards, cameras, and klieg lights in full force, removed any possibility of the spontaneous or unpredictable expression of emotions or embodied states occurring throughout the event[6].

2011: It is, then, an interesting and important moment in which to rethink earlier attempts to theorize what happens when we encounter live events presented as 'art,' and what happens when we write them into history. I am, among other things, struck by how my 1997–98 essay itself freezes the works it describes, turning them in the direction (if ever so slightly) of my thoughts and arguments. Is there a way to retain a sense of 'liveness' when writing about one's experience of durational art works?

It seems a lifetime ago, and at least three or four major shifts in my own thinking about how to think about writing histories of performance and live art, since ' "Presence" *in Absentia*' was published. I personally have developed my work on body art (since the 1998 publication of my book *Body Art: Performing the Subject*) to address issues of performativity in relation to the identifications of the artist, viewer, and the subject in general (in *Self/Image: Technology, Representation, and the Contemporary Subject*, 2006, and related essays), substantially expanding my own thinking about how most usefully to think about the relationship between performance and the visual arts. I have more recently, in fact, written explicitly about the issue of 'live art in history,' what happens when art history and performance studies come into contact, and have a large-scale book due out in 2012 which I have co-edited with performance studies scholar

Adrian Heathfield entitled *Perform, Repeat, Record: Live Art in History*[7].

Since the late 1990s I have been increasingly interested in addressing both the deep question of interpretation in terms of ephemeral acts and the correlative issue of how histories of art that accommodate such events get written. As I began to point to with this earlier essay, performance does something radical to structures of visual arts interpretation. I have worked to explore the different institutional structures of production and reception linked to performance and visual art, including the different assumptions at play in performance studies versus art history, criticism and curating. This is useful in figuring out new ways to question the tendency to force performance to become an 'object' or commodity – as is inevitably done in putting performance in visual arts institutions and in academic settings (as in fact I did in writing about specific performance events in this earlier article)[8].

The responses I have received when presenting this new work exploring conflicts and affinities across art history and performance studies in relation to the historicization of live art confirms a sea change in discourse – an increasingly fertile intertwining of concerns across these two disciplines, and a wholesale adoption of performance art by art institutions (for better or worse, as at MoMA), resulting in a huge wave of exhibitions on live art re-enactment and documentation[9]. And in the global art world an increasingly definitive shift has occurred since the early 2000s embracing the durational and relational (intersubjective) aspects of art introduced since the 1950s and refined with the development of Fluxus, Happenings, and performance, video, and installation art in the 1960s and 1970s. Sound byte terms such as 'relational aesthetics,' proposed by Nicolas Bourriaud in 1996, have both encouraged and responded to this trend. The notion of 'relational aesthetics' has become so popular that students of art and art history in Western Europe, North America, and the Antipodes are clamouring for courses and writing dissertations on 'relationality' and time-based art – themselves fired by a trend, rather than knowledgeable about the complex deep history of intersubjective and durational approaches to art making. The popularity of 'relational aesthetics,' or what artists and theorists since the 1960s have called 'intersubjective' or 'reciprocal' modes of opening up art as a process or exchange among artists and those who experience the work, points to a larger concern with understanding changes in the very basic structures of how art functions in contemporary society.

Perhaps this return to issues of reciprocity and durationality is the most important aspect of putting performance in the frame of art, as I began to explore in the 1997–98 article. Surely the artists, musicians, dancers, and others who turned to performance in the 1960s understood the value of exploding the then-current frames within which art was being made, evaluated, and positioned historically. It was no coincidence that many of the people who turned to the 'live' were otherwise marginalized from the existing power structures of the art world. While I address this connection between identity politics and performance in my 1998 *Body Art*, this connection remains to be fully explored and examined.

These final insights suggest that the most valuable thing that the intersection of 'presence' (or its claims) and 'art' can offer might be precisely the violent abutting of incompatible belief systems, an abutting that serves to expose the hypocrisies motoring the excesses of the art market. As well, thinking about performance or 'presence' in relation to history points to the limits of critiques of interpretation and meaning as these arose within postmodern theory in the 1980s and 1990s. It is easy enough in the abstract to note that performance, as a time-based act, points to the impossibility of ever fully knowing embodied experience, and thus of ever fully encompassing past events in the present – I have made these arguments in the article published here and elsewhere. It is a different story entirely, however, to insist on the political importance, even in the light of such 'impossibility,' of attempting to retrieve histories of live art (and, correlatively, of any events) from the past. Nothing, in this age of perpetual forgetting (wherein opponents can ignore the 'presence' of singular 'proof' of citizenship – the existence of a birth certificate – to argue that Barack Obama is not 'American') could be more important, in fact, than pushing ahead and continuing to write careful provisional histories in the face of such dangerous and purposeful erasures of evidence from the past.

'Presence' *in Absentia*: experiencing performance as documentation

Originally published in *Art Journal*, Winter 1997–98

I was not yet three years old, living in central North Carolina, when Carolee Schneemann performed *Meat Joy* at the Festival of Free Expression in Paris in 1964; three when Yoko Ono performed *Cut Piece* in Kyoto; eight when Vito Acconci did his *Push Ups* in the sand at Jones Beach and Barbara T. Smith began her exploration of bodily experiences with her *Ritual Meal* performance in Los Angeles; nine when Adrian Piper paraded through the streets of New York making herself repulsive in the *Catalysis* series; ten when Valie Export rolled over glass in *Eros/Ion* in Frankfurt; twelve in 1973 when, in Milan, Gina Pane cut her arm to make blood roses flow (*Sentimental Action*); fifteen (still in North Carolina, completely unaware of any art world doings) when Marina Abramovic and Ulay collided against each other in *Relation in Space* at the Venice Biennale in 1976 (Fig 11.1). I was thirty years old – then 1991 – when I began to study performance or body art[1] from this explosive and important period, entirely through its documentation.

Figure 11.1 Marina Abramović/Ulay, *Relation in Space*. Performed at Venice Biennale, 1976. © Marina Abramović. Courtesy of Marina Abramović and Sean Kelly Gallery, New York. DACS 2011. Ulay: © DACS 2011.

I am in the slightly uncomfortable but also enviable position of having been generously included in this special issue. Presented, in the words of the editor, as a sort of oral history, the issue is based on the premise that one had to be there – in the flesh, as it were – to get the story right. I was asked to provide a counter-narrative by writing about the 'problematic of a person my age doing work on performances you have not seen [in person].' This agenda forces me to put it up front: not having been there, I approach body artworks through their photographic, textual, oral, video, and/or film traces. I would like to argue, however, that the problems raised by my absence (my not having been there) are largely logistical rather than ethical or hermeneutic. That is, while the experience of viewing a photograph and reading a text is clearly different from that of sitting in a small room watching an artist perform, neither has a privileged relationship to the historical 'truth' of the performance (more on this below).

I have been accused on the one hand (by art historians) of not caring enough about 'the archive' and artistic intentionality (why didn't I 'get to know' Acconci before writing about his work so I could have a 'privileged' access to his intentions) and on the other (by artists) of not placing their needs or perceived intentions above my own intuitions and responses. At least for me personally I find it impossible, once I get to know someone, to have any sense of clarity about her or his work historically speaking (that is, as it may have come to mean in its original and subsequent contexts). Once I know the artist well, I can write about her or his work in (I hope) revealing ways, but ones that are (perhaps usefully, perhaps not) laden with personal feelings and conflicts involving the artist as a friend (or not, as the case may be). Furthermore, as noted, such relationships – especially if they are not positive – increase the logistical difficulties of writing and publishing on the work. The logistical problems are many: obtaining the documentation that is available; getting photographs to study and reproduce without blowing one's tiny budget; writing about the work without becoming entrapped in the artists' usually fascinating but sometimes intellectually and emotionally diversionary ideas about what the work is (or was) about, and so forth.

It is my premise here, as it has been elsewhere, that there is no possibility of an unmediated relationship to any kind of cultural product, including body art. Although I am respectful of the specificity of knowledges gained from participating in a live performance situation, I will argue here that this specificity should not be privileged over the specificity of knowledges that develop in relation to the documentary traces of such an event. While the live situation may enable the phenomenological relations of flesh-to-flesh engagement, the documentary exchange (viewer/reader document) is equally intersubjective. Either way, the twelve-person audience for the work may know a great deal or practically nothing at all about who the performer is, why she is performing, and what, consequently, she 'intends' this performance to mean. Either way, the audience may have a deep grasp of the historical, political, social, and personal contexts for a particular performance. While the viewer of a live performance may seem to have certain advantages in understanding such a context, on a certain level she may find it more difficult to comprehend the histories/narratives/processes she is experiencing until later, when she too can look back and evaluate them with hindsight (the same might be said of the performer herself). As I know from my own experience of 'the real' in general and, in particular, from live performances in recent years, these often become more meaningful when reappraised in later years; it is hard to identify the patterns of history while one is embedded in them. We 'invent' these patterns, pulling the past together into a manageable picture, retrospectively.

I will sketch out the problematic of experiencing performance or body art from an historical distance through a series of case studies, which will be interwoven with a discussion of the ontology of performance or body art. All of this material forms the backbone of my book *Body Art/Performing the Subject* (forthcoming from the University of Minnesota Press), which argues that body art instantiates the radical shift in subjectivity from a modernist to a postmodernist mode. Making use of a feminist post-structuralism informed by phenomenology, I argue this by reading this transfigured subjectivity through the works themselves (specifically: the works as documentary traces, and this goes even for those events I also experienced 'in the flesh'; I view these, through the memory screen, and they become documentary in their own right). I read body art performances as enacting the dispersed, multiplied, specific subjectivities of the late capitalist, postcolonial, postmodern era: subjectivities that are acknowledged to exist always already in relation to the world of other objects and subjects; subjectivities that are always already intersubjective as well as interobjective[2]. To the point, I insist that it is precisely the relationship of these bodies/subjects to documentation (or, more specifically, to re-presentation) that most profoundly points to the dislocation of the fantasy of the fixed, normative, centered modernist subject and thus most dramatically provides a radical challenge to the masculinism, racism, colonialism, classism, and hetero-sexism built into this fantasy.

Case Study 1: Carolee Schneemann's *Interior Scroll*, 1975

In Interior Scroll, *first performed in 1975, Schneemann performed herself in an erotically charged narrative of pleasure that works against the grain of the fetishistic and scopophilic 'male gaze' (Fig 11.2).*

Figure 11.2 Carolee Schneemann, *Interior Scroll* (1975).
      Performance photograph. Photo: Anthony McCall.

Covering her face and body in strokes of paint, Schneemann then pulled a long, thin coil of paper from her vagina ('like a ticker tape ... plumb line ... the umbilicus and tongue') (Schneemann 1979: 234)[3], unrolling it to read a narrative text to the audience. Part of this text read as follows: 'I met a happy man / a structuralist filmmaker ... he said we are fond of you / you are charming / but don't ask us / to look at your films /... we cannot look at / the personal clutter / the persistence of feelings / the hand-touch sensibility' (Schneemann 1979: 238)[4]. Through this action, which extends 'exquisite sensation in motion' and 'originates with ... the fragile persistence of line moving into space,' Schneemann integrated the occluded interior of the female body (with the vagina as 'a translucent chamber') with its mobile exterior, refusing the fetishizing process, which requires that the woman not expose the fact that she is not lacking but possesses genitals, and they are nonmale[5].

Movement secures Schneemann's momentary attainment of subjectivity (which coexists uneasily with her simultaneous situation as a picture of desire). The performative body, as Schneemann argues, 'has a value that static depiction ... representation won't carry'; she is concerned, she has said, with breaking down the distancing effect of modernist practice[6]. And yet, how can I, who experienced this work first through a series of black-and-white photographs published in Schneemann's More Than Meat Joy, then through a dissatisfyingly short clip in a video compilation of her work[7] – how can I speak of its disruption of the fetishizing effects of 'static depiction'? I 'know' this movement through the stuttered sequence of pictures, through the tiny fragment of performance on the videotape. I sit, still and quiet, and feel the movement pulse from picture to picture, along the slick surface of the magnetic tape.

The female subject is not simply a 'picture' in Schneemann's scenario, but a deeply constituted (and never fully coherent) subjectivity in the phenomenological sense, dynamically articulated in relation to others (including me, here and now in my chair), in a continually negotiated exchange of desire and identification. Schneemann plays out the oscillatory exchange between subject- and objectivity, between the masculine position of speaking discourse and the feminine position of being spoken. By 'speaking' her 'spokenness' already and integrating the image of her body (as object) with the action of making itself, Schneemann plays out the ambivalence of gendered identity – the

> fluidity of the positions of 'male' and 'female,' subject and object as we live gender in post-Freudian culture.
>
> Was (or, for that matter, is) there anything more 'present' than Schneemann, in her seemingly fully revealed sexual subjectivity, in Interior Scroll? Would I have been able to experience her sexed subjectivity more 'truthfully' had I been there (to smell and feel the heat of her body)?

One of the major conceptual and theoretical issues highlighted by body art as performance (which in this way, among others, is closely linked to the contemporaneous movements of Minimalism and Conceptualism), is that of the ontology of the art 'object.' Most early accounts of these practices made heroic claims for the status of performance as the only art form to guarantee the presence of the artist. Thus, in 1975 Ira Licht triumphantly proclaimed that bodyworks do away with the 'intermediary' mediums of painting and sculpture to 'deliver ... information directly through trans-formation' (Licht 1975: n.p.). And, in the early 1970s, Rosemary Mayer claimed body art to be a direct reflection of the artist's life experiences, while Cindy Nemser described the 'primary goal of body art' as 'bring[ing] the subjective and objective self together as an integrated entity,' which is then presumably experienced directly by the audience (Mayer 1973: 33–6 and Nemser 1971: 42).

More recently, Catherine Elwes argued that performance art 'offers women a unique vehicle for making that direct unmediated access [to the audience]. Performance is about the 'real-life' presence of the artist. ... She is both signifier and that which is signified. Nothing stands between spectator and performer' (Elwes 1985: 165). I have already made clear that I specifically reject such conceptions of body art or performance as delivering in an unmediated fashion the body (and implicitly the self) of the artist to the viewer. The art historian Kathy O'Dell has trenchantly argued that, precisely by using their bodies as primary material, body or performance artists highlight the 'representational status' of such work rather than confirming its ontological priority. The representational aspects of this work, its 'play within the arena of the symbolic' and, I would add, its dependence on documentation to attain symbolic status within the realm of culture-expose the impossibility of attaining full knowledge of the self through bodily proximity. Body art, finally, shows that the body can never 'be known "purely" as a totalizable, fleshy whole that rests outside of the arena of the symbolic' (O'Dell 1992: 43–4). Having direct physical contact with an artist who pulls a scroll from her vaginal canal does not ensure 'knowledge' of her subjectivity or intentionality any more than does looking at a film or picture of this activity, or looking at a painting that was made as the result of such an action.

Body art, through its very performativity and its unveiling of the body of the artist, surfaces the insufficiency and incoherence of the body-as-subject and its inability to deliver itself fully (whether to the subject-in-performance her/himself or to the one who engages with this body). Perhaps even more to the point than O'Dell's suggestive observations is Peggy Phelan's insistence on the way in which the body-in-performance puts forward its own lack:

> Performance uses the performer's body to pose a question about the inability to secure the relation between subjectivity and the body per se; performance uses the body to frame the lack of Being promised by and through the body – that which cannot appear without a supplement ... performance marks the body itself as loss ... for the spectator the performance spectacle is itself a projection of the scenario in which her own desire takes place.
>
> (Phelan 1993: 151–2)

Body art can thus be said to dislocate the modernist assumption of authorial plenitude (where the author, whose body is veiled but nonetheless implicitly male, is thought to be instantiated by the work of art and vice versa)[8]. Body art flaunts the body itself as loss or lack: that is, as fundamentally lacking in the self-sufficiency (claimed by Elwes et al.) that would guarantee its plenitude as an unmediated repository of selfhood. The 'unique' body of the artist in the body artwork only has meaning by virtue of its contextualization within the codes of identity that accrue to the artist's body and name. Thus, this body is not self-sufficient in its meaningfulness but relies not only on an authorial context of 'signature' but on a receptive context in which the interpreter or viewer may interact with this body. When understood in its full open-endedness, live performance makes this contingency, the intersubjectivity of the interpretive exchange, highly pronounced and obvious since the body's actions can be interfered with and realigned according to spectatorial bodies/subjects on the register of the action itself; documents of the body-in-performance are just as clearly contingent, however, in that the meaning that accrues to this action, and the body-in-performance, is fully dependent on the ways in which the image is contextualized and interpreted.

Seemingly acting as a 'supplement' to the 'actual' body of the artist-in-performance, the photograph of the body art event or performance could, in fact, be said to expose the body itself as supplementary, as both the visible 'proof' of the self and its endless deferral. The supplement, Jacques Derrida has provocatively argued, is a 'terrifying menace' in its indication of absence and lack but also 'the first and surest protection ... against that very menace. This is why it cannot be given up' (Derrida 1976: 154).

The sequence of supplements initiated by the body art project – the body 'itself,' the spoken narrative, the video and other visuals within the piece, the video, film, photograph, and text documenting it for posterity – announces the necessity of 'an infinite chain, ineluctably multiplying the supplementary mediations that produce the sense of the very thing they defer: the mirage of the thing itself, of immediate presence, or originary perception. Immediacy is derived. ... The play of substitution fills and marks a determined lack.' Derrida notes that 'the indefinite process of supplementarity has always already *infiltrated* presence, always already inscribed there the space of repetition and the splitting of the self' (Derrida 1976: 157, 163).

Derrida's insight explains the equivocal position of the body in modernist and postmodernist art discourse. Within the modernist logic of formalism, the body of the artist and of the interpreter – in its impurity – must be veiled, its supplementarity hidden from view. The formalist insists upon the 'disinterestedness' of his interpretations and such disinterestedness requires a pure relation between the art object and its supposedly inherent meaning (embedded in its 'form,' to be excavated by the discerning interpreter). The supplementarity of the body corrupts this logic. For the nascent postmodernists such as Nemser and Elwes who wish to privilege performance or body art as anti-formalist in its merging of art and life, its delivery of the body/subject of the artist directly to the viewer, the body must be seen as an unmediated reflection of the self whose presence guarantees the 'redemptive' quality of art as activism. I argue in my book on body art, however, that body art practices are never unequivocally anti- or postmodernist and certainly not guarantors of presence. Unlike formalist modernism, which veils the body of the artist to occlude its supplementarity (such that its transcendence – its masculinity – seems obvious and natural)[9], body art performances exacerbate the body's supplementarity and the role of representation in momentarily securing its meanings through visible codes signalling gender, race, and other social markers.

Case Study 2: Yayoi Kusama's Self-Portrait Photographs, c. 1960

> *There she is, enacting herself as pinup on one of her vertiginous landscapes of phallic knobs (woman-as-phallus meets phallus-as-sign-of-male-privilege): naked, heavily made-up in the style of the 1960s, she sports high heels, long black hair, and polka dots covering her bare flesh (Fig 11.3). As Kris Kuramitsu has argued, this photograph 'is only one of many that highlight [Kusama's] naked, Asian female body. These photographs, and the persona that cultivated/was cultivated by them is what engenders the usual terse assessment [in art discourse] of Kusama as "problematic"[10].*

Figure 11.3 Yayoi Kusama, Untitled. Photo Collage with photograph by Hal Reiff of Kusama reclining on *Accumulation No.2*. © Yayoi Kusama.

Kusama plays on her 'doubled otherness' (Kuramitsu, 1996: 2) vis-à-vis American culture: She is racially and sexually at odds with the normative conception of the artist as Euro-American (white) male. Rather than veil the 'fact' of her difference(s)(seemingly irrefutably confirmed by the visible evidence registered by her body), Kusama exacerbated it. (Intentionally? Would I have 'known' had I been there for her public 'performances' of self?) In a portrait of artists who participated in the 1965 Nul exhibition at the Stedelijk Museum, Amsterdam, Kusama sticks out like a sore thumb: there she stands, front and center – among a predictably bourgeois group of white, almost all male Euro-Americans (dressed in suits) – her tiny body swathed in a glowing white silk kimono[11].

Am I an object? Am I a subject? Kusama continues to perform these questions in the most disturbingly direct of ways, posing herself in 1993, dressed in polka-dotted fabric on a polka-dotted floor in front of a mirror reflecting a polka-dotted wall (her installation Mirror Room and Self-Obliteration). Now, her pose and garb remove her from us, camouflage shifting her into the realm of potential invisibility ('self-obliteration'). She still can't decide whether she wants to proclaim herself as celebrity or pin-up (object of our desires) or artist (master of intentionality). Either way, her 'performance' takes place as representation (pace Warhol, she's on to the role of documentation in securing the position of the artist as beloved object of the art world's desires); she comprehends the 'rhetoric of the pose' and its specific resonance for women and people of color. The pictures of Kusama are deeply embedded in the discursive structure of ideas informing her work that is her 'author-function'[12].

Rather than confirming the ontological coherence of the body-as-presence, body art depends on documentation, confirming – even exacerbating – the supplementarity of the body itself. Predictably, although many have relied on the photograph, in particular, as 'proof' of the fact that a specific action took place or as a marketable object to be raised to the formalist height of an 'art' photograph, in fact such a dependence is founded on belief systems similar to those underlying the belief in the 'presence' of the body-in-performance. Kristine Stiles has brilliantly exposed the dangers of using the photograph of a performative event as 'proof' in her critique of Henry Sayre's book *The Object of Performance*. Sayre opens his first chapter with the now-mythical tale of Rudolf Schwarzkogler's suicidal self-mutilation of his penis in 1966, a story founded on the circulation of a number of 'documents' showing a male torso with bandaged penis (a razor blade lying nearby). Stiles, who has done primary research on the artist, points out that the photograph, in fact, is not even of Schwarzkogler but, rather, of another artist (Heinz Cibulka) who posed for Schwarzkogler's entirely fabricated ritual castration (Stiles 1990: 35). Sayre's desire for this photograph to entail some previous 'real' event (in Barthesian terms, the *having been there* of a particular subject and a particular action)[13] leads him to ignore what Stiles describes as 'the contingency of the document not only to a former action but also to the construction of a wholly fictive space'[14]. It is this very contingency that Sayre's book attempts to address through his argument that the shift marked by performance and body art is that of the 'site of presence' from 'art's object to art's audience, from the textual or plastic to the experiential' (Sayre 1992: 5). Sayre's fixation on 'presence,' even while he acknowledges its new destabilized siting in reception, informs his unquestioning belief in the photograph of performance as 'truth.'

Rosalind Krauss has recognized the philosophical reciprocity of photography and performance, situating the two as different kinds of indexicality. As indexes, both labor to 'substitute the registration of sheer physical presence for the more highly articulated language of aesthetic conventions' (Krauss 1985: 209). And yet, I would stress, in their failure to 'go beyond' the contingency of aesthetic codes, both performance and photography announce the supplementarity of the index itself. The presentation of the self-in performance, in the photograph, film, or video – calls out the mutual supplementarity of the body and the subject (the body, as material 'object' in the world, seems to confirm the 'presence' of the subject; the subject gives the body its significance as 'human'), as well as of performance or body art and the photographic document. (The body art event needs the photograph to confirm its having happened; the photograph needs the body art event as an ontological 'anchor' of its indexicality.)

Case Study 3: Annie Sprinkle, *Post Post Porn Modernist*, 1990–93

Here's a performance I have seen in the flesh. Do I have some special access to its meaning or am I alternately distanced from/seduced by its embodied effects just as I would be through its documentation? (Note: I've also ingrained this piece, in other versions, into my memory by viewing photographs, slides, videotapes, and by talking to the artist.)

A sex worker, Annie Sprinkle moved into the art world with her 1985 participation in Deep Inside Porn Stars, a performance at Franklin Furnace in New York[15]. Since then, she has performed in art venues as a whore/performer turned art/performer, still with 'clients' to seduce and pleasure; one of the effects of Sprinkle's merging of 'sex work' with 'art work' is the collapsing of class distinctions (from lower-class whore/porn star to the cultural cachet of artist). She has also transformed her pornographic film career, moving into the production of self-help/'art' videos on female and transsexual pleasure[16]. Sprinkle's work is nothing if not about mediation. (Perhaps this is to be expected from someone who proffers her body regularly on the art and pornography markets; the body/self is most directly 'given' and yet never really 'there.')

Sprinkle's most incendiary performative act is part of her Post Post Porn Modernist performance; developed and performed over the last several years, the piece includes several different narrative segments. The most explosive moment occurs when Sprinkle displays her cervix to audience members: she opens her vaginal canal with a speculum and beckons audience members to file by and take a look, welcoming photography and videotaping. (It is, one senses, precisely through such acts of techno-voyeurism that Sprinkle can experience her own self-display.) Handing each spectator a flashlight to highlight the dark continent of the female sex, Sprinkle interacts with them as they file by (Fig 11.4).

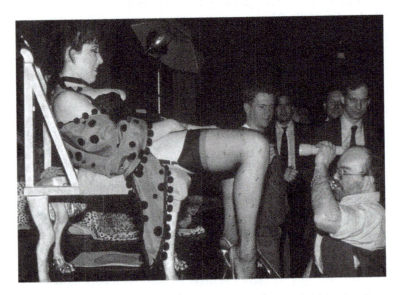

Figure 11.4 Annie Sprinkle, 'The Public Cervix Announcement,' from *Post Post Porn Modernist* (1990–93). Courtesy of the artist.

Looping back to Schneemann's self-exposure of the female sex, this moment of display explodes the conventional voyeuristic relation that informs the aesthetic (where the female body is represented as 'lacking' object of male viewing desire). Not only is the female sex in a general sense displayed – its 'lack' refused; also put on view are the internal female genitalia, including the paradoxically invisible, unlocatable G-spot (a primary site of female pleasure). The cervix-viewing portion of Sprinkle's performance also, in Lynda Nead's terms, destroys the containing mechanisms of the aesthetic: as obscenity, Sprinkle's presentation 'moves and arouses the viewer rather than bringing about stillness and wholeness' (Nead 1992: 2).

Or does it 'arouse'? Sprinkle certainly knows how to give pleasure to her audience/clientele. She has been professionally trained to do so. It is difficult, in fact, to view Sprinkle's cervix in an unequivocally self-empowering way (to pretend to possess an unmediated, dominating gaze of desire). Sprinkle's sex looks back: the subject of viewing is confronted by the 'eye'/'I' of the female sex.

This 'eye'/'I' is fully contingent whether I view it 'in the flesh' or 'on the page.' It operates as/through representation. For Sprinkle's body, in this particular scene distilled to the organs of her sex, is the image of Sprinkle as acting subject. I am no closer to 'knowing' the 'truth' of Sprinkle having seen and spoken to her than I would have been otherwise: She (re) presents herself to me as I sustain myself in a function of desire[17]. While Sprinkle can't illustrate herself as a full subject of pleasure and desire, she can situate herself in relation to us in such a way as to reclaim her own 'look' (the gaze of her cunt), if only momentarily, from the voyeuristic relation. Sprinkle's performance of self points to the always already mediated nature of embodied subjectivity as well as the sexual pleasure that gives this subjectivity 'life.'

In the final segment of Post Post Porn Modernist, *Sprinkle takes on the archaic-goddess persona of 'Anya' to bring herself to a twenty-minute long spiritual/sexual orgasm on stage. My first reaction on seeing this elaborately orchestrated performance of jouissance was to assert to my partner that she was faking it. My secondary response was to wonder why I needed to think that she was faking it. As Chris Straayer puts it, 'Whether Annie Sprinkle is acting (and/)or experiencing orgasms in her performances cannot be determined by us' – and, I would add, this is the case whether we view the performance live or not (Straayer 1993: 174)[18].*

In 1938 the Surrealist film actor, director, and playwright Antonin Artaud published his astounding collection of essays on performance called *The Theater and Its Double*. In his manifesto 'The Theater of Cruelty,' published in this collection, he articulates a passionate critique of realist theater, with its reliance on written texts and its 'servitude to psychology' and 'human interest' (Artaud 1958: 90). The theater, rather, must draw on its own 'concrete language' to 'make space speak':

We abolish the stage and the auditorium and replace them by a single site, without partition or barrier of any kind, which will become the theater of the action. A direct communication will be re-established between the spectator and the spectacle, between the actor and the spectator, from the fact that the spectator, placed in the middle of the action is engulfed and physically affected by it.

(Artaud 1958: 96)

I return in closing to Artaud's vibrant text, radical in its own time, to stress the point that such a desire for immediacy is, precisely, a modernist (if in this case also clearly avant-garde) dream. In this fin-de-millennium age of multinational capitalism, virtual realities, post-colonialism, and cyborg identity politics (an age presciently acknowledged and in some ways propelled by the radical body artworks noted here), such a dream must be viewed as historically specific rather than epistemologically secure. Body and performance art expose, precisely, the contingency of the body/self not only on the 'other' of the communicative exchange (the audience, the art historian) but on the very modes of its own (re)presentation.

Works cited

Artaud, A. (1958) *The Theater and Its Double*, translated by M. C. Richards, New York: Grove Weidenfeld.

Barthes, R. (1977) 'Rhetoric of the Image', in R. Barthes *Image-Music-Text*, translated by Stephen Heath, New York: Hill and Wang, 35–51.

de Beauvoir, S. (1970; [1949]) *The Second Sex*, translated and edited by H. M. Parshley, New York: Alfred A. Knopf.

Derrida, D. (1976) 'That Dangerous Supplement', in J. Derrida *Of Grammatology*, translated by G. C. Spivak, Baltimore MD: Johns Hopkins University Press, 141–64.

Elwes, C. (1985) 'Floating Femininity: A Look at Performance Art by Women', in S. Kent and J. Moreau (eds) *Women's Images of Men*, London: Writers and Readers Publishing, 164–93.

Foucault, M. (1977; [1969]) 'What Is an Author?', in M. Foucault *Language, Counter-Memory, Practice*, translated by D. Bouchard and S. Simon, Ithaca NY: Cornell University Press, 113–38.

Fuchs, E. (1989) 'Staging the Obscene Body', *TDR: The Drama Review*, 33:1, 33–58.

Heathfield, A. and Jones, A. (eds) (forthcoming, 2012) *Perform, Repeat, Record: Live Art in History*.

Jones, A. (1994) 'Postfeminism, Feminist Pleasures, and Embodied Theories of Art', in J. Frueh, C. Langer and A. Raven (eds) *New Feminist Criticism: Art, Identity, Action*, New York: Harper Collins, 16–41.

——(2008) 'Live Art in Art History: A Paradox?', in T. Davies (ed.) *The Cambridge Guide to Performance Studies*, Cambridge: Cambridge University Press, 151–65.

——(2011) '*The Artist Is Present*: Artistic Re-enactments and the Impossibility of Presence', *TDR: The Drama Review*, 55: 1, 16–45.

Juhasz, A. (1994) 'Our Auto-Bodies, Ourselves: Representing Real Women in Video', *Afterimage* 21:7, 10–14.

Karia, B. (ed.) (1989) *Yayoi Kusama: A Retrospective*, exh. cat., New York: Center for International Contemporary Arts.

Krauss, R. (1985) 'Notes on the Index', in *The Originality of the Avant-Garde and Other Modernist Myths*, Cambridge, MA.: MIT Press, 196–220.

Kuramitsu, K. (1996) 'Yayoi Kusama: Exotic Bodies in the Avant-Garde', unpublished paper submitted for Amelia Jones and Donald Preziosi's 'Essentialism and Representation' graduate seminar, University of California, Riverside/University of California, Los Angeles, Spring 1996.

Lacan, J. (1978) in 'Anamorphosis', in J-A. Miller *The Four Fundamental Concepts of Psycho-Analysis*, translated by A. Sheridan, New York: W. W. Norton and Co., 79–90.

Licht, I. (1975) *Bodyworks*, Chicago IL: Museum of Contemporary Art.

Mayer, R. (1973) 'Performance and Experience', *Arts Magazine*, 47: 3, pp. 33–6.

Nead, L. (1992) *The Female Nude: Art, Obscenity, and Sexuality*, London: Routledge.

Nemser, C. (1971) 'Subject-Object Body Art', *Arts Magazine*, 46:1, 38–42.

O'Dell, K. (1992) 'Toward a Theory of Performance Art: An Investigation of Its Sites', PhD. diss., City University of New York.

Owens, C. (1992) 'The Medusa Effect, or, the Specular Ruse', in S. Bryson, B. Kruger, L. Tillman, and J. Weinstock (eds) *Beyond Recognition: Representation, Power, and Culture*, Berkeley CA: University of California Press, 191–200.

Phelan, P. (1993) *Unmarked: The Politics of Performance*, New York: Routledge.

Poster, M. (1990) *The Mode of Information: Poststructuralism and Social Context*, Cambridge: Polity Press and Chicago IL: University of Chicago Press.

Poster, M. (1995) *The Second Media Age*, Cambridge: Polity Press.

Roth, M. (1983) 'The Amazing Decade', in M. Roth (ed.) *The Amazing Decade: Women and Performance Art in America 1970–1980*, Los Angeles CA: Astro Artz, 14–41.

Sayre, H. (1992) *The Object of Performance: The American Avant-Garde since 1970*, Chicago IL: University of Chicago Press.

Schneemann, C. (1979) *More Than Meat Joy: Complete Performance Works and Selected Writings*, edited by Bruce McPherson, New Paltz, NY: Documentext.

——(1991) 'Angry Women', in A. Juno and V. Vale (eds) *Angry Women*, San Francisco: Re/Search Publications, 163–76.

Sobchack, V. (1994) 'The Passion of the Material: Prolegomena to a Phenomenology of Interobjectivity', manuscript of an article forthcoming in Sobchack *Carnal Thoughts: Bodies, Texts, Scenes, and Screens* (Berkeley: University of California Press); published in German in C. Wulf, D. Kamper, and H.U. Gumbrecht (eds) *Ethik der Asthetik*, Berlin: Akademie Verlag, 195–205.

Stiles, K. (1990) 'Performance and Its Objects', *Arts Magazine*, 65:3, 35–47.

Straayer, C. (1993) 'The Seduction of Boundaries: Feminist Fluidity in Annie Sprinkle's Art/Education/Sex', in P.C. Gibson and R. Gibson (eds) *Dirty Looks: Women, Pornography, Power*, London: British Film Institute, 156–75.

Williams, L. (1993) 'A Provoking Agent: The Pornography and Performance Art of Annie Sprinkle', in P.C. Gibson and R. Gibson (eds) *Dirty Looks: Women, Pornography, Power*, London: British Film Institute, 46–61.

Notes, *Temporal Anxiety*

1 The Museum established a new department of 'Media and Performance Art' as recently as 2006. See the press release relating to this development, http://press.moma.org/images/press/PRESS_RELEASE_ARCHIVE/Media.pdf. Accessed 10 February 2011.

2 See my extended critique of this exhibition in Jones 2011.

3 The text on MoMA's website on the piece reads, similarly: 'Inspired by a trip the artist took to India, Joan Jonas's *Mirage* (1976/2005) was originally conceived as a 1976 performance for the screening room of New York's Anthology Film Archives. In it, Jonas carried out a series of movements, such as running as a form of percussion and as gestural drawing, while interacting with a variety of sculptural components and video projections. In 1994, the artist repurposed these elements – metal cones suggesting the form of volcanoes, videos of erupting volcanoes, wooden hoops, a mask, photographs, and chalkboards, among other items – as a discrete installation, which was itself reconfigured in 2005. At MoMA, the artist once again re-imagines the work in an installation that combines elements of ritual, memory, repetition, and rehearsal with games, drawn actions, and syncopated rhythms.' See www.moma.org/visit/calendar/exhibitions/1016. Accessed 10 February 2011.

4 In Jones 2011.

5 By commodified I mean both literally, as now glossy photographs, books, and other aspects from Abramović's work can be purchased, and figuratively in the sense that critics and art historians can authorize our own careers by writing about Abramović's work. Abramović, who has also founded a performance archive and a school of performance, has understood the way in which the *name* of an increasingly famous performer can itself have economic, cultural and social value. It is up to the art and performance communities to address such a case with critical acumen and by placing such efforts in a historical context, rather than, as has been the tendency so far, promoting Abramović and her work unquestioningly with hagiographic rhetoric.

6 The fact that websites, some sponsored by MoMA, sprung up documenting aspects of the piece – such as 'Marina made me cry' –

confirms the instantaneous fixing of the spectacle as 'Internet event' rather than its capacity to evoke unpredictable or otherwise interesting effects. See http://marinaabramovicmademecry.tumblr.com/. Accessed 10 February 2011.

7 See Heathfield and Jones forthcoming, 2012.

8 See Jones 2008.

9 See the extensive timeline of the publications, exhibitions, and art works relating to this shift in *Perform, Repeat, Record*.

Notes, Presence *in Absentia*

1 I use the term *body art* rather than *performance art* for several reasons. My interest in this work is informed by an embodied, phenomenological model of intersubjectivity; furthermore, the work that emerged during the period of the 1960s to the mid-1970s (before performance became theatricalized and moved to the large stage) was labeled 'body art' or 'bodyworks' by several contemporaneous writers who wished to differentiate it from a conception of 'performance art' that was at once broader (in that it reached back to Dada and encompassed any kind of theatricalized production on the part of a visual artist) and narrower (in that it implied that a performance must actually take place in front of an audience). I am interested in work that may or may not initially have taken place in front of an audience: in work – such as that by Ana Mendieta, Carolee Schneemann, Vito Acconci, Yves Klein, or Hannah Wilke – that took place through an enactment of the artist's body, whether it be in a 'performance' setting or in the relative privacy of the studio, that was then documented such that it could subsequently be experienced through photography, film, video, and/or text.

2 Mark Poster discusses the multiplicity of the subject in the age of multinationalism and cyborg identity politics in *The Mode of Information: Poststructuralism and Social Context* and *The Second Media Age*; see Poster 1990 and 1995. On the body/self as simultaneously subject and object, Sobchack 1994.

3 Schneemann has performed *Interior Scroll* three times: in 1975 at Women Here and Now in East Hampton, Long Island; in 1977 at the Telluride Film Festival in Colorado; and in 1995 inside a cave as *Interior Scroll – the Cave* (with six other women). This reading of Schneemann's piece is modified from my essay 'Postfeminism, Feminist Pleasures, and Embodied Theories of Art,' see Jones 1994: 30–32.

4 The audience for its original performance was almost all female, see Roth 1983: 14.

5 The first poetic descriptions in this sentence are from a letter sent to me by Schneemann (dated 22 November 1992), who encouraged me to revise my earlier, blunter readings of her work. Here is an example of my susceptibility to personal contact: I have been swayed by her powerful self-readings, changing my perceptions of the work. The term *translucent chamber* appears in Schneemann 1979: 234.

6 Schneemann states, 'my work has to do with cutting through the idealized (mostly male) mythology of the 'abstracted self' or the 'invented self' – i.e., work ... [where the male artist] retain[s] power and distancing over the situation'; in Schneemann 1991: 169.

7 The video, *Imaging Her Erotics*, was produced by Schneemann and Maria Beatty in 1995–96; the clip shown here is from the 1995 version of the performance. Schneemann informs me that all of the original footage of the earlier performances is in the possession of the documenter, who will not relinquish it for publication or study.

8 This marking of the body as absence is also exemplified in the photographic documents of Ana Mendieta's later *Silueta* series works, in which her body is enacted as *trace* (gash wounding the surface of the earth).

9 It is Simone de Beauvoir, in her monumental 1949 book, *The Second Sex*, who links the dream of 'transcendence' in Western aesthetics and philosophy to masculine subjectivity. Here, she reworks the dialectic between the self and other outlined by her partner, Jean-Paul Sartre (and more subtly transformed by Maurice Merleau-Ponty and Jacques Lacan), with an awareness of the mapping of power through gender in patriarchy. Beauvoir rereads Sartre's existentialist argument (in *Being and Nothingness*) that the subject has the capacity to project himself into transcendence (the *pour-soi*) out of the fundamental immanence of the *en-soi*, arguing that the *pour-soi* is a privileged potentiality open only to male subjects in patriarchy. See de Beauvoir 1949: especially p. xxviii.

10 See Kuramitsu 1996: 1, unpublished paper submitted for Amelia Jones and Donald Preziosi's Essentialism and Representation graduate seminar, University of California, Riverside/University of California, Los Angeles. Kuramitsu discusses this photograph of Kusama at some length. I am indebted to Kuramitsu for introducing me to this aspect of Kusama's oeuvre and for leading me to the best sources on the artist (see also Karia 1989). I should note here too that it was the large number of photographs such as these published as advertisements in magazines like *Artforum* from the mid-1960s onward that initially sparked my interest in body art. I am especially interested in the role these images play in enacting the artist as a public figure: they are performative documents. The only audience for the 'original' performance would have been the camera-person and whoever else was in the room.

11 The other artists in the portrait include Jiro Yoshihara, founder of Gutai, Hans Haacke, Lucio Fontana, and Günther Uecker. See the labelled photograph in *Nul negentienhonderd viff en zestig, deel 2 fotos* (1965, Part 2, Photographs).

12 On the rhetoric of the pose, see Owens 1992: 191–200. The term *author-function* is, of course, derived from Michel Foucault's 'What Is an Author?' See Foucault 1977: 113–38.

13 Henry Sayre's reading of Schwarzkogler's work can be found in Sayre 1992: 2.

14 See Barthes 1977: 44.

15 See Fuchs 198: 38–9. Chris Straayer stresses Sprinkle's links to 1970s feminist performance works by Schneemann and Linda Montano, Sprinkle's performance mentor, rather than her background as a sex worker. See Straayer 1993: 157.
16 Her films include *Linda/Les and Annie-the First Female to Male Trans-sexual Love Story* (1990), made in collaboration with Albert Jaccoma and John Armstrong, and *The Sluts and Goddesses Video Workshop, or How to Be a Sex Goddess in 101 Easy Steps* (1992), made by Sprinkle and Maria Beatty. See Linda Williams's discussion of how Sprinkle maintains in her pornographic videos (and, I would add, her 'art' videos) the 'intimate address' to the 'client' characteristic of the whore's 'performance,' in Williams 1993: 181.
17 This paraphrases Jacques Lacan, who writes of the subject 'sustaining himself in a function of desire' in 'Anamorphosis,' in Lacan 1978: 85.
18 See also Juhasz 1994: 11 for a discussion of Sprinkle's extended performance of orgasm.

Chapter 12

Here and now

Lynn Hershman Leeson and
Michael Shanks

Figure 12.1 Lynn Hershman signing in at *The Dante Hotel*, San Francisco, November 1973. Photo: Edmund Shea. Courtesy of the artist.

MICHAEL SHANKS: 1972: You were working in San Francisco, and you did a piece at the Dante Hotel.

LYNN HERSHMAN LEESON: Yes. I'd done a piece with sound at the museum, but they said media wasn't art and didn't belong in an art museum. So I thought, well, why not just use an environment, wherever it exists?

So, Eleanor Coppola and I created rooms in the Dante Hotel, which was a run-down place in North Beach. It was very simple. We rented the rooms – mine was rented indefinitely; hers was rented for two weeks. And I created a situation where people could look at presumed identities constructed from artifacts placed in the room.

MS: So, you put stuff in there?

LH: Yeah. I put goldfish in there. There was a soliloquy of Molly Bloom. There were books that the presumed people might have read, clothing that they might have worn. People were invited to trespass. It was open 24 hours a day; people could check in at the front desk, get the key, stay as long as they wanted, and displace it.

MS: Did anybody leave anything behind?

LH: Nobody left anything. They graffitied the mirror that was there, but nobody took anything. They really respected that space.

MS: Were you monitoring people coming and going?

LH: No, not really. It was left gathering dust and the flux of time as people traveled through. I was just starting to think of time and space as elements of sculpture at that point.

MS: And then the police came at some point, didn't they?

LH: Yeah – ha! Somebody reported a body in the bed, because there were these wax cast figures –

MS: – which had been there from the beginning?

LH: Yes. And the police confiscated everything in the room and took all the artifacts down to central headquarters, which, I thought, was really the apt ending to that particular narrative.

MS: And then thirty-two years later, Stanford acquires your archive of ninety-something boxes. The remains of your body of work – whatever hadn't been taken away by the police, I guess!

LH: Yes.

MS: As an archaeologist, I'm interested in what comes after the event, as it were. What you do with the remains of the past, to somehow try to get back to where they originated.

LH: I don't know that you can ever get back to that point, but you can go forward, using them as context for the future. The trail and the remains may be dormant, but they exist, waiting to be revived or resurrected into something else.

Figure 12.2 Lynn Hershman, *The Dante Hotel* (1973–74).
           Courtesy of the artist.

MS: Yeah, regenerated. This is one of our major points of contact.
    A lot of people think that archaeology – archaeologists –
    discover the past. And that's only a tiny bit true. I think it's
    more accurate to say that they work on what remains. That
    may sometimes involve, absolutely, coming across stuff from
    the past – maybe a trilobite fossil, or a piece of Roman pottery,

or, as my colleague Henry Lowood and I did, your boxes in the Stanford collection – but the key thing about archaeology is that it works on what's left. And that makes of all of us, really, a kind of archaeologist. We're all archaeologists now, working on what's left of the past.

And you're right, as we explore this stuff, we figure out how to bring it forward, first into the present, through our interpretation of it.

LH: Exactly. I didn't want the work to remain in boxes. Much as I love the Stanford Library and Special Collections, I wanted this to be more universally accessible. I suggested to Henry that, possibly, we could make a game, a mystery, or a film noir about the remains of this evidence of a life, which portrayed itself in various episodes. Henry suggested a possible adaptation into Second Life, which then became the 'Life to the Second Power' project.

MS: And it connects with the interest that we share in the nature of the archive. Boxes, in a collection, vitrines in a museum, they're often – and appropriately – seen as quite static.

LH: That's right. Static but charged.

MS: Unless there's a reason to reuse stuff, it'll fall out of use or be stored away; and, eventually, it'll end up in a landfill site, if you're lucky, or destroyed. So the question we share is how to re-animate the archive.

LH: Exactly. Revitalize the past, inserting it into the present, which gives direction to its future.

MS: Yeah. Displacement is another key feature of this archaeological sensibility. What happens when old stuff – remains – are shirted into new associations.

LH: And, it's particularly interesting because Second Life and some of these social-network programs involve notions of trespass that have no geographic boundaries. So it's taking the exact same premise of this project, the Dante Hotel, from thirty years earlier and transplanting it into something that allows a completely different, but yet related, experience.

MS: Yeah. There are parts of our contemporary attitude toward spaces and places that are very archaeological. It's about how we almost automatically and subconsciously look at spaces in terms of evidence. It's a forensic sensibility.

Archaeologists survey and excavate places. They document, map, collect, and categorize, seeking to identify what generated the remains – for example, past events, social or environmental changes. Archaeological evidence is thus treated as symptomatic traces of deep structures or events, archaeology is a hybrid science of material traces.

The detective, another nineteenth century invention, also connects evidence with event and place. But how do you know what might be the key evidence at the scene of a crime or an archaeological site? Anything might be relevant. Anywhere could be the scene of a crime. This is what I mean by forensic sensibility. Anything could be the trace of something that once happened there.

LH: But, now, with the forensic sensibility, there's also a digital demeanor that didn't exist before.

MS: Oh, right. 'Digital demeanor,' I like that.

LH: A digital demeanor of trespass using interaction to reveal the evidence.

MS: Yeah, which brings up implications for storage, for retrieval, and, of course, surveillance, looking, watching, and how these have become incorporated in all sorts of digital technologies. For two centuries and more, archaeologists have been developing a toolkit for working upon the traces of the past. They're concerned with a kind of genealogy – how the past, in its traces, has come down to the present, rather than the traditional sense of history as what happened in the past.

LH: This can involve the trauma of memory.

MS: Oh, yes. This is absolutely archaeological. We often feel separate from the past, and then, in that separation, we visit a room, such as the Dante, and we instinctively look to piece together what we see in front of us. Again, working on what remains.

LH: But, in the particular case of our project, Life Squared, you're able to see the evidence being looked at and to lurk inside and watch somebody else discovering the evidence and recreate endless narratives, as they repattern the same information and create yet another trail of how it's being seen, re-seen, recomposed, remixed, so that there are an infinite number of ways you can perceive it.

MS: And, I think, our digital demeanor, as you put it, precisely foregrounds us again. I mean I could argue that it's always been a component of what we do: taking up bits of the past, reusing them, reworking them, which absolutely implicates issues of memory.

LH: And erasure of ownership.

MS: Oh, yeah, absolutely. And I'm very keen on countering this notion that, in terms of the past, we need to somehow hang on to it and preserve it.

LH: How do you preserve it? How do you embalm time?

MS: Well, yeah. In this way, to preserve the past is to kill it off. Transformation, translation is essential if the past is to live.

LH: Yes.

MS: Just yesterday, I got an email announcing a website that essentially comprises virtual reality reconstructions of ancient sites – 3D models of the forum at Rome, or a basilica, or an ancient monument in Greece. These are CAD architectural models visualized in 3D, so you can walk through them. And they're realistic, in the sense that you can admire the textures, experience the spaces. It's meant to be a very engaging experience of the past – history reconstructed in some kind of photographic verisimilitude – so that it's present to you now. But I find them utterly, utterly empty and dead.

LH: Why?

MS: Well, to walk through a room, in this way, on a computer screen, doesn't necessarily elicit any reaction other than a distracting and superficial one, such as, 'Ooh, the texture of the floor is spot on .... Ooh, I like the light coming in through that window; it's just right.'

And what generates a sense of being there is not this kind of surface authenticity, but the fidelity of narrative. The narrative of these graphics is nothing more than taking a stroll.

These models can be very flashy, highly naturalistic and look 'real' but they don't help us make sense of and understand things – floor plans or the shape of ashlar blocks give little understanding about life in the past. This is the old illusion, that a faithfulness to the external appearance of things gives us a hold on reality.

And such models forget about engagement. Not just the experience of visiting old places, but the detective work that turns data into information and then into stories that engage people now.

I sometimes think that these elaborate models of the past are part of a contemporary optimism that a quantitative increase in data will somehow deliver a better understanding of the world. In this kind of digital archaeology I see the dream

Figure 12.3 The regenerated *Dante Hotel* in construction within Second Life for *Life Squared*. Photo: Gabriella Giannachi.

that eventually, and with so much data at hand, we will be able to relive the past. This is the impossible desire to bring back the dead. I say, look, the past is over and done, decayed, ruined, lost. We only have a few bits to work on. And this is what is fascinating.

Virtual reality archaeology is a project that brings to mind the movie *The Matrix* – the creation of a world that actually doesn't or didn't exist, though it is lived as reality.

LH: The closer you get to what you think something is, the more evident it becomes that it's also an illusion.

MS: Yes. Absolutely. It's a question of what truly constitutes evidence about who you are, about who I am.

LH: It's always apparent in the flaws. You know, it's in the crack in the wall, not the replication of it. I mean, that's where the truth is. It hides, waiting to be discovered.

MS: Yeah. It's in the gaps, in the stuff that gets overlooked.

So, anyway, that issue of authenticity, I think, is a big one. Considerable resources, research dollars, and institutional support are being devoted to this kind of VR modeling. And you know, it's …

LH: It's wrong.

MS: Well, it's illusory in the Matrix sense. And there's an authenticity there, because all of the stuff that's 'left over' is on show, in high res, so you can zoom in on it and look at it in considerable detail. But by no means is it 'The Past.'

It's an interesting negotiation between our current means and the ends we have in mind for archaeology. How we document the past connects, obviously, with all sorts of technologies and instruments now. Instrumentalities relating to information, information flow and organization. The whole field of documenting ourselves is changing as our tools change.

LH: The information age requires new tools, absolutely. I'm making a piece right now that deals with the five leading blog tags in the world. It's to see what people are thinking about, a global mind-reader. Software reads key words, tags them, and makes 'judgements' about the emotional range of information. So it lets us know at a glance the mood of the global mind, as seen in constantly evolving and morphing blogs.

So many things that used to be hidden are now evidenced and present. We're inverting the exoskeleton. For example, there are some wonderful ways to photograph and scan paintings to uncover their histories.

I like to pull forward the things that we've always thought should be invisible and make that a part of the communication structure, in fact, the whole nature of a work. So the invisible becomes the aesthetic itself. Because by revealing process, we reveal meaning.

MS: As you know, I have a deep interest in the history of archaeological approaches to the world, to evidence, to information, to documentation. And it's undoubtedly the case that a lot of this interest in ruination and the interest in decay – the gothic interest in the dark side of things – is very much an eighteenth century invention, or preoccupation at least.

It's the idea, the figure, of the undead, of the renegade. It's the perverse count in some ramshackle castle who's coming back to haunt us and thereby, you know, influencing the present.

LH: Was the creation of the undead simultaneous with the invention of electricity?

MS: Well, certainly it all goes together. There was a barrage in the age of reason, the development of experimental methods, of science, of rationality. And this accompanied, of course, a romantic fascination with the other side of reason. The irrational. Whether it's mental or social or cultural. The invention of modern notions of crime comes at this same time. So, deviation, crime, all goes with this hyper-rationalized approach to nature and the world. It was about separating the rational from the irrational.

LH: And deciding which is which.

MS: Yeah and trying to decide between the two, which is connected to another component: the demarcation of what it is to be human. What is human and what isn't human.

So, it's the machine and the human, or the inhuman and the human. Or the stuff that is often seen as accoutrement to us, separate from us, whether it's the information that we generate about ourselves, our relationships, or our stuff, our material things.

So, questions of: Is it me? Is it not me? Is this trail I leave in the world around me, this archaeological trace, is it me or is it something secondary? The things I use and own, do they constitute who I am? Or are they just the things that I use? This theme of, where do I end and where does the world begin and how am I, as a person, dispersed in the socio-cultural world? This is a classic theme that has worried us – in its modern guise – since the eighteenth century. And it goes with the invention of disciplines such as archaeology, anthropology, and human and social sciences.

LH: But now we're spawning a different kind of mutation, because we're able to reconceive ourselves virally and instantly put that morphed and evolving regeneration into the world specifically so that it can be adapted and changed. So, where does that mutation leave us? Is our sense of presence, and who we are, an appendage to how we are perceived?

MS: I always say that what archaeologists have to make them distinct is the long-term view of things. Absolutely, we're made very conscious of this now. But I see all of this, really, as just coming at the end of a long, long history. I don't think it's new. I think these issues have faced us for as long as we've been human. The phrase that I use is: For as long as we've been human, we've been cyborgs; we've been intimately connected with things, with goods.

In the early days – and I'm going back to 120,000 years ago – I think what made us human was an intimacy with goods, with things, in kind of 'machine-ic' assemblages, even though they weren't formal machines.

The temple and imperial administrative bureaucracies of the ancient Near East were what Lewis Mumford called mega-machines. They built the pyramids – 20,000 horsepower running for perhaps 600 years and capable of positioning a million stone blocks accurate to a fraction of an inch.

LH: So can autonomous agents even exist, do you think? Or do you think that everything is kind of tempered by these assemblages, this sampling and remixing? How would you determine whether something is independent, isolated? It can't be, in order to function.

MS: Yeah, yeah. I've been fascinated by the way your work explores the limits of what makes someone an authentic self. As an anthropologist I agree that authenticity is not best connected solely to internal properties of an autonomous individual. We find our authentic selves in others and in our relations with goods.

LH: Everything is defined by its relation to something else.

MS: Right – think of what's happening in this room right now. That is, in the future, looking back, what would be the definitive statement, representation, of the room here and now?

There's a conversation happening between you and me, but even that is influenced by where I've come from, where you've come from, and it will take us in different directions in the future. And, I don't know, maybe in a little bit of time I'll look back on this and say, 'Ah, that was when I realized my calling was not archaeology but the arts!' So, what happened in this room was – yes, a conversation – but that was coincidental to something else that I realized, only with hindsight, had happened.

But then you might say, what's happening in this room is that the air conditioning has been switched off and the patterns of heat transfer are now apparent. As a physicist, you have a very different view of things. As an investor, perhaps your perspective is that this is the last use of the building before they redevelop it and turn it into condominiums.

So, what's going on here has no bottom line. There's no definitive answer to say, this is what's going on here, and it can therefore be represented in one way.

So, the question becomes, how do you take photographs of all of that? How do you make a video out of it all? How would you document it? That is the classic issue, I think: What is the definitive record or representation of something, an event, an occurrence, a person?

There isn't one. Now, this is not disempowering, it's the opposite. It's actually empowering, because it opens the door to actually playing with it; to remixing, reworking the processes of documentation, of engagement, whatever.

LH: And invisibility, things we can't see now, that are embedded in time, even here in this room, waiting to reveal themselves. And there are many ghosts lurking unseen that it will take generations of inventive science to understand. Our perceptions are limited to the technologies we can access.

So you really can't discard anything. It's only a matter of time before we see what economies determine as being sustainable. It is going to be surprising, not at all what we expect, not at all linear.

MS: I think what you're looking for here, very appropriately, is what I would call the politics of legacy.

LH: Of presence.

MS: Yes – the politics of presence. What is made present and what is kept absent and invisible.

LH: But it's never completely invisible, because it can always be traced.

MS: Well, there, again, in my long-term perspective – it's a very melancholic one – I think that most of history is .... Well, we've just lost it all.

LH: Ahh.

MS: And I think there is a crucial issue in our current politics, now and for the future, which is what are we able to recall, to document, to trace, and also what should be documented and traced and not kept invisible.

LH: And who makes those decisions.

MS: Absolutely, it's about power over these processes. It's a crucial issue.

Figure 12.4 Visitors in Second Life occupy room 47 of the regenerated *Dante Hotel* in *Life Squared*. Photo: Gabriella Giannachi.

At the same time, as I say, there is a melancholy about our pasts in that so much has been deliberately destroyed or concealed or forgotten. It's the politics of the past. As we all know, it's the winners who write the history books.

But I think, with this digital moment, this digital demeanor – and behind it lies the utopianism of a lot of digital culture – the tools to uncover so much are in our hands; ours and those of people who haven't had access to this kind of cultural tool before.

LH: Our memories may be gone, but they're certainly recorded now in a way that was not possible before. They're retrievable. What will be preserved and archived will depend on the priorities, cleverness, politics, and rebelliousness of each generation.

MS: Right, you're talking about the will to conserve. It's a task to conserve, to rework, precisely in the way that we took that box of stuff connected to 1972 and reworked it in 2006, 2007. That's the only way the past is going to keep going. It has to be taken up and reworked. So, in the digital proliferation of all this stuff – from the mundane, the quotidian, the everyday of people's lives – we have to see value. The only way it's going to survive to give a new angle on the present, or be the basis for a new kind of understanding of the everyday history of the twenty-first century, is if people take it up in terms of those energies you've just described.

They've got to want to do it. Material preservation won't work. Information is a verb. You have to take things up and rework them, remix them.

LH: To make them alive.

MS: To make them live again. It's reincarnation, literally. You incarnate. You give them new material forms that you engage with.

There is all this stuff, so much stuff. I think the great prospect is that some unexpected components of today are going to be taken up and remixed and reworked. Not the great, grand stories of history, not the great accounts proffered by the victors and the great, powerful figures of today. But rather the mundane, the everyday, the stuff that really makes life what it is. That would be fascinating.

And, actually, this is what archaeological science has always offered – accounts of everyday life with which we can all identify and yet find uncanny. It may simply be a thumbprint upon an ancient pot that connects an inconsequential past moment with the present; it may be the evidence of the lives of those who built a place like Stonehenge. It is the archaeological focus on the everyday that many people find fascinating.

LH: Because these are the relics of ourselves.

Chapter 13

Photographic presence
Time and the image

Nick Kaye

> The thing was there, we grasped it in the living motion of a
> comprehensive action – and once it has become an image it
> instantly becomes ungraspable, non-contemporary, impassive
> [...] the present thing in its absence, the thing graspable
> because ungraspable, appearing as something that has
> disappeared, the return of what does not come back
> (Blanchot 1999: 418)

The Californian artist Chris Burden's *White Light/White Heat*
(1975) captures an experience of presence as processual and
performative. Directed toward phenomena emerging in the interval
or delay between expectation and appearance, Burden's work
provokes a speculation and projection toward his 'performance' in
which the opposition between the space, action and presence of
self and other becomes friable and unclear, yet in which the
experience of presence unfolds in a distinctive and direct way.
Entering an otherwise empty white gallery space, the visitor
encounters Burden's installation as a wide, white plinth suspended
below ceiling level. On the wall of the gallery room a discrete
statement indicates the form and event of the work. Burden's
contemporaneous description, issued by Ronald Feldman Gallery
in announcement of the exhibition, has subsequently been
published as its documentation and is thus reproduced here, as the
artist normally requires, adjacent to the photographic record of the
event.

Figure 13.1 © Chris Burden. Courtesy Gagosian Gallery

White Light/White Heat   Chris Burden

8 February to 1 March 1975
Ronald Feldman Fine Arts, New York, New York

For my one-man show at Ronald Feldman, I requested that a large triangular platform be constructed in the southeast corner of the gallery. The platform was ten feet above the floor and two feet below the ceiling; the outer edge measured eighteen feet across. The size and height of the platform were determined by the requirement that I be able to lie flat without being visible from any point in the gallery. For twenty-two days, the duration of the show, I lay on the platform. During the entire piece, I did not eat, talk, or come down. I did not see anyone, and no one saw me.

Relic: section of board
Case: 7 x 15$^1/_4$ x 10 inches
Collection: Noel Frackman, Scarsdale, New York

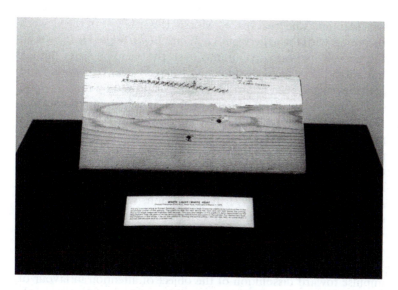

Figure 13.2 © Chris Burden. Courtesy Gagosian Gallery

White Light/White Heat	Chris Burden

8 February – March 1, 1975
Ronald Feldman Fine Arts, New York, New York

Relic: section of board
Case: 7 x 15$^1\!/_4$ x 10 inches
Collection: Noel Frackman, Scarsdale, New York

White Light/White Heat returns to the then well-established modes of minimal art installations by artists such as Robert Morris, Richard Nonas, and Donald Judd at a time in the mid-1970s when East Coast artists, including Vito Acconci, Dennis Oppenheim and others, were stepping out of 'live' performance (Acconci 1979) toward installation, architecture and video. In doing so, however, Burden's act crystallizes an address to experiences of 'liveness,' mediation and presence that finds a common thread through many of these developing forms and practices. Referencing the overt 'theatricality' of the white 'unitary forms' that had emerged from the early 1960s as sculptural interventions into the relational terms – in 'real time' and 'real space' (Morris 1993: 175) – of the viewer's encounter with the gallery object, *White Light/White Heat* casts an aggressively performative frame over the viewer's entry into a 'situation' in which distinctions between viewer, 'work' and performer have been radically eroded. Shadowed by the apparent, if self-imposed, urgency of his situation, which counterpoints and parodies the signature 'indifference' of the minimal object, Burden's proposition is aimed toward the awareness of a supplemental presence that might force 'the work' through its aesthetic frame to re-articulate the dynamic between viewer and viewed. In this respect, Burden's gesture carries an implicit logic of 'so-called minimalism' (Morris 1997) to conclusion, whereby, in directing sculptural form and function toward an intervention into the visitor's negotiation and awareness of their viewing, perceptual experience usurps the conventional place of the object. Here, too, *White Light/White Heat* is situated in relation to a post-minimalist impulse toward dissolution of the object of attention in favour of ephemeral processes and self-reflexive experiences. Such work is exemplified in installations by Bruce Nauman in the late 1960s and early 1970s (Nauman 2003) and the contemporaneous 'light and space' work of Southern Californian artists including Robert Irwin, Doug Wheeler and Michael Asher (Clark 2011). Taking such evacuations of the gallery space as a point of reference in his own analysis of the reading and experience of constructed space, the architect Bernard Tschumi argues that in this work conventional oppositions between subject and object are collapsed, as:

> By restricting visual and physical perception to the faintest of all stimulations, they turn the expected experience of the space into something altogether different. The almost totally removed sensory definition inevitably throws the viewers back on themselves. In 'deprived space' [...] the materiality of the body coincides with the materiality of space [and] the subjects' only 'experience their own experience'
>
> (Tschumi 1994: 41–2)

Yet the supplementary nature of Burden's presence complicates this mode of post-minimalist reflexivity. In contrast to the 'light and space' installations' extension of Frank Stella's celebrated maxim that 'what you see is what you see,' *White Light/White Heat* operates at a level of hypothesis, as a fiction or a conceit given material consequence by the viewer, for whom the question of Burden's presence presses forward. Resting on uncertainty, and focusing on the visitor's anticipation, Burden's act haunts the gallery in a will toward the immanence of the body and its performance. For Robert Horovitz, whose article 'Chris Burden' in *Artforum* in 1976 provided the first extended critical account of Burden's work, it is precisely this projection toward 'presence' in denials and withholdings through which '[t]he piece dominates its space effortlessly' (Horovitz 1976: 24). Here:

> The assumption that he is there alters everything – but I don't know for a fact that he really *is* there. I become 'it' in an unannounced game of hide-and-seek. I listen for telltale rustling, any breathing noises. The many small sounds that fill the gallery are magnified by my attention [...] The room is haunted.
>
> (Horovitz 1976: 24, original emphasis)

It is a haunting of space that also prompts an experience of 'presence' as divided and palimpsestual. Indeed, the uncanny effect and fascination this installation provokes perhaps lies less in the question of whether or not Burden 'is present,' so much as the visitor's realization that they may perceive only their projection of themselves. In this case, the phenomenon of Burden's 'presence' occurs in the sense of an interval, a difference, in the location of one's own presence in the installation. In retrospect, Burden recounted his own participation, too, as inhabiting the actions of those from whom he obscured himself:

> I participated kind of like a ghost, in everything that would happen in the gallery, because I could hear everything [...] I had day after day where the gallery opened up, and people would start coming in, and business would happen in the gallery, and I would participate in everything on a vicarious level.
>
> (Burden in White 1979: 15)

It is an approach to performance that also reflects the pre-occupations and tactics of earlier 'body art' work, which engaged with questions of the body's presence and its construction in and after the event. Thus for Dennis Oppenheim and Vito Acconci developing body-based artworks through live performance, video and photographic documentation in New York in the late 1960s and early 1970s, the body provided a 'de-materialized zone of psychological topology' (Oppenheim in Kaye 1996: 66) that would evade the limits of the 'object' in processual, excessive and ephemeral acts that also resisted reproduction. '[O]ne of the most catalytic aspects of Body Art,' Oppenheim later recalled, 'was this connection to the real world' (Oppenheim in Kaye 1996: 66), a connection that led him to emphasize the situated body and inter-connected phenomena in time. In turn, the visual expression and remainder of such events were frequently positioned as documentation displaced from the 'real time' centre of an act or event which may or may not have directly addressed a once 'present' audience. Indeed, Burden's own most notorious 'performances,' including *Shoot* (1971), *Trans-Fixed* (1974) and *747* (1973) occurred in the absence of knowing spectators, to be disseminated as carefully selected photographic remainders (Auslander 2006) seemingly charged by the 'real' acts to which they claim to be witness. Such methods work against both the conventional spectacle of performance and the binary opposition between performance and documentation. Consistently with this, in the event, *White Light/White Heat* provokes a heightened sense of simultaneous investment in and 'being before' Burden's action driven and shaped in his refusal to come to visibility. It is a gesture then reproduced in Burden's photographic documentation, in which his 'act' remains unavailable to view and in whose absence the image also obtains its peculiar charge.

In their emphasis on the relational dynamics in which the body is performed and perceived and the resistance of time-based processes to the documentary image, these engagements with presence may also be set against the influential poet and existentialist thinker Maurice Blanchot's association of 'the real' with ephemeral phenomena at once encountered and betrayed in their representation. Blanchot's attention to the act of reading and to modes of reflexivity in art and literature published in French from 1941 and disseminated widely in English from 1973 offer an articulation of the practice of writing, a privileging of experience and a scepticism toward the image that has had an overt influence on contemporary art engaging with presence as theme and phenomena[1]. Blanchot's emphasis, too, is consistent with the broad engagement with phenomenology that underpinned the emergence of the 'body art' practices in the 1960s and 1970s and in which latterly Burden's work participated. Thus, for Acconci, among others, approaches to the body in performance defined in the wave of post-minimal body work in the late 1960s were overtly influenced by then recent and contemporaneous publications by Maurice Merleau-Ponty (Blocker 2004: 27). Reflecting back on his steps into actions and performance from 1969, Acconci himself concluded in this phenomenological vein that: '[o]ne thing I learned through working with the body is that you can't think of it as an object' (Acconci in Nemser 1971: 21).

Approaching encounters with 'the real' as inseparable from a motion, an action or emergent process of comprehension that arrives, finally, at the stillness of the 'image,' Blanchot's writing emphasizes a dynamic relationship between sign and referent in which experiences of presence are shaped. In this context, Blanchot proposes in his essay 'Two Versions of the Imaginary,' first published in English in 1981, and echoing Emmanuel Levinas' phenomenology of an 'I' defined by 'infinity' and so openness to the 'other' (Levinas 1969: 26–7), '[t]he 'real' is that with which our relationship is always alive and which always leaves us the initiative' (Blanchot 1999: 418). Yet this phenomenon, he suggests, is grasped through art only in the very process in which the image – and so representation – emerges to obscure this 'living motion,' such that the image comes to announce 'the present thing in its absence [...] appearing as something that has disappeared' (Blanchot 1999: 418). For Blanchot, this leads to a formulation in which approaches to 'the real' in art come to be linked necessarily to art's interrogation of its own form and identity, and to an opening of itself to question. '[L]iterature,' Blanchot thus emphasizes, 'begins at the moment when literature becomes a question,' such that '[t]o make literature become the exposure of this emptiness inside, to make it open up completely to its nothingness' is to 'realize its own unreality' (Blanchot 1999a: 359–60). For Blanchot, also, this interrogation of means and forms is linked to the reader's agency, whereby, as the work negates itself, so '[t]he reader makes the work; as he reads it, he creates it; he is its real author, he is the consciousness and the living substance of the written thing' (Blanchot 1999a: 364–5). Read in relation to this account of the dynamic between action, event and image, Burden's *White Light/White Heat* offers the visitor an encounter defined in displacements of the image in favour of the viewer's agency and an emergent presence that anticipates and so precedes the spectacle of 'performance'.

This postponement and process, in which the viewer is installed as the agent of the work, and in which the artwork engages with 'the living motion of a comprehensive action,' is implicit not only to Burden's engagement with 'performance' in *White Light/White Heat*, but also in the relationship between this event and its photographic documentation. Where the experience of *White Light/White Heat* is prompted and unfolds in Burden's refusal to appear, so there is no straightforward opposition between Burden's event and the image and text that circulates as its remainder. Burden's descriptive text also provokes questions over this opposition, where, published in advance of the event, his account is written in the past tense, and so in anticipation of a documentary record. In these respects, the textual and photographic re-presentation of Burden's installation also marks the various tenses and intervals in which this work functions.

Indeed, as 'documentation,' Burden's account of *White Light/White Heat* participates more broadly in a genre of 'performed photography,' a mode of work that frequently announces itself in articulations of the intervals and slips of tenses and times between event, act and record. Invariably posing the question of where performance occurs or is constituted, and explicitly engaging with questions and experiences of presence, it is a mode of work, which, after Jon Erickson, the performance theorist Phillip Auslander considers to range from:

> Marcel Duchamp's photos of himself as Rrose Selavy to Cindy Sherman's photographs of herself in various guises to Matthew Barney's Cremaster films [...] These are cases in which performances were staged solely to be photographed or filmed and had no meaningful prior existence as autonomous events presented to audiences. The space of the document (whether visual or audiovisual) thus becomes the only space in which the performance occurs.
>
> (Auslander 2006: 2)

Here, it is the image's relationship with a past event that Auslander emphasizes, proposing that in this photography, 'performance' is constructed in the space and practice of the image itself, so revealing, after J. L. Austin's theory of speech acts, '[t]he performativity of documentation itself' whereby:

the act of documenting an event as a performance is what constitutes it as such. Documentation does not simply generate image/statements that describe an autonomous performance and state that it occurred: it produces an event as performance and, as Frazer Ward suggests, the performer as 'artist'.

(Auslander 2006: 5)

In this formulation, the 'performativity of documentation' presses toward the construction or reinforcement of a settled relationship between a past event and its definition in the space of a 'present' image.

As a category of work, however, 'performed photography' can readily be extended to embrace multiple relationships between performance and its remainder, many of which call into question oppositions between image and event. Thus the exhibition *Staging Action – Performance in Photography Since 1960*, presented at the Museum of Modern Art, New York, January to May 2011, embraced the 'documentation' of performed actions by Gunther Brus, Hermann Nitsch and the Vienna Actionists; the photographic record of events, actions and situations by Vito Acconci; as well as Cindy Sherman's untitled film stills, Ana Mandieta's *Untitled Facial-Cosmetic Variations* (January–February 1972) and Lucas Samaras' *Auto Polariod* (1960–71). This work ranges across radically different exchanges between image and performance: from photographic records of Nitsch's *Orgien Mysterien Theatre* and Brus' simulation of ritual actions on the body, to Acconci's elusive encounters or interventions into specific sites whose circulation has been primarily in their representation, to 'auto-performances' playing on the performativity of self and identity in which exposures of the act of self-representation intrude on various genres, including portrait photography, film and other media.

The range of work in *Staging Action* suggests that the dynamics between performance, image and record may equally serve to amplify or multiply the uncertainties over the identity of form and practice, rather than determine temporal and other relationships with a past event. Thus each of these images or image-sequences installs, announces and conditions its reception with reference to its multiple times: the times of action, record, staging, but also frequently production and reading. It is an incursion of the temporal that calls the image into question and that undermines its autonomy. In this respect, 'performed photography' may also serve to advance the impulse toward event and performance within much visual art, that has frequently aimed toward interrogating and unsettling rather than resolving the established terms of the object, text, or artist-viewer relationship. Recalling his own steps into 'live' work, Vito Acconci thus recalled, in 1989, that, far from asserting a new performative form, his eclectic engagements with situated events or acts sought to displace and disturb the place and role of artist, viewer and work, noting that: '[w]e hated the word "performance," because "performance" had a place, and that place by tradition was a theatre' (Acconci 2001: 358). Far from settling the identity of performance or making available an earlier event in another form, the 'documentation' of such activity frequently sought to further examine and complicate the field, time, and event of that to which it referred, as an extension of the original impulse and purpose. An analogous dynamic operates in Burden's record of *White Light/White Heat*. Where the 'performance' was 'itself' unavailable, so Burden's image renews and extends this gesture rather than render his act visible or construct a stable point against which the past event is redefined or positioned: Burden's image is empty, mute. Performance documentation, and performed photography, through this lens, may also extend the performativity of the 'event' in relation to the reader or viewers, opening further the field and eclecticism of the work.

Read in relation to Blanchot's analysis, such performativity also operates more radically again, toward the provocation and articulation of ideas and experiences of 'presentness'. Where phenomena of presence occur in time – and so where presence is processual – the experience of presence may be produced in mechanisms of refusal and delay; in provocations of anticipation and projection with regard to the emergence of the 'image,' of this 'limit next to the indefinite' (Blanchot 1999: 417). After Blanchot, then, it may be argued that the photograph, or more broadly the image, provokes experiences of presence in the very lack in which it obtains its relationship to its object: in the rhythm of appearance and disappearance in which a 'living motion' is recalled or produced, described and elaborated – in a self-negation that invokes and lends the viewer agency. Here, where 'performance' is deployed, represented or referred to in such a way as to effect a sense of a lack, gap, or interval in relation to the image, where the image 'becomes a question,' then this may itself become a focus for

Figure 13.3 Cindy Sherman, Untitled Film Still (1977).
Black and white photograph 8 x 10 inches (image size)
20.3 x 25.4 cm; 13$^5/_8$ x 16$^1/_8$ inches (frame size) 31.4 x 40.3 cm.
Edition of 10. Courtesy of the artist and Metro Pictures.

engagements with presence. In such photographic work, the figure of 'performance' conditions and informs the 'presence' of the image to the reader, rather than deferring to a performance past.

In these contexts, Cindy Sherman's celebrated untitled film stills can be seen to gain their uncanny effect precisely in the absence of the 'performances' to which they seem to refer. Originally exhibited in series, in which Sherman's role or identity is re-made in diverse, fragmented and ambiguous references to film genre, narrative and framing – and in overtly constructed moments of 'film performance' – these images also refer to and open the processes of their own making. Here, too, the performative quality of Sherman's gestures are revealed and extended in their presentation against overtly projected backgrounds that articulate the construction of the image, an effect amplified by these images exhibition in sequence. In these mechanisms, the 'presence' of 'Sherman' to the image is asserted in an overt layering and in separations that create the appearance of a doubling; a sense of the image standing before itself or in separation from itself. It is in these separations that these fabricated or imagined self-portraits also gain their charge of 'liveness,' and so a quality of 'documentation' and 'performance' that exceeds its film references. Such tactics amplify the sense of an act performed and now lost: an act that engages with these images' displacement to and from the performance, to and from the dramatic flow and film medium their composition and framing implies. Indeed these images' 'incompletion,' their reference out of frame, their gesture toward intermedia, all contribute to the rhythm that Blanchot describes: the movement toward and away from a resolution of the event into the image. Here, finally, it is in the articulation of the interval in which the performativity of the image arises, that a sense of an emergent presence is evoked.

Where Sherman's work emphasizes a recovery and representation of time, other contemporary photographic work has explored a performativity of presence in relation to images and constructions of space. For Doug Hall, whose influential work developed in the San Francisco Bay Area through performance, video and installation from the 1960s, including collaborations as T. R. Uthco and with the media collective Ant Farm, toward more recent large-format photography, the still image has provided a means of engaging with qualities and effects that lie beyond the conventional field of the photograph. Hall recalls that: 'I came to photography through the back door, *via* video and installation. As a result my original interests were less photographic and more spatial' (Hall 2000: 2). In his Anonymous Places series from 1989–91, comprising images of ostensibly 'empty' institutional interiors, and also his images of Archives, Museums and Opera Houses created in 1997 and 2002, Hall's work interrogated the architectural gaze and the 'spatial uncanny' (Hall 2010: 2) expressed in various dynamics between space, image and act. Here, too, his photography invariably pressed toward a doubling or layering of vision and perspective, in revelations of the camera's 'look' and, implicitly, the gaze of both artist and viewer. In relation to his work in 2002, in particular, Hall recalled:

> I became more and more aware of the scopic quality of the opera houses. What I mean by that is that, as I stood at centre stage and looked back toward the halls, I felt as if the halls themselves were looking back at me so that in a sense I was photographing not just the spaces, but the act of looking itself.
> (Hall 2005: 4)

This effect of a doubling is also driven at the level of meaning, and specifically in the assertion of an interval between the image and its significance; an interval advanced by the representation of

Figure 13.4 Doug Hall, *Teatro Dell'Opera*, Rome (2002). Courtesy of the artist.

ostensibly 'empty' spaces. Indeed, these images purposefully reproduce architectures that marshal the gaze and that are cultural sites created for the overt production of meaning and value in individual and communal acts of looking. In these respects, these works exemplify an effect that Hall identifies more broadly with his work, whereby large-scale still images of the everyday press toward 'allegory,' noting that: '[b]y 'allegorical' I mean that the photograph, in its stark literalness, distances itself from the world-as-fact.' (Hall 2003: 6). In this event, and in their 'stark literalness,' these photographs gain an uncanny effect in their sense of the image's distance from 'itself,' produced in the reader's impulse toward metaphor even as the 'empty' image remains mute. Here, where the interval between image and meaning intrudes upon and shapes the viewer's experience of reading the photograph, so the viewer's awareness of the time of reading, and the image as an index of the time of looking, intervenes into their experience. Yet the meaning of this image inevitably remains unresolved. Here, Hall's images work to capture in their 'emptiness' a layering of gazes in which the artist's own photographic act is reflected upon and amplified; an act that the auditorium seems to uncannily testify to and reproduce. Hall recalls that 'when standing on the stage and photographing the empty halls':

On more than one occasion, the ornate spaces seemed to be staring back at me. I felt as if I was caught in he gaze from a source I couldn't identify and that what I was actually photographing was not just a room, but the act of looking itself. I understand that on the surface this is completely logical: that centre stage where I was standing (and where the viewer of the photograph also stands) is the optical and perspectival hub to and from which all vision radiates. The result is that I, the photographer, and you, the viewer of the photograph, find ourselves at the centre of a world at least as it is defined by this interior. With the empty seats and vacant tiers of boxes arrayed before us, we are aware of ourselves as both the one seeing and the ones being seen.

(Hall 2005: 3)

In their introduction of the experience of layering, too, these images both reproduce and provoke, for Hall, a sense that 'I was photographing not just the spaces, but the act of looking itself' (Hall 2005: 4). It is here, then, that an uncanny sense of presence emerges in response to these photographs, as 'I,' the viewer, become present to 'my' reading of the image, and to the layering of gazes in which my looking is caught, so prompting a sense of agency in and before the image. It is also a presence and effect that moves closer toward the tactics engaged in Burden's installation. Hall records that:

The final twist to this and the thing that made it all a little unsettling was the distinct impression that I had been caught looking at myself by a presence that I can now only identify as being both myself and other than myself. An odd equation emerges: I see myself looking at myself looking at myself and the result is a real and perceptible unease.

(Hall 2005: 4)

Such engagements with presence and the image are also evident in the extended series of performance-related images, *Empty Stages*, by the UK-based photographer Hugo Glendinning created in collaboration with the writer, artist and artistic director of Forced Entertainment, Tim Etchells. Initiated in 2003 and continuing, Glendinning and Etchells' images draw directly on practices of theatre and performance documentation, to which Glendinning is

Figure 13.5 Tim Etchells and Hugo Glendinning, from *Empty Stages* (2003). Courtesy of the artists.

also extensively committed, yet the charge of these images lies precisely in the absences to which they claim to be witness and their carefully composed ambivalence toward the meanings of the spaces they present. Etchells recounts that:

> Each of the images shows some kind of raised platform in locations such as working men's clubs, village halls, amateur theatres and city squares – as well as grander prosceniums in theatres, opera houses and the like, in different parts of the world. Each of these stages is empty – no actors or technicians, and empty auditoria – but in a strange way I think of them as performance photographs. They're spaces of expectation and waiting, certainly, but also of imagining.
>
> (Etchells 2009)

Glendinning and Etchells' images invite, again, a sense of doubling, in which the reader becomes subject to the image's reproduction of the stage's demand for meaning, and its apparent anticipation of theatrical presence and purpose. It is an anticipation further provoked and amplified by the semiotics of the theatrical function and its cultural and aesthetic apparatus. Yet *Empty Stages* operates in a palpable denial of that which these spaces invoke. Laden with their meaning-making function, yet seemingly absent from the performance of this meaning, these images invoke their own uncanny double – becoming 'meaningful' in their very lack of signification; 'present' in their emphatic assertion of absence as the object of attention. In a recent interview with Gabriella Giannachi, Glendinning linked this gesture to that of Forced Entertainment's live performances and media work, which also pay close attention to the performance and modulation of presence, noting that:

> there's an impulse in his work with the company to view or underline the idea of the stage as a kind of container – a volume to be filled either literally or imaginatively in the performance. Many of the performances come back to this idea – the empty frame or container of the stage … a space of potential.
>
> (Glendinning in Giannachi 2011: 87)

This 'space of potential' marks the incursion of time and expectation into the viewer's relationship with the image, so reinforcing the event of the uncanny and the reading and experience of presence. Indeed, in these images, the sense that the still image captures and provokes a sense of the temporal, and a pressing forward to the future, toward an unrealizable potential, is an integral part of their effect. Glendinning himself concludes that it is here that the link to 'liveness' is most evident, noting that: 'I think the *Empty Stages* give you a kind of photographic space that's like the experience of being in a live performance, where you can imagine, wander in that space forward and backwards in time' (Glendinning in Giannachi 2011: 91).

Such tactics again bring performance forward in the functioning of the image, in modes of work that emphasize process and disjunction, memory and anticipation in the reading and production of 'presence'. Jon Erickson, writing in *The Fate of the Object: From Modern Object to Postmodern Sign in Performance, Art, and Poetry* (1998) observes the articulation of the performer's presence in disjunctive temporal relationships between the body, action, and language, noting: 'Presence' in the theater is a physicality in the present that at the same time is grounded in a form of absence. It is something that has unfolded, is read against what has been seen, and is presently observed in expectation as to what will be seen (Erickson, 1998: 62). Erickson concludes, '[p]resence has an inverse relationship to language,' arising in the moment where the body is *there* and yet '[o]ne is holding back the articulate meaning that the audience is expecting' (Erickson, 1998: 62). In these images, similarly, it is that which escapes representation or articulation, and so in a dynamic relationship between that which the image has stilled, and that which it denies, in which the layering of gaze and engagement provokes an uncanny sense of the presence of performance in and before the image. For Tim Etchells, too, and specifically with regard to performance, it is precisely through this introduction of the interval, the gap, and its consequences for viewing, that presence is articulated. In his interview in this volume, Etchells recalls that in witnessing Forced Entertainment's performance:

> I am aware of people on a number of levels, like I'm seeing past one layer of what they are doing to another layer and then maybe to another. Perhaps there's something important about this experience that we have, of seeing layers of information, the feeling that we are seeing through, from one layer to another to another. As watchers, we aggregate all of that information and we make a kind of map that allows us to say: there's somebody there. None of those layers is quite enough on its own – presence is to do with the combination.

In these contexts, and in amplifying the work of the 'reader' through layering or veiling, Etchells proposes, it is absence, lack, and even obstruction that drives the reading and so effect of 'presence'. Such tactics may clearly be set against the 'interval' in Blanchot, and so aligned with a scepticism toward the image that postpones its resolution in favour of the agency of the one who looks or reads.

chris burden

Figure 13.6 © Chris Burden. Courtesy Gagosian Gallery

While implicit in many of his photographic remainders of performances, Chris Burden's approach to audiences in the event of performance also incorporated this construction of the interval or difference. Where Burden's images of *White Light/White Heat* replay the muteness in which the original installation functioned, in other work the interval is installed as a primary mechanism of the event, which subsequently works against the attempt to

La Chiaraficazione   Chris Burden

5 May 5 1975
Galleria Alessandra Castelli, Milan, Italy

The Castelli Gallery consists of a series of rooms, all of different sizes and configurations. One room was unusual in that it had only one small entrance and no windows. In this room, I placed twenty-five chairs in four rows in the traditional manner of theater seating. I waited until eleven people had entered the room and then sealed off the entrance from the inside with particle board. An assistant placed a second panel on the other side which he painted white to match the gallery walls. The majority of the audience, about one hundred and fifty people, was locked out of the room and could only imagine what was happening within. Inside the room, I spoke to the eleven people in Italian and convinced them to stay in the room until someone broke in from the outside. I told them that they were the sculpture and the responsibility for the success of the piece rested with them. I had provided twelve bottles of mineral water, candles, and a makeshift toilet. After we had been in the room about an hour and half, the audience in the main gallery removed the outer panel and smashed the inner panel to gain access to the room. The room was left untouched for the remainder of the show.

separate the 'performance' from its record, or dissemination through 'performed photography'. Produced in Milan in the same year as *White Light/White Heat*, *La Chiaraficazione* thus operated in a series of deferrals of presence, as a performance never fully resolved into appearance to its audience or performers and whose principal remainder are charged yet 'empty' images.

Figure 13.7 © Chris Burden. Courtesy Gagosian Gallery

La Chiaraficazione   Chris Burden

5 May 1975
Galleria Alessandra Castelli, Milan, Italy

Relic: Hammer
Case: 5½ x 22¾ x 9¼ inches
Collection: Harvey La Tourette, Los Angeles, California

La Chiaraficazione poses the question of where its 'present tense' lies. Indeed, the 'presence' of this work is always subject to the interval and to difference, both in its 'original' operation and in its documentation. Thus Burden's spectator-collaborators await their audience, in anticipation of 'their performance,' only to discover, in their audience's appearance, that the event ends, to be displaced toward its remainders; the broken door, the description and Burden's photographs. In this moment, and through these remains, *La Chiaraficazione* works to cast a frame of performance in retrospect over these various 'audience's' actions; over the forcible intrusion; over the 'spectator-performer's' waiting and anticipation; which in turn becomes the past event to which the 'present' work defers. In Burden's expression of *La Chiaraficazione* in 'performed photography,' it is the 'absences,' too, that are re-staged, in a mode of presentation that extends this installation's capture of ephemeral acts within the everyday – acts framed retrospectively as in 'the real' and that cannot come to 'performance' or 'the image' without being transformed. Here performance, documentation and the photographic image each operate in the incursion of the interval, and the concomitant denial or resistance to the image – in explorations of a presence subject to 'other' times. In its 'documentation,' the performance of *La Chiaraficazione* does not remain, yet it is in this image's very refusal to bring its performance to appearance that the persistence of presence is felt and in which the potential of this event is most powerfully recalled and reproduced.

Works cited

Acconci, V. (1979) 'Steps Into Performance (And Out)' in A. A. Bronson and P. Gale (eds) *Performance By Artists*, Toronto: Art Metropole. 27–40.

——(2001 [1989]) 'Performance After the Fact' in G. Moure (ed.) *Vito Acconci: Writings, Works, Projects*, Barcelona: Ediciones Poligrafa, 358–9.

Auslander, P. (2006) 'The Performativity of Performance Documentation', *PAJ: A Journal of Performance and Art*, 28:3, 1–10

Blanchot, M. (1999) 'Two versions of the imaginary' in G. Quasha (ed.) *The Station Hill Blanchot Reader*, translated by L. Davis, P. Auster and R. Lamberton, Barrytown, NY: Station Hill Press, 417–28.

——(1999a) 'Literature and the right to death' in G. Quasha (ed.) *The Station Hill Blanchot Reader*, translated by L. Davis, P. Auster and R. Lamberton, Barrytown, NY: Station Hill Press, 359–99.

Blocker, J. (2004) *What the Body Cost: Desire, History and Performance*, Minneapolis MN: University if Minnesota Press.

Clark, R. (2011) *Phenomenal: California Light, Space, Surface*, Berkeley CA: University of California Press.

Erickson, J. (1998) *The Fate of the Object: From Modern Object to Postmodern Sign in Performance, Poetry, Art, Media*, Ann Arbor MI: University of Michigan Press.

Etchells, T. (2009) 'Tim Etchells on performance: the drama of an empty stage', guardian.co.uk 1 December 2009. Online. Available at: www.guardian.co.uk/stage/2009/dec/01/tim-etchells-photograph-empty-stage (accessed 12 June 2011).

Giannachi, G. (2009) 'The Making of *Empty Stages* by Tim Etchells and Hugo Glendinning – An Interview with Hugo Glendinning', *Leonardo Electronic Almanac*, 17:1, 84–99.

Giannachi, G. and Kaye, N. (2011) *Performing Presence: Between the live and the simulated*, Manchester: Manchester University Press.

Hall, D. (2000) 'Note to Andrew Grundberg Concerning His Essay for a Forthcoming Catalog' in D. Hall, *Short Statements*, 2–3. Online. Available at: http://doughallstudio.com/storage/On%20Opera%20Houses.pdf (accessed 12/06/11).

——(2003) 'Artist Statement for Atelier Books' in D. Hall, *Short Statements*, 6–7. Online. Available at: http://doughallstudio.com/storage/On%20Opera%20Houses.pdf (accessed 12 June 2011).

——(2005) 'Concerning the Opera Houses'. Online. Available at: http://doughallstudio.com/storage/On%20Opera%20Houses.pdf (accessed 12 June 2011).

——(2010) 'Paradise – Notes on Photographs'. Online. Available at: http://doughallstudio.com/storage/Notes%20on%20Paradise.pdf (accessed 12 June 2011).

Levinas, E. (1969 [1961]) *Totality and Infinity: An Essay on Exteriority*, translated by A. Lingis, Pittsburgh PA: Duquesne University Press.

Horvitz, R. (1976) 'Chris Burden', *Artforum* 14:9, 24–31.

Morris, R. (1993 [1978]) 'The Present Tense of Space' in R. Morris *Continuous Project Altered Daily: The Writings of Robert Morris*, London: MIT Press, 175–210.

——(1997) Interview with Nick Kaye, New York, 8 April.

Nauman, B. (2003) *Bruce Nauman: Theaters of Experience*, New York: Solomon R. Guggenheim Museum.

Nemser, C. (1971) 'An Interview with Vito Acconci', *Arts Magazine*, 5, 20–3.

Royle , N. (2003) *The Uncanny*, Manchester: Manchester University Press.

Tschumi, B. (1994 [1975]) 'The Architectural Paradox' in B. Tschumi *Architecture and Disjunction*, London: MIT Press, 27–52.

White, R. (1979) 'Interview with Chris Burden by Robin White' *View* 1:8, whole issue, Oakland: Crown Point Press.

Notes

1 See, for example, the video artist Gary Hill's discussion of his engagement with Blanchot's writing in Giannachi and Kaye 2011: 81–2. Hill's single-channel video *Incidence of Catastrophe* (1987–88) was inspired by Blanchot's novel *Thomas the Obscure* while other works have reflected his response to Blanchot's writing more broadly.

Chapter 14

Neither here nor there ...

Let's talk about adult matters ...

Mike Pearson

Figure 14.1 Me and her, Hibaldstow, January 1950.

I stood in the village churchyard with her, beneath the raucous rookery, on the carpet of fallen nest-twigs, over the grave of her grandfather Alfred Falkland Rogers, who was born in the Falkland Islands and who, though miles from any sea, wore his sailor's jersey to the end.

And she handed me the copy of my childhood psalter – *The Cathedral Psalter with Proper Psalms*; 'Michael Pearson, Age. 8 years.' inscribed in my late father's hand in the front. I opened it, and read these words:

For my days are consumed away like smoke,
and my bones are burnt up as it were a firebrand.
My heart is smitten down and withered like grass;
so that I forget to eat my bread.
For the voice of my groaning my bones will scarce cleave to
my flesh.
I am become like a pelican in the wilderness,
And like an owl that is in the desert.
I have watched and am even as it were a sparrow,
That sitteth alone upon the house-top.

Mine enemies revile me all day long;
and they that are mad upon me are sworn together against
me.
For I have eaten ashes as it were bread, and mingled my drink
with weeping.
And that because of thine indignation and wrath:
for thou hast taken me up and cast me down.
My days are gone like a shadow, and I am withered like
grass.

(Psalm 109, 3–11)

And I remembered singing, in the half-light of the church, incense decaying to its half-life in the cold, still air: trying to make sense of the dashes and asterisks, marks of pause and breath that score the text; understanding little of the jealousy and violence and rapture that soak the words. Remembered Reverend Clay's scrawny neck in his hard white collar. Remembered how close Evensong and the closing of day had seemed to the closing of life, as the cracked voices of the scattering of aged parishioners struggled to make anything but their own requiem from these great sad songs to a terrible and despotic god.

Wondered what a childish imagination had made of words of anguish and self-loathing, of despair and rage: words of longing and regret, of remorse, and of the smallest hope of deliverance and reconciliation.

Pause and sit[1]

She had just fallen. Had struck her head on the kitchen floor. Had somehow risen. Had broken nothing, this time. Had encouraged visitors to feel the lump – carers who were caring enough but not taking care. Who came to administer pills and sandwiches – pills that stop the trembles, that strengthen the bones – and to complete the forms that said they had administered the pills and sandwiches, pills that stop ... Who flitted in, and out, four times a day: markers of the passing of the daylight hours.

House bound, chair bound; her world, that just within reach. She would occasionally rise and shuffle, pushing the wheeled trolley, at which she ate, her preferred aid to locomotion: on missions already forgotten after the first few steps. The mats had been removed, impediments dispersed; she was warned to avoid the kettle.

She was off-balance, out of kilter: turning and reversing, arduous and fraught. For she had no self-defence, the slightest falter always a fall. First time was in Marks and Spencer's, standing on her scarf, in Blackpool, 'Fracture Capital of the North': obstacle course for elderly trippers. But they knew how to do it; screwed her hip together.

Second time was in the yard, struggling with the wheelie bin. Sat down, hard.

They did nothing. But her spine was rattled. The only relief, a beanbag heated in the microwave.

Then others, some witnessed, others unseen ... Recently she had lain helpless in the bathroom, through the hours of darkness, though she couldn't tell ... Her slippers had refused to slide, she said, pitching her forward. But safe, this time.

She was in peril, a danger to herself, in need of care and protection. Particularly at night: alone for twelve hours. Particularly after it had all begun to become one, without measure.

But they were locked down at the home, everyone sick, couldn't take her. Didn't want us coming round. So we spent a week together, mother and son reunited.

It was bleak, desperate; called upon to do all she had once done for me. And often silent ...

She slept much, her head far forward, her teeth sometimes slipping out; her waking schedule, the meals that she no longer relished.

I slept little, and once when I did, I failed her. She was wandering throughout the night, attending to this or that, that needed attending to; busy at jobs that evaporated as soon as started. And she fell often. Once I found her half out of bed, frozen in a moment of descending or ascending.

I listened out for sounds of impending disaster. I thought she was just talking in her sleep. It was a small cry for help. Next morning it was a crime scene: trolley overturned, clothes scattered, drawer pulled out. Her: slumped against the cupboard. 'I'm alright' she said. Safe, this time.

> She was a school cook. Every week she would arrive home with some terrible burn to the forearm, some new cut to the bone. The worst was when a catering-sized can of processed peas slipped from a shelf and hit her on the bridge of the nose, breaking it instantly.
>
> (*From Memory*, 1992)

And she talked – with workmates, with children, with her beloved mother – incessantly. Opinions proclaimed; thoughts for the day mulled over: fearless in correcting table manners, all manners. Now she went quiet, saying nothing without prompt, speaking only in response, though often recalling details at a stretch of memory, in moments of lucidity.

'I think she's got a urine infection' said a carer. 'Can you get a sample?' said a doctor. 'Use any domestic container.' I was out of my depth.

And then they said they could take her. She answered all their questions clearly – date-of-birth, likes and dislikes; wanted the hairdresser, the chiropodist, though unsure about seeing the vicar. 'I've got Parkinson's.'

As I lifted her into the car something cracked. She winced then said 'I'm alright'.

Brittle, fragile; I might break her.

Walter Benjamin once wrote:

> There used to be no house, hardly a room in which someone had not died. Today people live in rooms that have never been touched by death, dry dwellers of eternity, and when their end approaches they are stored away in sanatoria or hospitals by their heirs.
>
> (Benjamin 1992: 93)

I left. Out of sight, out of ... I felt elated.

Three days later when no one was paying particular attention – in broad daylight, when backs were turned – she fell, destroying her elbow. 'I'm alright' she said. But she wasn't, this time.

Next morning she wouldn't, couldn't, eat; drink. They dialled 999, summoning transport to a circle of hell. It would need wiring up, they said. Or she would forever remain in pain, they said. 'At least it's her bad arm' someone added – her hand closed with arthritis.

But infected, dehydrated, she was unfit to be operated upon. And as they pumped her with fluid, through the back of her good hand, it collected in her lungs. Pneumonia next.

By the time I got there, things were grave. They took me aside, into a room marked 'Quiet Room': consultant, doctor, matron – holy triumvirate. Asked me her history, her life history: of falls and eating habits. Told me about the drop in blood pressure. Prepared me for the worst, in an 'only to be expected', 'at her age' kind of way. But they would maintain for twenty-four hours. Thank God it was a weekend; twenty-four became forty-eight.

We started making ready, discussing the likely sequence of events. Grown ups at last: doing adult business.

It was a shock. I took flowers and took them away again. She was tiny. Tubes in her arm that she pulled at; tubes up her nose that rubbed it sore. Everywhere veins suddenly at the surface. Without her teeth, her face collapsed, skin drawn tight on her skull; her wispy white hair matted. 'You look more like *her* than your father' someone said.

> I am the family face;
> Flesh perishes, I live on,
> Projecting trait and trace
> Through time, to times anon,
> And leaping from place to place
> Over oblivion.
>
> The years-heired feature that can
> In curve and voice and eye
> Despise the human span
> Of durance – that is I;
> The eternal thing in man,
> That heeds no call to die.
>   (Hardy 1993: 103–4)

After a man has turned fifty, he wears the face he deserves.

Her breath came in the faintest pants and puffs, her chest fluttering, her mouth caked and dry, skin peeling from her lips.

Figure 14.2 Me and her, Hibaldstow, April 2000. During *Bubbling Tom* (2000).
Photo: Hugo Glendinning.

We held her hand; we stroked her cheeks; we whispered to her.

Sometimes she would tense, her arms mimicking a tree in some childish game. Often she tugged at her nightgown, and pointed to figures assembling on the bed.

Sometime she was with us, sometimes not, often betwixt and between: 'presence' and 'absence' bereft of meaning. Only once did she say 'I wish I was dead.' And then, echoing a distant conversation I barely registered, 'I wish I was in heaven too'.

Where was she? Often, eyes closed, she seemed to commentate on the private screening of a film: our voices become 'noises off' in the scene before her.

Sometimes she seemed to be with others: old, familiar faces in old, familiar settings. Often involving some imperative, something needing to be done: "Where shall I sit?' she said; 'I shortened her dress you know, and his suits. He was a short, little man.'

Once it was her mother. 'She never helped me' she said, some lasting moment of grievance or disappointment resurfacing, rankling.

Nan only ever trimmed her hair.
It grew below her waist,
Coiled round her head for work.
Then, just two weeks before she died,
They cut it all off, to make it more comfortable for her,
Or so they said.
I think it killed her.

(From Memory, 1992)

We brushed *her* hair. She smiled.

Others long passed, surely present again: her father who had very cold hands. He was the local bonesetter.

He was particularly good with lumbago, a typical farm labourer's complaint. I remember one Saturday afternoon, a young boy arriving from the village football team, the Hibaldstow Hotspurs, in great pain, his collar completely dislocated. Calmly, Grandad asked him to lie on the hearthrug and gently took him by the hand. And then he pulled!

Her mother-in-law who had muttered 'I never liked her' once, as she was leaving the home where the village elders sat a circle of armchairs, rarely speaking; after a lifetime together, there was nothing left to say ...

...Whose stories as the end approached became fewer and fewer, until finally only one remained. And this she repeated over and over. She must have been about five years old, preparing the dinner for the harvesters returning from the fields. But the tap on the beer barrel was blocked. 'Well Lillian' said her mother 'you'll just have to blow up it'. This she did, but it gushed back, giving her a mouthful of bitter ale. It was her first, and only, taste of alcohol.

... Who thought I was my father whom she'd forgotten she had already lost. 'I am the family face.'

My father who gasped once in the bed beside her:
And in his dream, was there sudden black,
The jolt of a fall,
Or just another page turning in the wind?

At Fred Machin's, she had bent down and kissed him on the cheek.

Only later would she stagger and wail
And here I can make no impersonation of my mother –

'He's not coming back to me'.
She had known him since she was six years old.

'Touch 'im, touch 'im, you 'ave to touch 'im', my grandmother had hissed. At the age of seventeen, she laid out her mother, washing, combing, dressing the body, in preparation for the gaze of others. Then later her father: shaving the face, scrubbing the hands. Just twenty years ago, it was the turn of her aged sister.

But she died wi' 'er mouth open duck, and a couldn't shut it.
I pushed and pushed.
But Harold Cox managed it, so that's alright.
Harold Cox was *her* village undertaker.

Sometimes her face would distort, and she would begin to cry at some personal anguish. 'Don't get fed up of me. Don't stop coming' she said.

Thinking she might need nursing care, I went in search. Descended into the second circle of hell: to places where payment is by degree of dementia, where the rooms are cellular, where residents sit in huge silent conclaves, where the social has already died.

And then … she rallied. 'Tough as old boots'; 'She's a fighter' they said, the usual platitudes. Twice every day then, the ritual of visiting and the alcohol handwash that some local places have removed because the desperate are stealing it to drink. The short anxious walk, not knowing what might await, what state of waking.

Telling her stories – about flowers, about the market: the mundanities of days become cyclic. Scraping the barrel.

'She's brightened up a lot'; 'She's a bit weepy'; 'She's eating quite well'; 'She had a bit of ice-cream' they tell me.

Finally, fit to operate: 'Nil by mouth' more a description than an instruction. First time they were ready to roll, the anaesthetist was unhappy. Pulled the plug.

Second time, they rang. 'The risks are high' they said. To go or not to go? 'Your decision.' 'Go then.' And whatever happens, it is the right decision, we agreed.

And they did it, put her back together: plated and wired the multiple breaks and cracks.

And now she's discharged, in a place of protection – 'I'm not bothered' she said.

Remembering what the surgeon had told her, but not the trip there a few hours before.

But I know she is frightened. Not of slipping into another state: already prepared for that. The advert on the kitchen notice board – cut from the parish magazine for 'Fred Machin: Funeral Directors' – amended in biro: 'Cremation only.'

But of the cracks she senses spreading and widening. In memory: once something is said, it cannot be repeated, already gone. In story: in all the *non sequiturs*, the unfinished sentences; in pauses, in silences; in 'I don't know...'.

'Just pull those wires out; those ones' she said. 'I got a lot of presents' she said. 'I think they're all drinkers here' she said. I laughed; she laughed; we laughed together. Out loud. Mother and son reunited.

I left her. Alone now. Good days. And bad. In unknown territory. Amongst the gaps and firm ground. Between presence and absence.

*   *   *

I spoke the words above in *Something happening, something happening nearby*, the performance that Mike Brookes and I presented on 27 March 2008 in several adjoining rooms at the *Performing Presence* conference in Exeter University.

It begins during a wine reception; I stand inconspicuously in the crowd. A door opens and Mike enters with a chair, then a microphone, then a second microphone, and finally a music stand. I sit and begin to cut the front of my shirt with a sharp knife, close to the lower microphone. People turn; gradually the room falls silent. From time-to-time over the next forty minutes as I deliver the text *sotto voce*, I shred my clothes further – shirt, suit, tie – in an act redolent of supplication. A waitress becomes disturbed, distraught even – she has not been forewarned, cannot understand why I am doing this. Some stay; others follow the cables, aware that something else may indeed be happening nearby. In the next room, Mike uses my amplified voice as one element in his live theatrical mix. On the wall: the large projection of a burning car – follow the cable outside and it is revealed to be a toy on fire. On the soundtrack: the insistent electric music of German-Slovene composer Robert Merdzo, and a disquieting rustling – follow the cable upstairs and in an empty room is a single microphone, placed over a box of chirping and rasping crickets. The complete audiovisual composition is only available in full in that place where Mike is. But some wander throughout. And I am surprised how many remain with me, in the presence of the one person who – even though I simply read and concentrate upon providing a sample for elsewhere – resembles a performer.

*   *   *

> The terrible gift that the dead make to the living is that of sight, which is to say foreknowledge; in return they demand memory, which is to say acknowledgement.
>
> (Sante 1992: 63)

A tone continues; the key is minor ...

It was a Monday. She had taken a turn for the worse during the night; she was not expected to last the day, they said. We rushed there, dutiful sons. Though she had already surrendered herself into the hands of others, she struggled on for a week.

On sitting with the dying: a form of gentle encouragement, of modest beseeching, of humorous cajoling; of quietly demanding presence; of summoning from a distance already unbridgeable ... .

Sometimes she seemed to see us, to see through us, transparent and breakable as glass. Her breathing was at times faint and fluttering in her bird-like chest, at others short and in sharp pants: speaking in syllables, in a tongue that sounded Latin.

On Wednesday, we combed her hair – though they had cut it, to make it more comfortable for her – and she smiled for the last time, and nodded her final acknowledgement: after that, little response. Our devotion? Our continued presence, and heat, human heat ... But the arc has only one trajectory.

On Sunday, the curtains were drawn, the bedside lamp switched on; no music played to keep her company. These were the signs of a routine, regularly performed. I should have read them, understood the full meaning of 'She's very poorly.'

And in the final moment, I was not there.

On sitting with the dead. I stroke her cheek, and brush her hair, and hold her hand, and kiss her forehead. They have placed a single daisy in her folded arms. Occasionally I whisper 'Goodbye' or 'Sleep well', but mostly am silent, no anticipated confessional outpouring: her overwhelming presence and absence, her profound silence and stillness, throwing me back on my own resources –

confused thoughts of angels and autopsies. Hours pass. I stroke her cheek, and brush her hair, and hold her hand, and kiss her forehead. She has her father's eyes, her mother's nose. 'Can I kiss her goodbye?' her carer asks. Hours pass. I stroke her cheek, and brush her hair, and hold her hand, and kiss her forehead. She is insistent; I cannot leave. Her awesome quietude absorbs me, this present-absence: she, both familiar and infinitely other. It feels cinematic; a pietà reversed.

The time is now set. Clocks are running: only a limited period in which all that needs to be said and done can, must, be said and done. But there is a confusion: who does what, is authorized to do what, can sign what? In the moment when discourse also dies – reduced to 'It was for the best', 'It was peaceful at the end' and such – process takes over: documentation, proof, certification. And it fails. Nobody's fault: it is a warm bank holiday, and we are not paying particular attention, some of us. Hours pass. The nurse who tests for signs of life gets the call late. She apologises. I know no better and am pleased for the hours.

Then Fred and his men arrive – in their van, a 'private ambulance' – and enter – in their dark suits – through a back door. I am shown out; they take over, those who stand between, deferential but workmanlike.

He was apprenticed as a wheelwright. With post-War mechanisation his trade diminished, but he could always find a little extra from his ration of wood. He became the local undertaker, the man who carries out much that only a generation before was still in the hands of the family, from laying out to carrying the coffin.

He has buried the 'big' farmers and village widows. He knows the whole community, the living and the dead. Intimately. He has passed on his business now, but is still requested, personally, by the elderly. Trusted. His straightforwardness matches the 'Primitive' that still lingers in the 'Methodist' here.

We sit in her house, in the *mise-en-scène* of a life. We barely know how to go on here, and there is no rehearsal for this. We seek advice and sanction from neighbours and others, conscious of a right way to do things, of answering claims barely articulate. But this in between is taking its own course: the bracket is opened, the momentum in a single direction. Then bank holiday confounds us: suspension, limbo ... . Monday passes.

Next morning the doctor is obliged to visit her at Fred's, to pass the final judgement. Once done, there is a renewed urgency to fulfilling legal, religious, communal responsibilities, though the fine detail of myriad meetings is now difficult to recall.

The registrar is suspicious that the doctor's form is not sealed. Have I tampered with it? Is Parkinson's Disease an actual cause of death? Whose signature is this? We're doing our best here. But as the computer programme fails to respond, and we show our professional appreciation, she relaxes. Reminded often enough, we collect the green form for Fred, that gives him permission to proceed.

The near-sighted solicitor is witty, particularly when speaking of the revenue, the reasons for her local popularity evident.

Full of old-style admonition, the vicar cautions against immediate feelings of guilt and anger: 'Banish them!' Reminds us that we are now orphans; that presentiments of our own mortality will surely follow. We agree on the ritual: one hymn, his favourite reading from Christina Rossetti ...

Fred is solicitous. Should she wear her own clothes? Should he remove her wedding ring? No need for ostentation we feel: for over-elaborate indexing, for creating an impression 'over-determined and controlled' (Pearson 1998: 40). But we follow his counsel: this is, after all, our first time, for him the several thousandth.

Others once intervened too: those 'who may prepare, flex, decorate, tend and carry the body, who grieve and who officiate at the graveside, who kneel to place objects ...' (Pearson 1998: 34). In west Wales, there are stories of the sin-eater who, upon eating a piece of bread placed on a plate of salt on the breast of the deceased, devoured all sins. 'He was utterly detested in the neighbourhood – regarded as a mere pariah – as one irredeemably lost' (Davies 1911: 45).

I become the bringer of news to the living: local relatives and friends. Those I barely know as an adult embrace me, hold my face and kiss me. 'It's the end of an era' say two enigmatically. But talk quickly turns to other matters: beautiful and intricate recitations of genealogies; of the sequence of marriages in the Baptist chapel; of who farmed where; of who did what, to whom, when. To disability: 'He's not a very handy lad.' To the trials of aging: 'They ought to rub us out and draw us again; only they'd probably draw us the same.' A ninety-three year old aunt is still the dramatic storyteller: 'I tried suicide' she said sardonically, relating how she had tipped over the wardrobe, trapping herself on the bed. 'I thought I've got to get out.' Pulling out her leg, she took the skin off her shin. 'Me head was bleeding.' Somehow she managed to crawl to the phone. Later in a moment of contemplation she said: 'We had fun – me and Wilf and Sheila.' What will disappear here is not only accent, but a way of regarding the world: a matter-of-fact resignation in face of the vagaries of survival and of passing. And the ways of telling that lessen the impacts ...

Then we become forgetful, negligent, as – unexpectedly – imperatives of kinship take over. We ignore those others who attended, who also invested here – in friendship, companionship, neighbourliness, in caring; in *our* absence.... This ignorance I regret, but our instincts are those of strangers in a strange land.

It was foreseen. In the rummaging that inevitably begins the search for clues and answers, we find scraps of paper upon which she had monitored her own decline – strings of numbers to prove she could remember. And a hand-written letter to be opened in *her* absence, in a private act, anticipated, between her and us. Only. She affirms that everything is in order; directs us to bank accounts, and to the small stashes of notes that came as comfort, even after the burglary – the stigma of not being able to pay for one's own funeral perhaps echoing down the years. She informs us that we'll both receive the same, advises us to keep what we can of furniture and belongings, but cautions us against fighting over them. She beseeches us to stay good pals, and bids us farewell. 'Let Mr Machin of Kirton take over' she ends ...

We choose a single bouquet of the white arum lilies that she carried at her wedding.

*   *   *

Fred drove up slowly and parked for a few moments outside the house, in a tradition ancient, or recently invented. Either way, it came as a surprise: we stood awkwardly. Then the cortège of two proceeded.

Discrete strands came together at the crematorium: in the manifestation and demonstration of communal obligations and personal commitments – vicar, mourners, us, her; in an imbrication of how she would want to be remembered, how we want to remember her, and how things should be done.

We did the best we could: an improvised choreography of following and leading, sitting and standing. We were deployed: the ultimate demand of the dead upon the living. As expected, we showed decorum. And our focus was unswerving, her presence 'serving to disattend out-of-frame activities' (Davies 1911: 36).

The committal was short, but seemed appropriate. We sang Psalm 23 to Crimond. I gave a tribute, ending ...

> Canon Lilley asked us about her interests; we scratched our heads. She took up painting at one point; she liked dressing up for Kirton fête. But I think her main hobby was people – she loved meeting people; listening; and talking. And that's why people loved her – her ease with others; her sympathetic ear; and the reassurances she could give with a few words: usually quietly, but unafraid to speak out if she felt something wrong or unjust. This I think she got from her mother, a belief in human decency and dignity; an old-school commitment to the common good. In a changing world, she still had faith in the importance of civility, of tending to relationships, and of showing compassion for the trials of others.

And I read from Paul's First Letter to the Corinthians, Chapter 13, concluding: 'And now faith, hope, and love abide, these three; and the greatest of these is love.'

A curtain closed, a final curtain. Outside, flowers shone and wilted: 'The discarded paraphernalia of mourning' (Davies 1911: 32).

Later, we provided tea; had bought far too much cake. And people came and talked, as they have always talked here – familiar stories, new revelations, startling re-workings; passing on bits of this and that; setting the record straight. Once more.

*   *   *

'Neither here nor there ...' is the last in a series of practical and scholarly works set in rural communities of north Lincolnshire, that have addressed and involved interpenetrating themes of dwelling, place, memory and landscape. In 1992 I created *From Memory*, a solo performance in response to the death of my father James Frank Pearson, and it seems right to conclude here with the passing of my mother Sheila Marjorie Pearson on Sunday 30 August 2009.

I have written intimately about family, and I have included biographical material. The result is a blurring of distinctions between writing *for* performance and writing *about* performance, and between academic and artistic modes. What has frequently disappeared is citation, as the genealogy of people supplants the genealogy of intellectual argument. As in the recent work of anthropologists Kathleen Stewart (2007) and Daniel Miller (2009) and historian Karl Schlögel (2004), opinion and expertise and allusion can be palpable without being explicitly stated: evident in signature style, and in the dramaturgy of textual composition.

These communities are in essence conservative: old ways still haunt social attitudes and practices. But the reproofs and approbations of communal life, for better or worse, weaken. And ways of describing the world, of making sense in face of daily travail, now hover on the brink of extinction. One small ambition of my protracted attention has been to highlight its insights – in its humour and its resignation – as it fades. Or perhaps it is just a personal desire to recall and note some of the energy of post-War aspiration, and the survival of traces of earlier attitudes and ways of going on not quite extinguished in the rush to the modern.

After the performance in Exeter, several colleagues described the work as 'provocative' and 'challenging.' Gratifying to know that performance can still address adult matters, can still attempt to deal with, to come to terms with, the most personal and poignant experiences of presence and absence: the ultimate non-presence – death; and the ever-presence of the departed – in memory.

The text for *Something happening, something happening nearby* includes direct quotation from *From Memory* (1992); it also draws upon the section in *Theatre/Archaeology* (Pearson and Shanks 2001: 169–72) concerning my paternal grandmother.[2]

Works cited

Benjamin, W. (1992) 'The storyteller', in H. Arendt (ed.) *Illuminations*, London: Fontana Press, 83–107.

Davies, J. (1992 [1911]) *Folk-Lore of West and Mid-Wales*, Burnham-on-Sea: Llanerch Press.

Hardy, T. (1993 [1917]) 'Heredity', in T. Hardy *Selected Poems*, London: Penguin, 103.

Miller, D. (2009) *The Comfort of Things*, Cambridge: Polity Press.

Pearson, M. (1998) 'Performance as valuation: early Bronze Age burial as theatrical complexity', in D. Bailey (ed.), *The Archaeology of Value*, Oxford: BAR International Series 730, 32–41.

Pearson, M. and Shanks, M. (2001) *Theatre/Archaeology*, London: Routledge.

Sante, L. (1992) *Evidence*, New York, Farrar: Straus and Giroux.

Schlögel, K. (2004) *Moscow*, London: Reaktion Books.

Stewart, K. (2007) *Ordinary Affects*, Durham and London: Duke University Press.

Notes

1 Citations and indications of pause did not appear in the performance; eccentricities and irregularities of punctuation result from the compression of a working script, conceived originally for performance as stanzas of short phrases and lines.

2 My considerable thanks are due to Dr Dee Heddon (University of Glasgow) and my departmental colleagues Dr Carl Lavery and Margaret Ames for their close and critical reading of this text, for their advice on adjustments and amendments, and above for all their encouragement to proceed.

Index

Please note that page references to non-textual content such as illustrations will be in *italics*, while the letter 'n' will follow references to Notes.

Lightning Source UK Ltd.
Milton Keynes UK
UKOW05f0808100517
300882UK00018B/192/P